LENZ

THREE PLAYS

OBERON BOOKS ★ LONDON ★ ENGLAND

LENZ

THREE PLAYS

THE SOLDIERS
Translated by Robert David MacDonald

THE NEW MENOZA
Translated by Meredith Oakes

THE TUTOR
Translated by Anthony Meech

These translations first published in 1993 by Oberon Books Limited
521 Caledonian Road
London N7 9RH
Tel: 071 607 3637
Fax: 071 607 3629

ISBN 1 870259 33 5

Printed by Longdunn Press, Bristol
Cover design: Andrzej Klimowski

Oberon Books Limited
Managing Director: Charles Glanville
Publisher: James Hogan
Associate Editor: Nicholas Dromgoole MA [Oxon], FIChor

CONTENTS

INTRODUCTION, by Nicholas Dromgoole   7

THE SOLDIERS, translated by Robert David MacDonald   29

THE NEW MENOZA, translated by Meredith Oakes   77

THE TUTOR, translated by Anthony Meech   135

INTRODUCTION

Nicholas Dromgoole

What is surprising about Lenz is how little impact he has made on English letters and English drama. Most of us would class him with Sir Walter Scott as largely unreadable and certainly unread. By 1978 he had still not made it to the *Oxford Companion to the Theatre*. This makes it difficult for us even to begin to grasp his importance, not just for German, but for European drama. Jakob Michael Reinhard Lenz was found on 24th May, 1792, at the age of 41, lying dead in a Moscow street. His death is a mystery. His family had no idea what country he was in, or whether he was even alive. He was staying with a freemason, at a time when the Russian secret police were inquiring into freemasons as a threat to state security. Lenz was an unpredictable, at times almost crazy personality, liable to say anything anywhere. It is not beyond the bounds of possibility that he was murdered by his own circle as a security risk. At his death, whatever literary career he had achieved lay in ruins. He was unremarkable and unremarked. He died in poverty without position or financial prospects. The only certainty remains those sightless eyes staring unseeing at a Moscow sky.

Yet he had originally been hailed by some of the finest minds of his generation as "the second German Shakespeare after Goethe." He formed an intense friendship with the young Goethe and shared a room with him. He was among the leading dramatists of that strange movement known as *Sturm und Drang*, taking its name from a play by Klinger, a movement that anticipated the political idealism of the Romantic Movement, espousing the rights of the individual, a Rousseau-esque return to nature, the championing of Shakespeare's freedom in dramatic writing, as opposed to the dramatic unities, and scurrying back down the corridors of time to find themes for plays in other countries and even more importantly, in distant epochs. This involved the first attempt at some kind of historical realism in stage settings and costumes. Almost every theme that was to launch Romanticism as a major shift in European sensibilities was to be found in *Sturm und Drang*.

Even in this group Lenz stood out as being different. For the modern reader his plays seem addressed to an audience several generations after they were actually written. For his contemporaries they must have been baffling indeed. He was constantly being rediscovered throughout the 19th and 20th centuries. Georg Büchner wrote a novella on Lenz's descent into near madness, a sort of middle class Woyzeck, and Lenz's impressive theoretical work *Anmerkungen übers Theater* [Oberservations on the Theatre, 1774] might be seen almost as a blueprint for Büchner's dramatic approach in *Danton's Death*, 1835, and *Woyzzeck*, 1836. Playwrights like Hebbel, Bleibtreu and Halbe acknowledged his influence on them. The German Naturalists in the 1880's claimed him as a spirit. From 1910 Arthur Kutscher, director and critic, gradually kindled public enthusiasm for Lenz with exciting stagings of his plays, and since then they have been regularly performed as a small part of the standard repertory of German theatre. Bertolt Brecht adapted Lenz's *The Tutor* for the Berliner Ensemble in 1950. Yet if anything flashed before Lenz's eyes in his last moments on that Moscow street, it was more failure than success. His radically different play, *The Tutor*, had two performances in Hamburg, one in Berlin and over a decade a mere eleven in Mannheim. After that it was not performed for over a century.

Before we can make any attempt to assess or analyse Lenz's contributions to European drama, we must recognise that we stare back at him across a historical divide. He was born in 1751, and like Wordsworth was a young man as the forces that were creating the French Revolution in 1789 gathered impetus, when "bliss was it in that dawn to be alive, but to be young was very heaven." We now know about the French Revolution, we know about its aftermath, and even more importantly, we know about that whole shift in European attitudes and assumptions that we attempt to describe with the label Romanticism. If we are to grasp Lenz's importance, we should be aware of what the Romantic movement involved to create such a separation.

Western culture's dominant ideology remains firmly bound up with that same Romantic Movement, we are still enmeshed within the same cultural change, so it is extraordinarily difficult for us even to attempt any kind of analysis. The patient still on the operating table is in no state to arrive at a dispassionate assessment of his condition, much less attempt an impartial prognosis. Yet somehow if we are to make any sense of what has happened to our values and attitudes in the last two centuries, that is what we must attempt to do.

If we talk of a particular generation, imbued with a vague but powerful sense of political purpose, a sense that somehow "the system" had failed them and had to be rejected and largely dismantled so that it could be built afresh, a generation that wore its hair long, and clothes that scandalised its elders, a generation consciously welcoming a laxer lifestyle, a different set of values, a generation that experimented with drugs, questioned sexual tabus, dropped out, most readers will think of the 1960's. But every single one of these attributes applied just as forcibly to the 1840's. Almost every European capital except London experienced violent political upheaval and revolution in 1848. The student revolts of the 1960's were very small beer in comparison.

When we attempt to deal with major shifts in European ideology, such as the impact of Christianity on the pagan world, or the Renaissance which was in a strange reversal, the impact of a long dead pagan world on Christianity, and then the next major change that is Romanticism, it is dangerously easy to generalise. Romanticism changed the way we perceived the world, ourselves, our relations with each other, society and all the arts. Value systems altered and are still changing.

A few examples make the difference clear. There is a passage in one of Jane Austen's letters where she refers to the Peninsula campaign being conducted by the British army under the man who would in due course be the Duke of Wellington. She did not consider the Napoleonic war to be of sufficient importance to refer to it in any of her novels. In her letter she notes the heavy casualties suffered by British troops. Our troops. Her troops. "What a blessing", she says cheerfully, "that one does not care a jot for any of them!" This is the authentic voice of pre-Romanticism, sane, rational, assured. It shocks us. Even if we do not actually care a jot for victims in the latest air crash or train disaster, we feel we ought to. We would not dream of admitting that we did not. We belong to the Romantic Movement.

Or take attitudes to Nature. The very fact I have to spell it with a capital is revealing. If I could take readers and drop them down on the top of Cader Idris, that much admired mountain in North Wales, on a glorious sunny day, I could be fairly sure of everybody's reaction in the 1990's. Deep lungfuls of pure air, a sense of exhilaration at the view, increased spiritual well-being in communing with unspoilt scenic wonders. Nothing in the view around has changed since people were there in the 14th, 15th or 16th centuries. But their reactions, as far as we can tell, would have been quite different. Surrounded by a "horrid waste", they would have been anxious to get back to civilisation. Or let me put it another way. Faced with a particular valley, a soldier looks at it with the eye of a professional, defence is possible here, troops will be vulnerable there, positions can be dug there and so on. A farmer has different, but equally professional eye. This land can be drained, that is only good for pasture, this could make arable. A typical twentieth century individual, faced with the same valley, is more likely to experience undifferentiated emotion. "How pretty! How unspoilt!" We have not gone soft in the head. We have gone Romantic. Even Shakespeare looked at Nature with the expert, understanding eye of the true countryman. It is just that expertise we have lost.

Is *Sturm und Drang* in any sense to blame for any of this? Not really, or only partly. There were at least two Romantic movements, and because we are at the end of a process which has incorporated both, these differences no longer seem important. To return to the analogy of the patient on the operating table, he does not care very much whether his cancer came from smoking or from chemical additives. All he cares about is the cancer. Perhaps it is not a very good analogy because I do not want to suggest that society has acquired a terminal disease. But whatever it is we have, *Sturm und Drang* helped to give us. It started us smoking, let us say. It took the industrial revolution to provide the chemical additives. And now the analogy is making more sense because Romanticism was spawned as much by the industrial revolution as by anything.

Let us take the *Sturm und Drang* Romantic Movement first. This was a healthy development of the rationalism of the 18th century. Towards the end of the 17th century, instead of being overshadowed by the past achievements of the Greeks and Romans, and the whole Renaissance had been devoted to picking up where the Greeks and Romans had left off, thinkers and artists began to imagine they were not only as good as, but possibly better than their illustrious predecessors. Newton had demonstrably taken science further than Aristotle. Dryden could only defend Shakespeare by setting aside classical dramatic rules about the unities of time, place and action. The 18th century embarked on that most dangerous of paradoxes a blind faith in the power of human reason. It would only take so long before the scientists and the thinkers would find the necessary solutions to all the outstanding problems. Given time, we would lay bare the secrets of the universe, remodel nature in man's image, reconstruct reality, etc., etc. Wonderfully heady stuff. Rousseau in the 1760's and 70's shifted the emphasis to the "*moi*", edging the individual and his own response to his own predicament into the centre of the new world reason was itching to create. His *Social Contract*, wildly unhistorical but enormously influential, indicted the "system" for failing to honour the supposed contract by which free individuals supposedly bargained themselves into a society. "Man is born free and is everywhere in chains." Even more heady stuff. We have just been celebrating the bicentenary of the end result of this blind faith in the power of reason, the French Revolution.

Studying the interminable debates among the so-called experts in 1789 who set about that epoch-making event in European political and cultural history, their conceit, their naivety, their assurance in their own ability to replan the world is what *Sturm und Drang*, among other influences, has to answer for.

There is a depressing little parallel among the architects of the 1930's, 40's and 50's. They too thought they knew best and could cheerfully destroy in order to replan. "Bliss was it in that dawn to be alive" for architects among the municipal corruption and shoddy building of the booming 1960's. Middle-aged architects now have a hunted expression. After 1789 French politicians were lucky to make middle age at all. One of their many supposed solutions to social problems was the guillotine, and seldom have so many theorists had to endure so quickly and so rudely the end results of their own theoretical solutions. Many of us would like to condemn architects to live on the top floor of their vandalised tower blocks where the lift is semi-permanently out of order. Many of the most vehement French seekers after liberty, equality and fraternity, found neither liberty nor fraternity, but only the nastiest kind of equality as the guillotine reduced them to the final indignity of becoming a mere statistic.

Had anybody told French thinkers at the close of the 17th century that the coming century would prove to be a battle for supremacy between England and France, which England would win, to enjoy the fruits of victory throughout the 19th century, they would have found it too unlikely even to feel insulted. France was the undoubted leader of the arts, of thought and of military might. Spain was already looking back regretfully on a noble past. Venice no longer counted for much. Germany was a gaggle of independent little principalities.

What were the long term effects of the French Revolution, succeeded as it was by Napoleonic tyranny, the attempt to conquer Europe? It certainly helped the rise of nationalism, largely as a reaction against the French. Nothing made a German, an Italian, or a Spaniard feel more nationalistic than a French army lording itself on their land and their goods. But the main change was ideological. In spite of all the Congress of Vienna could do in 1815, a new kind of political idealism and revolutionary fervour arrived which not even the most frantic efforts of the *ancien régime* could suppress. Democracy, as a principle, became part of the political fabric of Europe after the French Revolution, replacing the feudal world that had lingered since the middle ages. Expediency might resist democracy, but its gains were all short term.

Ideas are ultimately defeated only by better ideas, and the idea of democracy survived its appalling failure in the French Revolution to continue to win the hearts and minds of Europe. That is the main achievement of the intellectual ferment in the second half of the 18th century which *Sturm und Drang* reflected and advanced. Democracy was not, of course, anything new. Even accepting that most of the ancient Greek and Roman world was based on slavery, a background against which Pericles' funeral speech rings a shade hollow to modern ears, democracy was a Greek word and a Greek idea. It was also the last gift of the Renaissance to modern Europe. And it started the Romantic movement.

The term Romantic, although based on the English word, was first used in its currently accepted sense by the German critic Friedrich Schlegel, who managed so to muddy the water over its definition, that nobody has been quite sure exactly what it means ever since. The English word was, of course, already loaded with meaning, echoes and associations long before Schlegel hijacked it for art criticism. His use of *romantisch* can fluctuate in meaning even within the confines of a single work. In *Gespräch über Die Poesie* [Conversations about Poetry], having accepted that ancient and Romantic represented almost opposite areas of feeling, he says: "*indessen bitte ich Sie doch, nur nicht sogleich anzunehmen, dass mir das Romantische und das moderne völlig gleich gelte*" [I beg of you, however, not to jump to the conclusion that the Romantic and the modern are entirely synonymous to me]. He comes close to narrowing things down in his much quoted: "*ist eben das Romantische, was uns einen sentimentalen Stoff in einer phantastischen Form darstellt*" [What shows emotional subject matter in an imaginative form is Romantic]. He then when on equate Romanticism with Christianity until nobody was quite sure what he meant by the word at all. The debate and the problem of definition took some time to reach English literary criticism. Carlyle wrote in 1831: "we are troubled with no controversies on Romanticism and Classicism.

But while French and German thinkers were enthusing over Rousseau, something quite different was happening in England. We were about to step onto the centre of the world stage for our moment of glory. The agricultural and industrial revolutions literally changed the face of the land. The total population of England in 1720 was about five million, most of them living in villages. Throughout the 18th century land enclosures revolutionised peasant lifestyle. More food was grown with much less labour, driving surplus labour into the cities at the very time improved agriculture was providing more food to feed them. In the cities, jobs were becoming available for the new surplus labour as the factory system got under way. Steam engines provided power and improved communications enabled the capitalist system of a market economy, obeying the laws of supply and demand with as little government interference as possible, to spread octopus-like tentacles everywhere.

It is difficult for us to grasp the extent of the change which occured within the span of a single lifetime. My father is a hale and hearty 103. Born in 1890, he has seen Britain, which in his early manhood owned a quarter of the globe in the largest empire known to mankind, shrink to a small, relatively unimportant island off the coast of Europe, now anxious to strengthen its links with the rest of the European Community in order to compete with the new super powers. He has survived two world wars. He has seen the advent of the combustion engine, the diesel ship, the aeroplane, the telephone, radio, film, television, computers, word processors, space exploration. Yet the shape and pattern of the city in which he has spent his life, while altered, has not really altered that much. Trains are still there. Railway stations have hardly changed. Horse-drawn buses have given way to petrol engines, but they still trundle up unaltered streets. Houses have changed to flats, but they are still the same houses. Shops are still shops. Many of the branded goods have been on sale most of his life. Public libraries, museums, theatres, concert halls, even public houses are all unchanged. Yet take the London of Wordsworth, who could stand on Westminster Bridge as a young man and write:

Earth has not anything to show more fair.
Dull would he be of soul who could pass by
A sight so touching in its majesty.
This city now doth like a garment wear
The beauty of the morning. Silent, bare
Ships, towers, domes, theatres and temples lie

Open unto the fields and to the sky;
All bright and glistening in the smokeless air.

Wordsworth too lived to a ripe old age. Had he been taken back to
Westminster Bridge in the last year of his life, the London of his youth would
have almost completely disappeared. He could probably not have seen
anything anyway, because the new bridge on which he was standing would
probably have been enveloped in a dense, man-made fog from all the factory
and domestic chimneys belching smoke from the new city built all around
him. There were no fields, nothing bright and glistening in the smokeless air.
Historians tell us of the appalling living conditions of the early industrial
workers. England paid a high price in human suffering for being the first to
industrialise. A lifestyle that had suited village life did not adapt easily to the
overcrowded living conditions of the factory system. Overcrowding, polluted
water and minimal sanitation meant that life was nasty, brutish, short and
cheap. Even London did not acquire Bazalgette's gravity sewage system until
the 1860's. Before that it was a matter of carts, stench, along with cholera and
other diseases. Marx and Engels working in London as it changed all around
them, saw the exploitation, the poverty and the ghastly living conditions and
came to conclusions about capitalism containing the seeds of its own decay,
which while they seriously underestimated the resilience of the system, were
all too understandable.

It would make a neatly fitting mechanism of cause and effect, although
history is anything but mechanistic, to read into these terrible changes in the
environment the causes of the sense of alienation from society that is such a
marked feature of Romanticism. Sadly, with examples stretching as far back as
Lenz and the *Sturm und Drang*, or early versions of Goethe's *Faust*, this
alienation is discernible even before industrialisation created a more hostile
environment. Undoubtedly the industrial revolution helped, but perhaps it was
the growing status and importance of the artist, who was therefore able to
make much more of his neurotic sense of being different, which Freud
maintains is one of the mainsprings of artistic activity anyway, that better
explains the growth of alienation as Byronic artists paraded their separateness
through a host of artistic creations.

We need historians to tell us about the terrible living conditions because
the arts were almost unanimously silent about the epoch-shattering changes
taking places in society. The arts were going Romantic. It is as if collectively

the arts turned their face to the wall and tried to pretend the industrial revolution simply was not happening. There are noble exceptions like Dickens' *Hard Times*, but not many. The arts became preoccupied with other cultures, other periods, Nature, anything to escape from what was taking place around them. The most popular British novelist as the Romantic Movement got under way was Sir Walter Scott. The bogus medievalism of such novels as *Ivanhoe* and *Quentin Durward* make him depressingly unreadable today, but his influence here and in the rest of Europe was incalculable. Reading Scott's poetry or prose, it would be difficult to grasp that the industrial revolution was changing the whole fabric of society:

Tunstall lies dead upon the field
His life blood stains the spotless shield.

What had shields and obscure medieval battles to do with factories, child labour, sewage pollution, the railway network, canals, the frantic search for markets, the booming economy, the poverty of the slums? Perhaps it was just because they had nothing to with these realities that they appealed.

As the arts retreated from the real world, the status of the artist changed too. Artists had acquired prestige in the Renaissance. One of the ways rulers and lay governments showed off their power was through the arts. It became important which court finally attracted Leonardo da Vinci, but artists still needed a patron, still remained subservient. With Romanticism artists finally achieved independence. It is instructive to look at Haydn's contract. He was a senior servant in an aristocratic household, wore its livery, was responsible for a group of musicians who played at family occasions, was entitled to a seat at the upper servants table and so forth. He was also a composer with a European reputation. His pupil, Beethoven, also had contracts. They were with his publishers. In one generation Beethoven achieved the kind of independence that was impossible for Haydn. The market for the arts was changing. The industrial revolution was a period of intense social mobility. The middle class expanded enormously.

It is not always appreciated just what a trap this must have been for the women in the emerging middle class. A generation earlier in the peasant village economy, women were probably working harder than men and playing a pivotal role in the family economy. The lucky ones who emerged into the middle class in the subsequent industrial revolution found things quite otherwise. The men in the family were still working hard in factories and offices in the helter-skelter of the new industrial economy. They were able to buy fine houses for their families to live in. It was possible to drive from central London to the Crystal Palace passing almost nothing but these fine new houses for the new middle classes.

But what of the women inside them? They were now fine ladies. They had hordes of servants to do the actual work. They were not allowed to seek a career or a vocation. They were anyway worn out in the endless business of procreation, producing surprising numbers of children to underpin the population explosion. Ill-educated, with no chance of a career, waited on hand and foot, they had to find ways of passing the time. Hence the growth of Mudies' circulating libraries, of the four volume novel, of sheet music, magazines, of theatre, of a whole entertainment industry. Artists made large profits meeting this new demand from a newly emerging class of consumers. But as profits rose, standards fell. This is the key to the depressing lowering of standards in all the popular arts throughout the Victorian period. The new consumers, one or two generations away from the village economy, were largely female, with time on their hands, ready to be exploited. The first mass market for the arts had arrived. With it came the hallmarks of Victorian art; sentimentality, hypocrisy and sensationalism. Ghosts and the supernatural generally, much as they must have done in the tales told round the evening fire in the village, popularised the "thrill of horror." Disembodied hands clutched from behind the wainscot, maidens were immured in turrets, listening as grisly things slowly climbed the stone stairs towards them, young women died of love in almost every chapter and every play, and the arts became steadily more and more divorced from the actual, practical ways in which people lived and behaved. When we read of young middle-class girls toying with their food at the dining table and genteely eating almost nothing, then tucking into a large tray in the privacy of their own room afterwards, art was clearly reshaping life with a vengeance.

Most of these aspects of Romanticism are still with us. Sentimentality, hypocrisy and sensationalism are as much the hallmark of our own time as of the Victorians. The industrial revolution in due course produced a more prosperous working class who in their turn became the new consumers waiting to be exploited. The tabloid press, sentimental horror films, lurid computer games, nightly violence on television are as symptomatic of our period as the first excesses of Romanticism were for the Victorians. Our journalists, scriptwriters, and film crews grow fat on the proceeds just as the first artists of the industrial era did. A Disneyland erected in the middle of a France full of real castles, wonderfully beautiful and historic, yet with crowds packing in to see gawdy imitations, is symptomatic of the same process.

We now view Lenz with perceptions that cannot help taking account of all that has happened since he wrote his plays. It may have been "very heaven" to be young at the beginning of Romanticism, but these days Romanticism has been around too long for us to show the same naivety. We view Lenz's early enthusiasms with a slightly jaundiced eye. What we can see is that much of what Lenz stood for was disregarded or discarded as the Romantic movement gathered impetus. Indeed in a sense, by playing a part in the *Sturm und Drang* movment, he was presiding at his own literary funeral. He set out to write a new and radically different form of ironic drama at the very moment when Romanticism was about to rush off in almost every direction but the one he wanted to take. No wonder his plays met with a poor response at the time and were steadily neglected for a century after they were written. His friend Goethe was a sufficiently major artist both to encompass early Romanticism, be an influence within it, and still maintain many neo-classic attitudes and interests that were light years away from what Romanticism stood for. Lenz sank almost without trace. Happily he still spoke to a select few, and increasingly this century we have come to realise that he is remarkably well worth listening to.

Lenz can still surprise us. He was almost as much of a pioneer in the theatre as William Blake was in painting and poetry. Lenz's contribution was threefold. He set about creating what amounted to a new theatrical form. He was among the first writers anywhere, long before Marx, to perceive the importance of social class in human relationships. He seems to have been among the very first creators of fiction attempting both to depict and analyse the emotional tensions, unspoken but shatteringly powerful, that exist in various disguises within the domestic family circle, particularly between parent and child, sister and brother. These gifts did not come to him piecemeal. They are all apparent in his very first play, *The Tutor*.

This was partly the result of his own personal experience. Germany in the 18th century was in a state of growing social crisis. It is of course impossible to talk of Germany in the 18th century. The Holy Roman Empire, which was, as Talleyrand neatly noted, neither holy, Roman, nor an empire, consisted of a patchwork quilt of little independent states, kingdoms, dukedoms, fiefdoms, ruled by all-powerful little despots, each supporting a court and a local aristocracy, depending as it had since feudal times on a labouring peasant class. Yet the increasing efficiency of the educational system was producing a middle class for which there were very few jobs, very little chance of status and position. This created a growing social tension which was only gradually resolved as industrialisation and increasing prosperity in the 19th century absorbed and greatly increased the new middle classes. In the 1770's it looked as though there was nowhere for the tiny, upstart middle class to go.

Lenz was very much a victim of this social process. Gifted, intelligent, educated, he spent his first year in Strasbourg as a "lackey cum companion" to the von Kleist brothers, sons of a local aristocrat, and a humiliating year it must have been. It was during this year, 1771, that he wrote *The Tutor*. At the same time he was gradually coming into closer contact with Goethe, Jung-Stebbing, Klinger, Wagner, Herder and Salzmann, the group which later became labelled as *Sturm und Drang*. They did not behave as later artistic groups were to do, the pre-Raphaelites in England or *Das Junge Deutschland* or the Naturalists in Germany and issue a *pronunciamento*, form a society, publish a periodical, agree a basic set of principles. Rather it seems as though meeting with each other sharpened and intensified that vital emphasis of Romanticism, the awareness of the self as an individual, subjectively relishing and exploiting the uniqueness of a single imaginative vision. Perhaps nowhere else in Europe was the middle class so frustrated, so aware of its emasculated state as the aristocrats comfortably controlled the levers of power and authority. Even so it was a major achievement for the young Lenz to grasp objectively the role of the aristocracy as a social class and present it in a dramatic form that made the concept so apparent to his audience.

Läuffer, the tutor of the play, is humiliated by the aristocrats he works for. When he expresses an opinion about a ballet dancer, contrary to the Count's, he is publicly rebuked and sent to his room. His salary is arbitrarily reduced without consultation. He is never given the use of a horse as promised. Yet perhaps the key point is the blundering reply of the major when his brother, von Berg, asks why he has a tutor for his children. The major clearly has a tutor because he feels his social position calls for it, a matter of class vanity, rather than because he knows or understands the purpose of education, much less cares about what is actually being taught to his children, nor does his wife. Läuffer's father, although prosperous will not pay for him to achieve a university post. Von Berg will not consider him for a teaching post at the local school. The major is unwilling to use his influence to get Läuffer a post in the civil service. Läuffer is at their mercy, humiliated and helpless. The moment when Läuffer's bitter mood is transformed to servility as he sees the von Berg brothers come down the street, and they in turn fail to notice him at all [as aristocrats they only see other aristocrats], is exactly paralleled, is indeed made the central point of Gogol's novella *The Overcoat*. Yet Gogol was published in 1842. Lenz is making the same point, and getting his audience to think objectively about it in the early 1770's.

In the same way his insight into family relationships would seem to stem from his own experience. Büchner, although medically qualified, was only 23 when he wrote his novella, *Lenz*, giving an account of Lenz's descent into near madness. This account was closely based on the notes of Pastor Oberlin with whom Lenz was staying at the time in 1778. For a post-R. D. Laing generation it is clear from this detailed account that Lenz was schizophrenic. It has even been suggested that much of Laing's insight into this condition stemmed from his own mental struggles. Büchner, although trying imaginatively to be sympathetic and certainly telling the story from Lenz's point of view, was writing in 1835 and could not begin to grasp the emotional and mental complexities with which he was dealing. A closer study of Lenz's plays might have helped him. Lenz shows the kinds of insight into family behaviour that Laing's psychiatric studies in *The Self and Others* and *The Divided Self*, have now made more familiar territory. Laing was writing in the 1960's, Lenz in the early 1770's.

What are we to make of the major's wife's clear need to control and humiliate the tutor before she can feel at peace with herself? Von Berg, while shown as an upholder of new and liberal ideas about education, is quite unable to take the pastor's point about young middle class men being victims of the system because that would have meant confronting the aristocracy's refusal to relinquish any of its powers. And how quickly von Berg reverts to type when he discovers his son, Fritz, and his niece, Gustchen, are in love. Lenz sees the members of a family as being in conflict with each other, a conflict they can neither understand nor control, particularly those differences between the parents' view of their role and the emotional needs of their children. Von Berg sees the affair which has flourished in secret as a threat to his authority as a father, which he immediately sets about re-establishing. Having made the lovers feel small by making fun of them [effectively translated by Antony Meech] he then imposes impossible conditions. They are not to meet in private and he is to read their letters when Fritz is away at university. Punishment at disobedience will be severe. Fritz will join the army, Gustchen will go to a convent. At one level he appears to be controlling their love in their best interests, but he is in effect destroying it in such a way as to make it seem that the collapse of the affair will be their own fault.

As Edward McInnes has pursuasively pointed out in a perceptive paper on *The Tutor,* what a contrast this represents between the man who has extolled the power of choice to educational growth and the father setting out to destroy any possibility of choice for these two lovers. He never attempts to see things from their point of view. It is his sense of how things should properly be arranged that is outraged. Father and son are locked in conflict for the rest of the play, although they do not see this consciously, because the victims of family conflict in Lenz never seem able to communicate their feelings of fear and emotional distress, much less analyse the process by which those they are supposed to love oppose their deepest wishes. This is familiar Laing territory, but in 1771? The major's family relationships read even more like a Laing case study. A conservative and proud officer, he cannot cope with a sexually dominant wife and as a result bullies his son, thus demonstrating his authority to her which she increasingly undermines. This creates an ever widening spiral of emotional tension. He compensates by expecting too much for his daughter and fantasising about her future so that she is made to feel inadequate. Where else in the 1770's can we find these kinds of perceptive understanding?

Surely what we are dealing with here is the stuff of tragedy. It is perhaps in his awareness of the need for a new dramatic form through which to present his insights that Lenz is at his most revolutionary. And he had few models. No member of the *Sturm und Drang* had published a play when Lenz wrote *The Tutor.* Goethe had started *Götz von Berlichingen* and had probably discussed it with Lenz. And that year saw the first mention of *Faust* as a project. Only in 1776 did Leisewitz's *Julius von Tarant,* Klinger's *Die Zwillinge* and *Sturm und Drang,* and Wagner's *Die Kindermörderin* or Lenz's own *Die Soldaten,* begin to give the group some dramatic credentials. Lenz was a pioneer.

In 1774 Lenz published his major theoretical work *Anmerkungen übers Theater*, a paean of praise for Shakespeare, seen not only as the best dramatist of the modern age, but as genius and prophet of all that was best in Christian culture. Above all, Shakespeare was praised for his creation of the outstanding individual, heroic before an awesome destiny, embodying individual will and representing mankind's endless striving towards the spiritual. Lenz was nothing, if not committed. Gerstenberg in his *Literaturbriefe*, 1766, and Goethe in *Shakespeare-Rede*, 1771, had praised Shakespeare's ability to create believable individuals in believable situations. Lenz sees the development of the individual hero interacting with events and other characters as the essence of Shakespeare's drama. The hero as individual is the play's very stuff and justification. The old Aristotelian unities should be replaced by a new, single unity, the unity of character. And a central figure alone could be the unifying force that held a drama together. This for Lenz was the essence of tragedy.

Lenz did not grasp the secret of the effectiveness of Renaissance tragedy. The old sense of social order and religious certainty was breaking up, but was still powerful. The new sense of individualism, of a testing of the limits of the possible, an exploration of new experiences and a demand for new meanings as the old retreated, created a fascinating tension between old and new that was at the heart of Elizabethan tragedy. By the 18th century, the age of rationalism, the old medieval certainties had lost too much of their hold. The tension was gone. Where in Elizabethan plays, rank implies a social hierarchy, a view of order and justice, by the 18th century at best this had narrowed down to sympathy and pity between private persons. Pope was simply out of date when he praised Addison's *Cato* as:

A brave man struggling in the storms of fate
And greatly falling with a falling State.

Addison's tragedy was a hollow facade based on earlier models. The greatness, the sense of social order and religious certainty the State used to mean, had crumbled away. Cotes was nearer the mark:

What pen but yours could draw the doubtful strife
Of honour struggling with the love of life?

Raymond Williams, who contrasts both these quotations in his *Modern Tragedy*, goes on to talk of bourgois tragedy as not being social enough:

For with its private ethic of pity and sympathy it could not negotiate the real contradictions of its own time between human desire and the new social limits set on it... We hear the first weak accents of man the victim: the old far-reaching heroism has gone.

Williams suggest that it is not enough to look at the isolated martyr, but rather we should look at the social process of his martyrdom:

And at this point we reach the profoundly ambiguous question, is it not a sin against life to allow oneself to be destroyed by cruelty and indifference and greed?

Writing on Brecht he says:

In most modern drama, the best conclusion is: yes, this is how it was. Only an occasional play goes further, with the specific excitement of recognition: yes, this is how it is. Brecht at his best reaches out and touches the necessary next stage: yes, this is how it is, for these reasons, but the action is continually being replayed and it could be otherwise. The trap at this last moment is the wrong kind of emphasis on the undoubted fact that it could indeed be otherwise. To make it clearly otherwise by selecting the facts... is to go over to propaganda or to advertising.

What was so prescient about Lenz was his recognition in 1771 that Renaissance tragedy no longer worked, and a new theatrical form was required. The theatre needed a new kind of play, not hopefully the bourgeois tragedy that involved the "first weak accents of the victim", but a look at the "social process." He called his first play a tragedy, but by the time of publication after much heart searching and playing with alternatives he opted for the word comedy. This and his later plays are certainly concerned with the human condition, but it is a social condition. In a series of short scenes he invites his audience to consider the social forces that produce a given set of characters. And yet he is almost Shakespearian in his skill at bringing his characters to life as believable individuals in believable situations. And there is an unspoken corollary. If the social conditions were to change, "it could be otherwise."

When he wrote *The Tutor* he was dealing with a given audience accustomed to a given kind of theatre. The idea of a comedy on education must have reassured them, particularly with its subtitle, *The Tutor* or *The Advantages of Private Education* suggesting a mildly satiric view of a particular profession along such well-worn lines as Lessing's *Der junge Gelehrte*, 1747, Krüger's *Die Candidaten*, 1748, or *Die Geistlichen auf dem Lande*, 1743, and Mylius's *Arzte*, 1745. Specific plays on education like Moliere's *Ecole des Femmes* or Gottsched's *Die Hausfranzösin* had already paved the way. Yet once Läuffer begins to reveal his true feelings the effect on the modern reader is surprisingly similar to Jimmy Porter's effect on British audiences in Osborne's *Look Back in Anger* in 1956; in spite of its shortcomings, it is still a saying of things that needed to be said, a breaking of a conventional tabu of silence, a facing up to changing circumstances. Porter was castigating a middle class establishment, Läuffer was taking a hard look at the aristocrats. *The Tutor's* actual performances were few and unsuccessful, unlike Osborne's play, but it was, nevertheless, published, read and discussed.

The plot soon gathers impetus. As we realise that Läuffer and Gustchen are caught in the same kind of trap, both longing for what they cannot have, both alienated by their very longings from the actual pressures that surround them, they have a sexual encounter. Nothing could be further from the grandeur of Romantic passion. Neither grasps the reality of the partner as another person, they clutch at each other as a brief escape from the real world which imprisons them. Neither shows much comitment or loyalty to the other. As soon as their guilty secret is discovered they flee in different directions, Läuffer to Wenzeslaus, a village schoolmaster, Gustchen to a blind beggar woman in the forest. The action of the play is now divided. Parents are separated from children, children from each other. The major searches for Gustchen. Gustchen, unable to carry the burden of her guilt at having a child, throws herself into a lake. Läuffer comes across the supposedly orphaned child and, overwhelmed by guilt, castrates himself. Fritz, learning that Gustchen is dead and was seduced by the tutor, is overwhelmed with guilt just as Läuffer was. The audience knows that Gustchen is not dead at all, which adds a fresh touch of absurdity to the whole proceedings. The readiness of everybody to shoulder guilt for what has not even happened, when the play is showing us just the opposite, that the characters, far from imposing themselves on events and taking responsibility for their actions, are themselves the uncomprehending victims of a social system they have no hope of controlling adds yet another layer of absurdity. Nobody is in control, nobody is a free agent. Lenz then adds a final icing to the layer cake. Against all the odds everything turns out happily. Patus, Fritz's friend, wins heavily in a lottery and can pay both their debts and bring them home. The major arrives at the lake precisely as Gustchen throws herself in. And from nowhere a beautiful girl dedicates herself to a spiritual love and life with Läuffer.

We know about Lenz's theory of comedy because he rote about it, not only in his *Anmerkungen übers Theater*, but in his article, *Recension des Neuen Menoza*, which appeared in the *Frankfurter gelehrte Anzeiger* in 1775. Lenz sees characters in comedy as being at the mercy of the plot, structured around a crisis which Lenz calls a *Sache*, and swept along as the complications develop. He also claims that comedy can be a form dramatists can use to present both grim and upsetting facts to an audience intent only on enjoying themselves. Whether the characters are controlled by the twists of the plot, or by a social system that imprisons them in a given set of class responses, the point is that in comedy they have little or no chance to assert themselves as individuals, much less impose themselves on events. Lenz sees this as the crucial difference from tragedy. In a tragedy the hero grows before our eyes, acquires new insights, changes and matures as a person, controls, or at least attempts to control the course of events. In a comedy the characters achieve no insight, cannot change. Von Berg remains the same father at the end of *The Tutor* as at the beginning. He accepts his son's apology. He never sees that he himself has precipitated disaster. Nothing is resolved except the plot – and the more arbitrarily that is managed, the more effectively Lenz is making his point. It is of course a humourous ironic point. German critics are notorious for having difficulties with humour, particularly irony. They have struggled with Lenz' ending to the *The Tutor* and, in general, dismally failed to understand it. In England Sheridan in *The Critic* does much the same as Lenz, at much the same time, in the conclusion to his glorious subplot, when true identities are revealed. "This is your father, this your mother, these your uncles, these your aunts, these your cousins." English critics happily responded to an equally improbable parody of theatrical form and, incidentaly, a gorgeous send-up of the critic's role. German audiences, readers, critics have been less responsive to Lenz. Even Brecht, in his adaptation of *The Tutor*, irons out much of the irony. Lenz deserved better of his countrymen.

The Soldiers, published in 1776, the very year a middle class America was doing rather well against an aristocratic Britain, is an easier play. It is the most accessible of all Lenz's plays and because parts of it seem old-fashioned and dated, audiences can comfortably patronise it and find it charming without being too upset by it. Eighteenth century views of women, views of chastity, views of pre-marital sex, views of the married state, now sound archaic. The *Weltanschauung*, the mind set, of a society close to the 21st century has moved on and left most of this unnecessary baggage behind.

Yet just as in the ballet *Giselle*, created in 1841 and loaded with Romantic flummery, but still holding its place in the ballet repertory, there comes a moment of recognition as the aristocrat, Albrecht, deceives the peasant girl, Giselle, and one can almost hear the women in the audience thinking "yes, that is what men are really like, they'll lie and cheat and deceive, they're all after the same thing!" So *The Soldiers* has its moments of recognition.

The soldiers are aristocrats, officers. They amuse themselves with seducing pretty tradesmen's daughters, ruining the girls' reputations in the process, but tempting them with dazzling prospect of marriage into the aristocracy. And the girls pursue the bubble reputation even in the cannon's mouth. Lenz is consciously inviting his audience, not only to see the officers as representatives of an aristocratic class, but much more importantly to think about the role of that aristocratic class in society as a whole. Chaucer shows us bad priests. He never expects us to question the role of priests. Lenz was pushing his audience into asking far more searching questions about the social responsibilities of the aristocracy. The French revolution was still thirteen years in the future, and Lenz's play was in many ways a revolutionary tract. Yet his characters are not cyphers. Once again he has a gift for sharp observation, for creating believable characters in believable situations, so that Marie, the daughter of a fancy goods dealer in Lille, is all too believable as an ambitious flirt, dazzled by the material things of life, only too ready to play with fire.

Once again, Lenz deliberately overplays his ending. We can perhaps still take the melodrama as her original lover poisons the man who has done her wrong. But when the father, faced with a woman whom he suspects to be a prostitute, begins fearfully to apprehend he may be talking to his own fallen daughter, "was your father a dealer in fancy goods?" is a line which deserves to rank with "out, out, into the cold snow" as one of the mightier clichés of melodrama. And how well Robert David MacDonald's translation catches exactly Lenz's intentions. Once again, nobody changes, nobody grows and matures before our eyes, nobody gains fresh insights. Once again they are the creatures of chance and social conditioning. A freak combination of circumstances brings them together. By stressing the implausibility at the end, Lenz is nudging us into a recognition of the sheer absurdity of the human condition with out responses fixed by the way society has conditioned us, immersed in events we cannot hope to control. The shock of recognition here is a jolt to complacency even in the 20th century. In the 18th it must have seemed considerably more than that.

The New Menoza, 1776, is a less accessible play, more difficult to read, more difficult to stage. It represents more of a challenge, because in it Lenz is looking not so much at life as at the theatrical conventions of his time. It is as though, rather than hold the mirror up to nature, he starts playing tricks with the mirrors. We must remember the predominance of theatre as a medium for fiction in Lenz's day. In England the words poet and playwright were almost interchangeable even at the end of the 17th century. The novel was only beginning its long rise to dominance as a literary form. Cinema, radio, television lay far in the future. Not only writers, but audiences had almost nowhere else to go for imaginative fiction. Lenz could therefore count on the audience recognising the conventions he was making fun of.

The title is based on a Danish novel by Pontoppidan, translated into German in 1742, using the then popular formula of an oriental visitor looking at European customs as a method for objective social comment. Once again it is easy to see why the Naturalists rediscovered Lenz in the 1880's. Although they are characters in scenes which are poking fun at the different theatrical genres of the day, the characters still come vividly to life, flaring into believable existence before our eyes in a brief moment of theatrical glory. They are not really naturalistic at all, since as the same characters appear in different plots they adapt into the style of each.

The diversified plot is gorgeously complex. It is not intended to be taken seriously, yet in its own crazy way it hangs delightfully together and makes a bizarre kind of sense. Naumburg is recognisably small-town Saxony; philistine, affluent fathers misunderstand melancholy scholarly sons. Wilhelmina is beautiful, naive, unspoilt as heroines should be. Across this basic setting a variety of subplots burst like coloured streamers, each highlighting a particular kind of theatre. This is extraordinarily difficult to translate and Meredith Oakes has found the dramatic language for Lenz's intentions. Prince Tandi represents the "Europe as seen through the eyes of a foreign visitor" approach. He travels to seek enlightenment. The young men Herr Zierau and Master Beza visit him to discuss philosophy, and of course we marvel at the superior wisdom he brings from exotic foreign lands. He falls for Wilhelmina, and courteously agrees to wait five years in Germany until she decides to return with him to Qumba. In mid-drama we are led to believe the Prince and Wilhelmina are actually brother and sister, but a further revelation is in store. Wilhelmina is a changeling and all will therefore turn out for the best.

The Donna Diana subplot is fairly standard Spanish melodrama. Passionate and wicked, she poisons her father, steals her mother's jewels and elopes with the seducer Count Chameleon to Dresden. The Count, after failing to get his manservant Gustav to kill her, flees to Herr von Biederling, tells him he has killed a man in a duel, and is allowed to hide secretly in a house in the garden. Donna Diana tracks him down because Gustav, the manservant, is in love with her. She kills the Count and Gustav hangs himself. Donna Diana is not really a Spanish aristocrat, but a von Biederling.

The Count Chameleon subplot is again a tilt against the power of the aristocracy. The Count ruthlessly uses the von Biederlings, making Frau von Biederling fall for him because he is in love with Wilhelmina and needs her mother's help to obtain the daughter's hand in marriage. Prince Tandi challenges him to a duel, but the Count in typically villainous style will not fight. The Count throws a masked ball, ostensibly for Wilhelmina's pleasure, but really so that he can take her into a side room and rape her. Here the theatrical convention of changed identities and masks is used delightfully. Wilhelmina does not go to the party, Donna Diana takes her place, the Count finds himself raping the very woman he wants to avoid, Donna Diana stabs him, the various subplots have all interlocked in fine style and the play ends with Herr Zierau complaining at the sheer monotony of life in Naumburg.

Lenz became a sad victim of increasing mental instability. He was the son of a pastor and studied theology at Dorpat and Königsberg. He had a depressing tendency to fall in love with women associated with men around him whom he should have avoided antagonising. At Strasbourg he made advances to Friederike Brion, an affair of Goethe's, and Cleophe Fibich, a fiancée of one of the von Kleist brothers. In 1775 he convinced himself he was in love with Henriette von Waldner, an aristocrat engaged to someone else, although she was scarcely aware of Lenz at all. In 1776 he seems to have behaved so tactlessly and oddly that he had to leave Weimar and seems to have lost the respect and affection of Goethe, who wrote in *Dichtung und Warheit* of Lenz's general instability. After becoming more and more unstable, he had to return in 1778 to his family in Riga, probably not exactly a calming environment, and three years later Lenz went to Russia, first to St. Petersburg and then to Moscow where he died eleven years after leaving his Baltic homeland. He wrote other plays [the long lost manuscript of one of them was found in Hamburg in 1971] and his works were first collected and published in Germany 1828, again in 1900 and again in 1967. The letters were published there in 1918 and again in 1969. His poems were published separately there in 1968. This volume brings together three of Lenz's plays in English for the first time.

London, 1993

THE SOLDIERS
[Die Soldaten]

TRANSLATED BY
ROBERT DAVID MACDONALD

This translation was commissioned by the Citizens Theatre, Glasgow, and first performed at the Edinburgh International Festival, 1993.

DRAMATIS PERSONAE

Marie, daughter of Monsieur Wesener
Charlotte, daughter of Monsieur Wesener
Stolzius, a cloth-merchant in Armentieres
His **Mother**
Desportes, a nobleman from Hainault, in the French service
Monsieur Wesener, a fancy-goods dealer in Lille
Count von Spannheim, Desporte's Commanding Officer
Eisenhardt, Field Chaplain
Count de la Roche, cousin to Spannheim
His **Tutor**
Major Hardy★
Lieutenant O'Murphy★
Madame Wesener
Captain Pirzel
Lieutenant Rammler
Mademoiselle Zipfersaat
Wesener's Mother
Aaron, a Jew.
Countess De La Roche, the young Count's Mother
Desporte's Gamekeeper
Gilbert
Madame Bischof
Mademoiselle Bischof, her niece
Ladies, Gentlemen, Officers, Servants, Townspeople, etc.

The play takes place in the French part of Flanders.

★These two names have been changed [from Haudy and Mary respectively in the original] to avoid ambiguity, of pronunciation among other things, not least a confusion with the name of the heroine.

ACT ONE

Scene 1
Lille

Marie: [*Writing a letter, her chin on her hand*] Sister, do you know how you spell "Madame?" M.A. Ma... D.A.M. Damm... M.E. Meuh?

Charlotte: [*Sitting spinning*] That's right.

Marie: Listen, I'll read it to you, see whether it's all right what I've written: "My dear Madamm-e! We arrived safe God be praised back in Lille"... Is that right? Two R's in "arrived"?

Charlotte: That's right.

Marie: "We do not know how we are deserving the kindness with which we have been overwhelmed wish only however to be placed in a position"... is that all right?

Charlotte: Just read it all, so I get the sense.

Marie: "...a position as to repay your kindness and courtesy to us. However, since it is not yet in our power to do so, then only beg for further continuation of same.."

Charlotte: *We* only beg for further..

Marie: Oh, do stop interrupting all the time.

Charlotte: It's "*we* only beg for further continuation.."

Marie: Oh, what are you talking about, I'm doing it the way Pa would.

[*She folds the letter, and makes to seal it*]

Charlotte: All right, read to the end.

Marie: The rest doesn't concern you. You always want to be cleverer than Pa; only the other day Pa was saying it isn't polite, always writing "We" and "I" and that sort of thing. [*She seals the letter*] There, Stephan, take that to the post. [*Gives the SERVANT money*]

Charlotte: Why didn't you want to read me the end? Something pretty about your Monsieur Stolzius, I suppose.

Marie: Nothing to do with you.

Charlotte: Oh, really, am I supposed to be jealous? I could just as well have written it as you, I just didn't want to rob you of the pleasure of showing off your handwriting.

Marie: Listen, Lottie, I'm telling you, just leave me in peace about Stolzius, or I'll go straight downstairs and complain to Pa.

Charlotte: Hoity-toity, do you think I care? Father knows very well you're in love with young Stolzius. You can't bear to hear his name in anyone else's mouth.

Marie: Lottie!

[*She starts to cry and runs downstairs*]

Scene 2
Armentières

Stolzius: [*With a bandage round his head*] Mother, I'm not well.

Mother: [*Stands for a moment looking at him*] You've got that wretched girl on the brain, that's what's the matter with you. You haven't had a cheerful moment since she went away.

Stolzius: Seriously, Mother, I'm *not* well.

Mother: Well, if you ask nicely, I think I might be able to cheer you up a little. [*She produces a letter*]

Stolzius: [*Springing up*] Has she written?

Mother: Read for yourself.

[*STOLZIUS tears it from her hand and devours it with his eyes*]

Mother: Listen, the Colonel is wanting that cloth measured out for the regimentals.

Stolzius: Let *me* answer the letter, Mother.

Mother: You big, daft thing, you're going to measure the cloth the Colonel ordered for the regiment. Come along, now..

Scene 3
Lille

Desportes: What are you up to, divine Mademoiselle ?

Marie: [*Scribbling on a sheaf of blank paper in front of her. She hastily sticks the pen behind her ear*] Oh, nothing, nothing, Monsieur - [*Smiling*] I'm much too fond of scribbling away..

Desportes: If I could only be fortunate enough to see one of your letters, one single line from your fair hand.

Marie: Oh, please, I haven't got a fair hand at all. I'd be ashamed to show you anything I'd written.

Desportes: Anything from such a hand would have to be fair.

Marie: Oh, Monsieur le Baron, pray don't go on so, I know those are just compliments.

Desportes: [*On his knees*] I swear I have never seen so perfect a creature as you in my whole life.

Marie: [*Knitting, her eyes on her work*] My mother told me... What a two-faced person you are.

Desportes: *Moi?* Two-faced? Can you believe that of me, divinest Mademoiselle? Was it two-faced of me, having sold my half-year's leave, to steal off from my regiment, just to be with you? And now, if anyone discovers I am not with my parents, as I gave out, I risk being thrown into jail, all for the happiness of seeing you, most perfect of creatures - am I two-faced?

Marie: [*Looking back to her work*] But my mother's always telling me I'm not really properly grown up yet: I'm at an age where girls are neither pretty nor plain.

[*Enter WESENER*]

Wesener: Why, look who's here! Monsieur le Baron, your most obedient. Another visit! To what do we owe the honour? [*Embraces DESPORTES*]

Desportes: I am just here for a week or so - visiting a relative of mine who has arrived from Brussels.

Wesener: You will forgive my not having been at home, my little Marie will have been boring you, and how are your worthy parents, they will have received the snuff-boxes by now -

Desportes: No doubt, I have not seen them. We must settle up, *cher ami*.

Wesener: Oh, time enough for that, it isn't as if it was the first time. Your good lady mother didn't come down for carnival this year.

Desportes: She is not awfully well - many dances?

Wesener: So, so, sprightly enough - as you know, I go to none, and my daughters to fewer.

Desportes: But, Monsieur Wesener, can that be right, to deny your daughters all their pleasures, how can they stay healthy?

Wesener: Oh, let them work, they'll stay healthy enough. My little Moll wants for nothing, God be thanked, and she always has good red cheeks.

Marie: Pa won't be told - sometimes I feel so tight about the heart, so edgy I hardly know now to stay in the room.

Desportes: You see, you allow your daughter no entertainment; it will turn her melancholic sooner or later.

Wesener: Rubbish, she has entertainment enough with her friends; when they get together, you can't get a word in edgewise.

Desportes: Allow me the honour of escorting Mademoiselle to the play some time. They are giving a brand new piece this evening.

Wesener: No - no, certainly not. Monsieur le Baron, do not take it amiss, but let us have no more words on the matter. My daughter is not accustomed to going to the theatre, there would only be talk in the neighbourhood - with a young military gentleman to boot.

Desportes: But I am not in uniform. Who would know me?

Wesener: Never mind! Once and for all, not with any young man. She's hardly been confirmed yet, and would she be going to the play and acting the fine lady? In short, Monsieur le Baron, no. I do not permit it.

Marie: But, Pa, if nobody's going to recognise Monsieur le Baron?

Wesener: [*In an undertone*] Hold your tongue, will you! "If nobody is going to recognise him"... so much the worse if nobody does. [*Aloud*] You will forgive me, Monsieur le Baron, much as I should like to accommodate you, in any other matter you have but to command.

Desportes: *A propos,* my good Wesener, could you show me some hair ornaments?

Wesener: At once! [*He goes out*]

Desportes: Listen, my angelic, my divine little Marie, we are going to play a trick on your father. It is no good today, but the day after tomorrow they are giving an excellent piece, *Woman After Wit,* and *The Deserter* as a curtain-raiser - have you a good friend locally? Someone you're allowed to visit?

Marie: Madame Weyher.

Desportes: Where does she live?

Marie: Just round the corner, opposite the fountain.

Desportes: You visit her - I shall meet you there - and we shall all go to the play together.

[*WESENER enters with a large box full of hair combs. MARIE smiles and makes a sign to DESPORTES*]

Wesener: Here we are now, at all prices. These are a hundred Thalers, these fifty, these a hundred and fifty, to suit all tastes.

Desportes: [*Looks at one after the other, and shows the box to MARIE*] Which would you have?

[*MARIE smiles and, as soon as her father is busy getting a comb out, she makes a sign to DESPORTES*]

Wesener: This one makes a good effect, my word, yes.

Desportes: It does indeed. [*Holds it up to MARIE's hair*] Just see the effect against the colour of her hair! Look, Monsieur Wesener, it suits your daughter so well, would you not do me the honour of allowing her to keep it?

Wesener: [*Handing the comb back with a smile*] Forgive me, Monsieur le Baron, that would never do - my daughter has never yet in her life accepted a present from a gentleman.

Marie: [*Her eyes fixed on her knitting*] I would never have been able to wear it anyway, it's too big, with my hair done this way.

Desportes: [*Wrapping it up carefully*] Then I shall send it to my mother.

Wesener: [*Packing up the remainder, mutters to MARIE*] Big or small, you won't get to wear a thing like that in your hair; it's no fashion for the likes of you.

[*MARIE silently gets on with her knitting*]

Desportes: I shall take my leave, Monsieur Wesener! We must settle up before I go back to my regiment.

Wesener: Time enough for that, Monsieur le Baron, time enough for that, perhaps you will be so kind as to honour us with another visit before then..

Desportes: If you will permit me. Adieu, Mademoiselle Marie!

[*He goes out*]

Marie: Pa, what on earth is the matter?

Wesener: What have I done? You know nothing of the world, you silly little girl!

Marie: But I'm sure Monsieur le Baron is a gentleman.

Wesener: Just because he paid you a few pretty compliments and so on - one's as bad as the next, don't try and teach me anything about young military gentlemen. Strutting through all the concerts and cafés, boasting of this and that, and before you know where you are, whissh!, some poor girl has become the talk of the town. Oh, yes, yes, Mademoiselle This is no longer any better than she should be, and Mademoiselle That, I know her too, she wouldn't mind doing it with him, and Mademoiselle The Other..

Marie: Pa! [*Starts to cry*] You are always so coarse!

Wesener: [*Patting her cheek*] Don't mind me, you're the only joy I have, you little silly, that's why I'm so concerned for you.

Marie: If you'd just let me be concerned for myself for once. I'm not a child any more.

Scene 4

Armentières

[*Colonel the COUNT von SPANNHEIM at table with EISENHARDT, his chaplain; the young COUNT de la ROCHE, his cousin, with his TUTOR; Major HARDY, Lieutenant O'MURPHY and other OFFICERS*]

Count: Think we'll get a good troupe of actors here soon?

Hardy: Devoutly to be wished, especially for our younger gentlemen. They say Godeau was to come here. Can we wait?

Tutor: It is indeed not to be denied that the playhouse is a well-nigh indispensable adjunct to a garrison, *c'est-à-dire,* a playhouse where good taste prevails, as, *par exemple,* the French.

Eisenhardt: I really fail to see where the necessity lies.

Spannheim: You only say that, my good Chaplain, because of those two white tabs under your chin. You know, in your heart of hearts, you think otherwise.

Eisenhardt: Forgive me, Colonel. I have never been a hypocrite, and, were hypocrisy a necessary condition of our calling, then I would have thought that Chaplains in the Field might be exempted from it, seeing they have to deal with men in more realistic situations. I am very fond of the theatre; I like a good play, but I do not on that account believe it is a healthy institution for an officer corps.

Hardy: For God's sake, Monsieur le Curé, or Father, or Preacher, or whatever you call yourself, just tell me how many excesses are encouraged or provoked by the theatre. Officers require diversion, do they not ?

Eisenhardt: In moderation, Major! Rather you tell me how many excesses are *not* encouraged by the theatre.

Hardy: Just a lot of talk. In a word, Sir, I maintain... [*Leaning with both elbows on the table*] ...here, that a single play, even the grossest farce, does ten times more good, and I don't mean just among the officers, or the enlisted men, but throughout the whole country, than all the sermons you and your kind have ever preached or are ever likely to preach in your entire lives.

Spannheim: [*With an angry gesture to HARDY*] Major!

Eisenhardt: Were I a man prejudiced in favour of my office, Major, I might be annoyed. However, since I consider neither you, nor most of these gentleman remotely capable, should they live to be a hundred, of judging the actual function of that office, let us leave all that aside. Let us stay with the theatre, and reflect on the astonishing benefits it is supposed to bring to the gentlemen of the corps. Answer me one question, pray, what do you suppose these gentlemen learn at the theatre?

O'Murphy: Oh, come now, does one always have to be instructed? We amuse ourselves, is that not enough?

Eisenhardt: Would to God amusing yourselves was all you did, and *not* learning anything! But you ape the things you see there, and bring unhappiness and disaster on whole families.

Spannheim: My dear, good Chaplain, your zeal does you credit, but, if I might say so, it smacks somewhat of the cloth. What family is ever made unhappy through the action of an officer? A girl sometimes has a child, *bien sur*, probably no better than she should be..

Hardy: A whore always turns out a whore, whatever hands she falls into: if she doesn't turn out a soldier's whore, then it's a preacher's whore.

Eisenhardt: Major, the way you continually drag ministers of religion into your arguments irritates me, since it prevents me from answering you frankly. You may find an element of personal spite in what I say; if I become heated, I promise you, it is because of the subject matter, not because of your insulting and suggestive remarks. The dignity of my office can hardly be affected by witty observations of that sort.

Hardy: Go on then, speak, speak up, hold forth, that's what we're here for. Who's stopping you?

Eisenhardt: What you said just now would have been worthy of the soul of a Nero, a Vlad the Impaler - and even then, might have given rise to some horror at its first utterance. "A whore always turns out a whore." Are you really so well acquainted with the opposite sex?

Hardy: Let us just say, *mon père*, I shall learn nothing of it from you.

Eisenhardt: You doubtless study it closely in "private collections", but allow me to inform you, whores are made, *not* born. The urge is there in all Mankind, but every girl knows she will owe all her future happiness to the application of that urge, and would she sacrifice her future happiness, unless somebody were to trick her out of it?

Hardy: Was I talking about respectable girls?

Eisenhardt: It's the respectable girls who have most to fear from the theatre, where you learn the art of taking away their respectability.

O'Murphy: Who would harbour such wicked thoughts?

Hardy: You've a damned uncivil tongue in your head when you're talking about officers – God damn it, if anyone else talked to me like that... Perhaps, sir, you are of the opinion that we cease to be gentlemen the minute we enter the service?

Eisenhardt: I wish you every happiness in that conviction. And as long as I continue to see kept women and ruined daughters of respectable families, I am unable to retract my opinion.

Hardy: You need a punch in the mouth.

Eisenhardt: [*Rising*] Monsieur, I wear a sword.

Spannheim: Major, please... The Chaplain is not in the wrong, what do you expect of him? The first man who insults him... sit down, Eisenhardt, he will apologise.

[*HARDY goes out*]

Spannheim: But you go a little far all the same. No officer is unaware of what honour demands of him.

Eisenhardt: When he has time to think about it. But when the latest comedies display the grossest infringements, painted in the most glowing colours, of the sacred rights of fathers and families, and the most venomous practices have their stings so removed, that the villain is presented as if he had just fallen from Heaven, does that not discourage, does that not indeed stifle every scruple of conscience that can have been brought from the parental home? The betrayal of a vigilant father, the corruption of a innocent girl – these are the things that the theatre rewards and applauds.

Hardy: [*With other officers in the anteroom, as the door opens for a moment*] Damned preaching fellow..

Spannheim: Let us retire, Eisenhardt, you owe me my revenge at chess – Adjutant, request Major Hardy not to leave his quarters today. Tell him I shall return his sword in person tomorrow morning.

Scene 5

Lille

[*WESENER sitting at dinner with his wife and elder daughter. MARIE enters, very dressed-up*]

Marie: [*Falls on her father's neck*] Oh, Pa!

Wesener: [*Talking with his mouth full*] What is it, what is the matter?

Marie: I can't hide it from you. I went to the theatre. What a thing it is!

[*WESENER pushes his chair back from the table, and turns away*]

Marie: If you'd just seen what I have, you wouldn't be angry, really not, Pa! [*Sitting on his lap*] Dearest Pa, the things that go on, I shan't be able to sleep the whole night I'm that excited. Monsieur le Baron is so kind!

Wesener: Are you saying the Baron took you to the theatre?

Marie: [*Somewhat apprehensively*] Yes, Pa - dearest Pa!

Wesener: [*Pushing her off his lap*] Get away from me, you slut! Are you proposing to become the Baron's mistress?

Marie: [*Her face turned away, half in tears*] I was with the Weyhers - we were standing by the door - [*Stammering*] - and he came and spoke to us.

Wesener: That's right, lie, lie away, lie the ear off the Devil - get out of my sight, you godless little slattern!

Charlotte: I was going to tell Father that's how it would end. They've always had secrets together, her and the Baron.

Marie: [*Crying*] Hold your tongue, can't you!

Charlotte: Not for you I won't. Ordering us around, behaving like that.

Marie: Just watch yourself with that Monsieur Heidevogel of yours. If I behaved as badly as you do..

Wesener: Be quiet the pair of you! [*To MARIE*] Go to your room this minute, nothing to eat for you this evening - wretched girl!

[*MARIE goes out*]

Wesener: And you can hold your tongue too, you're no angel. You imagine nobody knows why Monsieur Heidevogel hangs around the house all the time?

Charlotte: It's all Marie's fault! [*Bursts into tears*] God-forsaken town harlot, she wants to bring decent girls into disrepute because that's how her mind works.

Wesener: [*Violently*] Hold your tongue! Marie has far too good a nature to talk about you, but no, you must be jealous of your own sister; you're not as pretty as she is, so you might at least try to behave a bit better. You should be ashamed! [*To the MAID*] Take it away, I'm not hungry any more.

[*He pushes away his plate and napkin, throws himself into an armchair, and sits there sunk in thought*]

Scene 6

MARIE's room
[*She is sitting on the bed, with the comb in her hand, looking at herself in a mirror, in a dream. As her father enters, she starts and tries to hide the comb*]

Marie: Oh, dear God...

Wesener: Now, now, don't be such a child. [*He paces up and down a few times then sits with her*] Listen, Moll! You know how much I love you, just be honest with me now, it won't do you any harm. Tell me, did the Baron say anything to you about love?

Marie: [*Mysteriously*] Pa! - he is in love with me, it's true. Just look, didn't he give me this comb?

Wesener: What comb?! Damnation! [*Takes the comb*] Didn't I tell you not to..

Marie: But Pa, how could I be so rude as to refuse it? I tell you, he carried on like a madman when I wouldn't accept it. [*Runs over to the cupboard*] And here's some poetry, he wrote it for me. [*Hands him a piece of paper*]

Wesener: [*Reading aloud*]

"Thou, highest object of my purest passion,
I worship Thee in true, undying fashion,
My guarantee of faith and love, you light my way,
Fairest of the fair, new-born with each new day!"

Fairest of the fair my backside!

Marie: No wait, let me show you something else. He gave me a little heart, all set with little stones in a ring. [*She goes over to the cupboard again. Her father looks at the ring without interest*]

Wesener: [*Reading again*] Thou, highest object of my purest passion! [*Puts the poem in his pocket*] His intentions might be honourable. Listen, Marie, I'm telling you, I won't have you accept any more presents from him. I don't care for his giving you so many presents.

Marie: He is so kind-hearted, Pa.

Wesener: And give me the comb, I'll send it back to him. Just do what I say, I know what's good for you. I've lived in this world a lot longer than you, daughter, and you can go to the theatre with him again, only take Madame Weyher with you whenever you do, and don't let anyone see I know of it. Just tell him to keep it a dead secret, say I'd be very angry if I were to hear of it. And above all, no more presents from him, child, for the love of God!

Marie: I know my Pa would never give me bad advice. [*Kisses his hand*] You'll see, I'll follow your advice, to the very letter. And I'll tell you everything afterwards, trust me.

Wesener: Very well then. [*Kisses her*] You might end up a real lady, you little stupid. You never know what's in store for you.

Marie: [*Quieter*] But, Pa - what is poor Monsieur Stolzius going to say?

Wesener: Now you mustn't scare young Stolzius off right away, you understand. - I'll tell you what to write to him. Meantime, sleep tight, Monkeyface.

Marie: [*Kisses his hand*] Good night, Pappuschka! [*When he has gone, she heaves a deep sigh, and goes over to the window, as she loosens her stays*] My heart is so heavy. I think it's going to thunder tonight. If lightning were to strike.. [*Looks up into the sky, her hand on her breast*] Oh, God! have I done something wrong? - - Stolzius - I do still love him - but if I can better myself - and Pa gave me the advice himself - [*Draws the curtains*] - if it strikes, it strikes, I shouldn't be sorry to die. [*Blows out the lamp*]

□

ACT TWO

Scene 1

Armentières

[*HARDY and STOLZIUS are walking by the River Lys*]

Hardy: My dear good fellow, you mustn't allow yourself to be panicked so soon. I know Desportes, he's a naughty boy, after nothing but his own amusement. But that doesn't mean he is after your girl.

Stolzius: But all the talk, Major! The whole town is full of it, and the country too! I could throw myself into the river this minute just thinking about it.

Hardy: [*Taking his arm*] You mustn't take it so to heart, for Heaven's sake. We must all put up with being gossiped about in this world. I am a good friend, you can rely on me, and I would certainly tell you if there were any danger. But there isn't, you're imagining it. Just make sure the wedding can be sometime this winter while we're still quartered here, and if Desportes gives you the slightest trouble, I'm your man; blood will flow, I can promise you. Meanwhile, pay no attention to all the talk, you know quite well the most respectable girls attract the stupidest gossip - it's only natural the young fools who haven't been able to get near them should want their revenge.

Scene 2

The Coffee House

[*EISENHARDT and PIRZEL in the foreground, on a sofa, drinking coffee. In the background, a group of officers is chatting and laughing*]

Eisenhardt: [*To PIRZEL*] It is ridiculous, the way they all swarm round the wretched Stolzius like flies round a honeypot. One tweaks him this way, another nudges him that, someone else takes him for a walk, another takes him for a drive in his carriage, and yet another plays billiards with him - like hounds on the scent! And his cloth business has taken off amazingly, ever since it became known he was going to marry the young lady from Lille who was doing the rounds here lately.

Pirzel: [*Seizing EISENHARDT's hand, energetically*] Why should this be so, Chaplain? Why do people not think? [*Rises and strikes a highly picturesque* *attitude, half turned towards the group at the back*] An absolutely perfect being exists. This absolutely perfect being I can either insult - or not insult.

One of the group: [*Turning*] Is he off again?

Pirzel: [*Eagerly*] If I am able to insult this absolutely perfect being - [*Turning right round to the group*] - then it ceases to be absolutely perfect.

Another of the group: Pirzel, you're right, you're absolutely perfectly right.

Pirzel: [*Turning quickly to the Field Chaplain*] If I am unable to insult it - [*Grabs his hand and remains stock still, deep in thought*]

Two or three of the group: Devil take it, Pirzel, are you talking to us or not?

Pirzel: [*Turning to them, seriously*] My dear comrades, you are worthy creatures of God's creation, I cannot therefore but respect and venerate you.

Someone: Just what we'd advise you to do.

Pirzel: I too am a creature of God's, you cannot therefore but hold me in respect. [*Turning back to EISENHARDT*] Now..

Eisenhardt: Captain, I am of your opinion on every point. Only the question at issue was how people could be persuaded to leave the wretched Stolzius in peace, and not sow jealousy and suspicion in two hearts that just might have made each other happy ever after.

Pirzel: [*Who has meantime sat down, gets up again hastily*] As I had the honour and pleasure of telling you, Chaplain, it is because people just do not think! Thinking, thinking is what Man is, that is my point. [*Takes him by the hand*] Look, here is your hand, but what actually is it, skin, bone, clay?! [*Feels his pulse*] There, there is where it is, the rest is just the scabbard. The sword is there, in the blood, in the blood -

[*PIRZEL looks round suddenly, at the noise caused by HARDY entering shouting*]

Hardy: I've got him! The sacrificial lamb itself! [*Roaring*] Madame Roux! Get the glasses washed right away, and make us some decent punch! He'll be here any minute, and, please, I beg you, behave yourselves with the fellow.

Eisenhardt: [*Leaning forward*] And who, Major, if one may enquire -

Hardy: [*Without looking at him*] Nobody, good friend of mine.

[*The whole group throngs round HARDY*]

One of them: Did you ask him, is the wedding going to be soon?

Hardy: You have to leave it all to me, or you'll be spoiling the whole game. I'm telling you, he trusts me like the prophet Daniel, and if one of you sticks his nose into things, the whole business will be in the shit. He's jealous enough without any help, poor soul, Desportes is giving him a vast deal of

trouble; it's just been all I could do to stop him throwing himself in the
river. My game - just for your information, so you don't go stirring, and
spoiling things for me - is to persuade him to trust the girl - he must know
her well enough by now to know she isn't one of your bullet-proof sort.

Rammler: What are you talking about, I know him better than you, he's got
a good nose on him, believe you me.

Hardy: And you've a better, I note.

Rammler: You think the way to get under his skin is to flatter the girl to him.
Well, you're wrong, I know him better, it's just the opposite. He'll pretend
to believe you, and remember everything, but if we were to make him
suspicious of her, then he'd believe we were being honest with him -

Hardy: Manoeuvres, manoeuvres! Wait till you've been under fire, rednose!
Want to send the man out of his wits? You don't think he's got maggots
enough in his head already? And if he jilts her, or hangs himself - where
does that leave you? A human life is not nothing, am I right, Monsieur
le Curé?

Eisenhardt: I desire no part in your council of war.

Hardy: But you must admit, I'm right.

Pirzel: My worthy brothers and comrades, do ill to no man. A man's life is
an estate wherewith he is endowed, that he has not made for himself. No
man, however, has the right to an estate given him by someone else. Our
life is such an estate -

Hardy: [*Taking him by the hand*] Yes, yes, Pirzel, you are the worthiest fellow
of my whole acquaintance - [*Sits between him and the Chaplain*] - but the
Jesuit - [*Embracing EISENHARDT*] - wouldn't mind being the only cock
on the midden himself.

Rammler: [*Sitting on the other side of the Chaplain, and hissing in his ear*]
Chaplain, just watch me take the Major down a peg.

[*STOLZIUS enters. HARDY jumps to his feet*]

Hardy: Ah, my dear chap! Come in, come in, I've ordered us a good glass of
punch, that wind was going through us like a sword. [*Leads him to a table*]

Stolzius: [*Raising his hat to the others*] Gentlemen, you'll forgive my boldness,
it was at the Major's command.

[*All raise their hats with great politeness, and bow. RAMMLER stands up and
approaches them*]

Rammler: Your most obedient - this is a signal honour.

Stolzius: [*Raising his hat again, somewhat distantly, and sitting next to HARDY*] The wind outside is so keen, I really think we are going to have snow.

Hardy: [*Filling his pipe*] I think so too. You smoke, don't you, Monsieur Stolzius?

Stolzius: Now and then.

Rammler: I can't imagine what's happened to our punch, Hardy - [*Rising*] - what's taking that damned woman so long?

Stolzius: Oh Major, I should be deeply sorry to cause you any inconvenience.

Hardy: Not in the very least, my dear friend. [*Offering him the pipe*] That wind off the river really does one no good whatsoever!

Rammler: [*Sitting at the table with them*] Any news from Lille recently? How is your bride-to-be?

[*HARDY glares at him. RAMMLER remains sitting, with a smile on his face*]

Stolzius: [*In some embarrassment*] At your service, Monsieur - but you must excuse me, I know nothing of any fiancée, I haven't one..

Rammler: Mademoiselle Wesener, from Lille. Is she not your fiancée? Desportes wrote to me, said you were engaged.

Stolzius: In which case, Monsieur Desportes knows more about it than I.

Hardy: [*Smoking*] Rammler never stops nattering away, without a notion of what he says or what he wants.

One of the group: I assure you, Monsieur Stolzius, Desportes is an honest man.

Stolzius: I never doubted it for an instant.

Hardy: You fellows know nothing about Desportes. If anyone knows him, then it must be me. His mother put him under my wing when he joined the regiment, and he's never done anything without consulting me. Still, I can assure you, Monsieur Stolzius, Desportes is a man of feeling, both personal and religious.

Rammler: We were at school together. Never saw a man so at a loss with women in my whole life.

Hardy: That is true, you're right there. The moment a female bestows a kind glance on him, he's incapable of saying a word.

Rammler: [*With studied artlessness*] I really believe - unless I'm gravely mistaken - no, it's true, he still corresponds with her, I read a letter the day he left, to a young woman in Brussels, whom he was astonishingly infatuated with. My guess is he'll be marrying her pretty soon.

One of the Group: What I can't make out is - why does he spend so much time in Lille?

Hardy: God damn it, what has happened to our punch? Madame Roux!!!

Rammler: In Lille? Ah, now, the only person who can explain that is me, I know all his secrets. But they're not for public consumption.

Hardy: [*Irritable*] Out with it, you fool! What are you doing keeping it up your sleeve?

Rammler: [*Laughing*] All I can say is - there's a certain party he's expecting there who he's going to make off with on the quiet.

Stolzius: [*Rising, putting down his pipe*] Gentlemen, allow me to take my leave.

Hardy: [*Startled*] Whatever - my dear friend - the punch will be here any moment.

Stolzius: Please - don't take it amiss - something has just come over me.

Hardy: But what? - The punch will do you good, no, really.

Stolzius: I do not feel at all well, my dear Major. You must forgive me - allow me - but I really cannot stay here a moment longer, or I shall faint -

Hardy: That's the air off the river - or was the tobacco too strong?

Stolzius: Goodbye.

[*STOLZIUS staggers out*]

Hardy: That's done it! Bunch of arseholes!

Rammler: Hahaha! [*Thinks for a space, walking up and down*] You idiots, don't you see, I contrived it all? Chaplain, didn't I tell you?

Eisenhardt: Leave me out of it, if you please.

Hardy: You have the tactical sense of a duck, I'll wring your neck!

Rammler: And I'll break both your arms and legs and throw you out of the window. [*Struts theatrically*] You've no idea the tactics I've got up my sleeve.

Hardy: As full as them as an old fur is full of fleas. You and your contriving make me puke.

Rammler: If I could be bothered to put my mind to it, I'd be more than a match for you and the whole lot of you in this Stolzius business.

Hardy: Listen, Rammler! It's just sad you've come by a little more wit than is good for you, and it'll be the ruin of you. You're like a bottle that's so full, when you turn it upside down, not a drop comes out because they're all jammed in the way of one another. So - move along - and when I get a wife, you have my full permission to sleep with her, *when* you can persuade her to it.

Rammler: [*Walking rapidly up and down*] All right, then, the whole pack of you, see what I'm going to make of that Stolzius!

[*RAMMLER goes out*]

Hardy: That man's so stupid he gives me indigestion! All he can do is ruin other people's plans.

One of the Group: Absolutely. Always has to stick that nose in everywhere.

O'Murphy: He's always got a head full of schemes and intrigues, and imagines other people as incapable of living without them as he is. The other day I asked Reitz, confidentially, could I borrow his spurs for the next day, and blow me if Rammler didn't tread on my heels the whole day, asking me to tell him, for the love of God, what it was we were plotting. He really is a great loss to politics.

Another officer from the group: The other day I stopped in front of a house, to read a letter in the shade. He immediately assumed it had been thrown to me from the house, and was prowling round the place till midnight! There's an old Jew of sixty lives in the house, and Rammler had posted sentries all down the street, to tip him the wink if I went in. I got the whole story from one of the fellows for three livres. Laugh? I thought I'd die!

All: Hahaha!, and he thought there was a pretty girl in the house!

O'Murphy: No, wait, for a really good laugh, we should warn the Jew there's someone with designs on his money.

Hardy: Yes, yes! Brilliant! We'll go there right away. It should be as good as – better than a play! And O'Murphy, you must gradually put the idea in his head that the most beautiful woman in all Armentières lives there, and that Gilbert told you in strictest confidence he was going to see her there tonight.

Scene 3

Lille

[*MARIE in an armchair, crying, a letter in her hand. To her, DESPORTES*]

Desportes: What is the matter, Marie? What is it?

Marie: [*Trying to hide the letter in her pocket*] Ohh!

Desportes: For Heaven's sake, what sort of letter is it that can cause such tears?

Marie: [*More collected*] Just look what that Stolzius has written, as if he had any right... [*In tears again*]

Desportes: [*Reads the letter to himself*] Impertinent ass! Why do you exchange letters with a block like that?

Marie: [*Drying her eyes*] All I can say, Monsieur le Baron, is it's because he proposed to me, and I'm as good as sort of promised to him.

Desportes: He proposed – to you? That jackass! How dare he! I'll answer that letter.

Marie: Oh, yes, Monsieur le Baron! And you can't imagine what I have to put up with from my father, always on at me about how I shouldn't squander my good fortune.

Desportes: Good fortune – with an oaf like that? What are you thinking of, my dearest girl, and what is your father thinking of? I know the fellow and I know his circumstances. Anyway, you weren't meant for a person of that class.

Marie: No, Monsieur le Baron. You're just trying to get round me. Nothing can come of this. These are just empty hopes. Your family would never give their consent.

Desportes: Let me worry about that. Just wait and see. Do you have pen and ink? I want to reply to that lout's letter.

Marie: No, I'll write it myself.

[*She sits at the table, and prepares the pen, while DESPORTES comes to stand at her shoulder*]

Desportes: Then I'll dictate it.

Marie: No, you won't.

[*She begins to write*]

Desportes: [*Reading over her shoulder*] "Monsieur Stolz"... Clodhopper you mean.

[*He dips a pen in the ink and tries to write it in*]

Marie: [*Shielding the paper with her arms*] Baron!

[*They start teasing each other: the moment she lifts her arm, he makes a move as if to write. After a lot of laughter she wipes him across the face with the pen. He goes over to the mirror to wipe it off, while she goes on writing*]

Desportes: I'm still watching you.

[*He comes closer, she threatens him with the pen. Finally she stuffs the paper into her pocket, with him trying to stop her; they wrestle together, she tickles him, he lets out a pitiable shriek, till finally he falls, half out of breath, into the armchair*]

Wesener: [*Entering*] Now then, now then, what is going on? We'll have the whole street here.

Marie: [*Getting her breath back*] Pa, you can't think what sort of letter that coarse creature Stolzius has written me. He calls me unfaithful! Just look! As if we'd been herding pigs together. But he's going to get an answer he won't expect, the great pillock.

Wesener: Show me the letter – oh, whom have we here? Mademoiselle Zipfersaat. I'll read it downstairs in the shop.

[*He goes out. Enter MADEMOISELLE ZIPFERSAAT. MARIE bobs curtseys round her mischievously*]

Marie: Mademoiselle Zipfersaat, I have the honour to introduce to you a Baron who is in love to death with you. Monsieur le Baron, here is the young lady you took such a mortal shine to at the play the other evening.

Mlle Zipfersaat: [*Embarrassed*] I really don't know what's come over you, Moll.

Marie: [*With a deep curtsey*] And now you can declare your undying passion!

[*She runs out, slamming the door behind her. MADEMOISELLE ZIPFERSAAT, deeply embarrassed, goes over to the window. DESPORTES casts a contemptuous glance at her, and listens for MARIE, who opens the door a chink from time to time, finally sticking her head right in.*]

Marie: [*Mockingl*] Well, are you nearly done?

[*DESPORTES tries to get his foot in the door, but MARIE fends him off with a long pin. He cries out and suddenly runs off to get to the next room by another door. MADEMOISELLE ZIPFERSAAT leaves with considerable ill-grace, while shouts and laughter issue from the next room. Wesener's aged MOTHER creeps into the room, spectacles on nose, and sits in the window corner, knitting, as she sings - or rather croaks - in her harsh, old voice*]

Mother:

No one can foretell just how
Young girls, like, dice, will fall:
My little rose from Hennegau
Is purest of them all.

[*Counts her stitches*]

Dear child, though you are smiling now,
There's soon a cross to carry;
My little rose from Hennegau
You'll find a man to marry.

Oh, child of mine, I feel such fears,
To see you laughing gaily;
To think of all the thousand tears
You'll soon be weeping daily.

[*Meanwhile the uproar from the next room continues. The old woman goes in to scold them*]

□

ACT THREE

Scene 1

Armentières. AARON's House

[*RAMMLER enters with several disguised men, whom he places in positions*]

Rammler: [*Speaking to the last of his men*] If anybody goes in, cough - I'll hide below the steps, so I can be right behind him. [*Creeps into hiding under the staircase*]

Aaron: [*Looking out of the window*] Gott, what for ein terrible conspiracy unter mine own haus?!

[*O'MURPHY, muffled in a greatcoat, comes down the alleyway. He stops under the Jew's window, and gives a low whistle. AARON calls down to him quietly*]

Aaron: Iss dot you, gnaediger 'Err?

[*O'MURPHY gives a signal*]

Aaron: I am at vunce opening the door.

[*O'MURPHY goes up the steps. One of the men coughs quietly. RAMMLER creeps after him, unnoticed. The Jew opens the door and both RAMMLER and O'MURPHY go in. The scene changes to AARON's room, in pitch darkness. O'MURPHY and AARON whisper together. RAMMLER tiptoes round them, keeping his distance and darting back every time one of the others makes a movement*]

O'Murphy: He's in here somewhere.

Aaron: Oy weh mir!

O'Murphy: Just keep quiet, he'll do you no harm; just let him do whatever he wants, even if it means tying you up. I'll be back here with the watch in a brace of shakes, and he will pay dearly for his actions. Lie down on the bed.

Aaron: But if he is taking of my life, eh?

O'Murphy: Have no fear, I shall be back in a moment. It's the only way we can apprehend him - *in flagrante*. The watch is standing by below, I only have to call them. Lie down -

[*He goes out. AARON lies on the bed. RAMMLER creeps nearer*]

Aaron: [*Through chattering teeth*] Adonai! Adonai!

Rammler: [*To himself*] I do believe it's a Jewess. [*Aloud, attempting to imitate O'MURPHY's voice*] Ah, my little darling, it's so cold outside. [*Takes off his coat and tunic*] I think we'll be having snow, it's that cold.

[*O'MURPHY bursts in with a whole crowd of officers with lanterns, who collapse with loud laughter. AARON starts up in terror*]

Hardy: Have you gone out of your mind, Rammler? Or are you planning something unnatural with the Jew? Tut tut.

Rammler: [*Stands as if turned to stone. Finally he draws his sword*] I'll cut the lot of you to ribbons!

[*He runs out in disorder. The others only laugh the louder*]

Aaron: [*Stands up*] Ach, I am, Gott he knows, half tot already.

[*The officers run out after RAMMLER, AARON following them*]

Scene 2

STOLZIUS' house.

[*STOLZIUS, his head bandaged, a letter in his hand, is sitting at a table, with a lit lamp on it. His MOTHER stands beside him*]

Mother: [*Suddenly showing temper*] Get off to bed! Godless creature! Just say, just tell me what the matter is. The little tart wasn't good enough for you. What are you doing, whining after that - soldiers' whore!

Stolzius: [*Rising from the table in a towering rage*] Mother!

Mother: Well, what else is she? - you - you too, associating with such creatures.

Stolzius: [*Taking both her hands*] Dear Mother, don't speak ill of her, she is not to blame, that officer turned her head! Remember the way she used to write to me. I think I'll go mad! Such a sweet-hearted girl.

Mother: [*Stamping her foot*] Sweet-hearted slut! Go to bed at once - I mean it! What's to come of all this, how's it going to end? I'll show you, young man, show you I'm your mother!

Stolzius: [*Striking himself on the chest*] Oh, my little Marie - but she isn't that any more, she's not the same any more - [*Jumping up*] - Leave me alone!

Mother: [*In tears*] Where are you off to, you God-forsaken boy?

Stolzius: To the devil who corrupted her - [*Falls onto the bench, his strength gone, hands in the air*] - oh, you will pay for this, you will pay *me* for this. [*Coldly*] One day is much like another, but what today does not bring, tomorrow will, and what comes slowly, comes surely. How does the song go, Mother, if a bird comes every year to take a grain of sand from the mountain, sooner or later it will have taken the whole mountain.

Mother: You're wandering - [*Feels his pulse*] - go to bed, Karl, for God's sake, please. I'll tuck you up all snug, what's to come of all this, Dear God in

Heaven, you're burning with fever... all for a little tart like that..

Stolzius: Sooner or later - sooner or later - - one grain of sand every day, every year ten, twenty, thirty, a thousand... [*His MOTHER tries to lead him out*] Leave me alone, Mother, I'm perfectly all right.

Mother: Come along, now. Don't be silly! [*She takes him out forcibly*] I'm not letting go of you, believe you me.

Scene 3

Lille

Mlle Zipfersaat: [*To the Wesener's MAID*] She's in, but not at home to anyone. Fancy that now, we *have* turned grand.

Maid: She says she's things to do, she's reading - a book.

Mlle Zipfersaat: Just say I've something to tell her she won't want to miss.

[*MARIE enters, carrying a book. She speaks indifferently*]

Marie: Good morning, Mademoiselle Zipfersaat. Why didn't you sit down?

Mlle Zipfersaat: I just came by to tell you that your Monsieur le Baron Desportes ran away this morning.

Marie: [*In great agitation*] What did you say?

Mlle Zipfersaat: It's true, believe me. He still owes my cousin over seven hundred Thalers, and when they got to his quarters, they found everything gone, just a note on the table saying they shouldn't trouble to follow him, because he'd resigned his commission, and was going to enlist with the Austrians.

Marie: [*Rushes out, sobbing and calling*] Pa! Pa!

Wesener: [*Offstage*] What is it?

Marie: Come here, quick! Pa!

Mlle Zipfersaat: Officers and gentlemen. Now you see what they're like - I wanted to tell you from the start.

Wesener: [*Entering*] Well, what is it ? Servant, Mademoiselle Zipfersaat.

Marie: Pa, what are we to do? Desportes has run away.

Wesener: Now, now, now, who's been telling you silly stories?

Marie: He's seven hundred Thalers in debt to her cousin - the silk merchant! - and he left a note on the table saying he wouldn't ever come back to Flanders as long as he lived.

Wesener: [*Very angry*] Just what sort of wicked, evil-minded tittle-tattle is this... [*Striking himself on the chest*] I shall stand surety for the seven hundred Thalers, you understand, Mademoiselle? And for as much again, if needed. I've been doing business with the Baron's family for more than thirty years; it's all the fault of God-forsaken, malicious..

Mlle Zipfersaat: Well, if you're prepared to take it on yourself to retrieve the Baron's reputation, it will be a great relief to my cousin.

Wesener: I shall go with you right away. [*Looking for his hat*] I shall stop the mouths of those who have the gall to bring the good name of my house into disrepute, you follow me.

Marie: But Pa...! [*Impatient*] Oh, I wish I'd never set eyes on him!

[*WESENER and MADEMOISELLE ZIPFERSAAT leave. MARIE throws herself into the armchair; after sitting for a little, sunk in thought, she calls out nervously*]

Marie: Lotte! Lotte!

Charlotte: [*Entering*] Well? What is it? Shouting like that.

Marie: [*Going to her, stroking her face*] Lottie - my darling Lottie!

Charlotte: Gracious Heavens, wonders will never cease.

Marie: You are my dearest, darling Charlotte.

Charlotte: You want to borrow money again.

Marie: I'll do anything you want.

Charlotte: Oh, rubbish! - I've no time for all this.

[*Makes to go. MARIE holds on to her*]

Marie: No, listen - just for a moment - can you help me write a letter?

Charlotte: I've no time.

Marie: Only a few lines - I'll give you my beads, they cost six livres.

Charlotte: Who to, then?

Marie: [*Ashamed*] Stolzius.

Charlotte: [*Starts to laugh*] Guilty conscience?

Marie: [*Half in tears*] Oh, don't -

Charlotte: [*Sitting at the table*] Well, what do you want to say? - you know I hate writing.

Marie: My hands are shaking - put at the top... or all on one line, oh, whatever you like - "My dear, dear friend"..

Charlotte: "...dear friend"..

Marie: "In your last, you had occasion to reproach me, since my honour has been attacked.."

Charlotte: "... attacked"..

Marie: "However, not all my expressions are to be weighted in the balance, but have regard to the heart that"... Oh - how shall I put it?

Charlotte: How am I supposed to know?

Marie: Tell me the word I want.

Charlotte: I'd know, wouldn't I?

Marie: ..."That my heart, and"...

[*She begins to cry, flings herself into the armchair. CHARLOTTE looks and laughs*]

Charlotte: Well, what am I supposed to put?

Marie: [*In tears*] Oh, whatever you want.

Charlotte: [*Writes and reads it out*] ..."that my heart is not so changeable as you suppose"..

Marie: [*Jumps up and reads over her shoulder*] Yes, that's it, that is it. [*Embracing her*] Dear, dearest old Lottie!

Charlotte: All right then, let me finish.

[*MARIE walks up and down a few times, then suddenly runs up to CHARLOTTE, tears the paper from her and rips it into pieces*]

Charlotte: You slut! – just when I'd got it right – you are a real slattern!

Marie: Slattern yourself!

Charlotte: [*Threatens her with the inkwell*] You –

Marie: You're only trying to make things worse, when I'm wretched enough anyway.

Charlotte: Silly slut, then, why did you tear it up, it was in my best writing!

Marie: [*Quite heated*] Don't you raise your voice at me.

Charlotte: [*Half in tears as well*] Why did you tear it up, then?

Marie: Am I supposed to tell him lies?

[*MARIE begins to cry violently, and throws herself into a chair, burying her face in the cushions. WESENER comes in. MARIE looks up and runs to him, flinging her arms round his neck, trembling*]

Marie: Pa! Oh dear Pa! What's happening – for Heaven's sake, tell, tell.

Wesener: Don't be such a goose, he's not vanished into thin air. You're behaving like a fool.

Marie: But if he's left..

Wesener: If he has left, then he will have to come back. Even if you have lost your senses, you're not going to make me lose mine. I've haven't been dealing with his family since yesterday, they aren't going to want anything like this hanging over them. Send over to our lawyer, see if he's in; I want that note of credit I signed for Desportes certified, along with a copy of the promise of marriage, and I'll send the whole lot to his parents.

Marie: Oh, Pa! Dear Pa! I'll run over this minute myself and fetch him.

[*She runs out at breakneck speed*]

Wesener: God forgive me, that girl could take the heart out of an emperor. But that is no sort of behaviour of Monsieur le Baron's, I'll see he gets proper treatment from his father, just you see. - Where has the girl got to? [*He goes out after MARIE*]

Scene 4

Armentières. A promenade by the disused city moat

Eisenhardt: [*Strolling with PIRZEL*] Lieutenant O'Murphy intends spending his leave in Lille, what do you suppose that implies? He has no family there, that I know of.

Pirzel: Nor is he the brightest man in the world. Grasshopper mind. The Colonel, now, there's a man, if you will..

Eisenhardt: [*Aside*] (Oh dear, oh dear, metaphysics again...) [*Aloud*] In my opinion, if you want to understand men, you have to start by understanding women.

[*PIRZEL shakes his head*]

Eisenhardt: [*Aside*] (He has too little of what the others have too much of! Oh, the soldiers' art and the dreadful celibacy it entails. What gargoyles it makes of men!)

Pirzel: Women, you think? Tantamount to beginning with sheep. No, no, as far as men go - [*Lays a finger to his nose*]

Eisenhardt: [*Aside*] (He will philosophise me to death!) [*Aloud*] It has come to my notice, that in the last few weeks one has not been able to set foot outside the house without seeing a soldier kissing a girl.

Pirzel: That comes from people not being able to think.

Eisenhardt: Do you not sometimes find thought interfering with your military duties?

Pirzel: Not in the very least, all that is entirely mechanical. As for the others, they don't think either, just see pretty girls swimming in front of their eyes all the time.

Eisenhardt: That must have odd results in battle. An entire regiment under such delusions should perform great deeds.

Pirzel: All entirely mechanical.

Eisenhardt: Yes, but you also march mechanically. The Prussian bullets must have given you a rude awakening.

[*They walk on*]

Scene 5

Lille. O'MURPHY's quarters

O'Murphy: [*Sketching, looks up*] Who is it? [*Looking hard at the newcomer, then getting up*] Stolzius?

Stolzius: Yes, sir.

O'Murphy: Where in Hell have you sprung from? Why are you in uniform? [*Turns him round*] You've changed - you're so thin, so pale. You could have told me a hundred times you were Stolzius, I'd never have believed you.

Stolzius: It'll be the moustache does that, sir. I heard your honour required a batman, and as the Colonel thought me reliable, he gave me permission at least to help you raise a few recruits, and to act as your servant.

O'Murphy: Bravo! Excellent fellow! It's good you're in your sovereign's service. What's the point of civilian life, anyway? Boring. And you have the advantage of having a bit extra to live on decently, so you can make your way in the world. I'll look after you, never fear. Come along, I'll see about quarters for you right away; you can spend the winter with me, I'll see you alright with the Colonel.

Stolzius: So long as I pay someone to do guard duty for me, no one will be able to touch me.

[*They go out*]

Scene 6

Lille

Madame Wesener: It's a disgrace the way you carry on with him. I can't see it's any different from the way you carried on with young Desportes.

Marie: Well, what else am I to do, Ma - he is Desporte's best friend, and the only one we can get news of him from?

Charlotte: You'd be very different with him if he didn't give you all those presents.

Marie: Am I supposed to throw his presents back in his face? I have to be polite, don't I - he's the only one who's still in touch with Desportes. If I scare him off, there'll be a fine mess; he gets hold of all the letters Pa writes to Desportes' father, and stops them reaching him, you know that.

Madame Wesener: Once and for all, I will not have you going out with that man!

Marie: Then come with us, Ma! He has ordered a horse and carriage! Is he to send them back?

Madame Wesener: Nothing to do with me.

Marie: Then you come, Lottie. Oh, what am I to do? Ma, you don't know how much I put up with for your sake.

Charlotte: And pert with it.

Marie: Just be quiet, you!

Charlotte: [*Sotto voce*] Soldiers' whore!

Marie: [*Behaving as if she had not heard, continues doing herself up at the mirror*] If we offend Lieutenant O'Murphy, we'll have no one but ourselves to blame.

Charlotte: [*Aloud, as she runs out of the room*] Soldiers' whore!

Marie: [*Turning round*] You see, Ma! [*Clasps her hands*]

Madame Wesener: You ask for it, the way you behave.

[*Enter O'MURPHY. MARIE assumes a cheerful expression and goes up to him with the greatest good humour and friendliness*]

Marie: Your servant, Monsieur O'Murphy! Did you sleep well?

O'Murphy: Incomparably, dearest Mademoiselle! I witnessed last night's fireworks all over again in my dreams.

Marie: They were really lovely.

O'Murphy: They must have been to earn your approbation.

Marie: Oh, I'm no expert in such things, I'm just repeating what I heard you say.

[*He kisses her hand, and she drops a deep curtsey*]

Marie: You find us all in disorder; my mother will be ready in a moment.

O'Murphy: Madame Wesener is coming with us?

Madame Wesener: [*Drily*] And why not? Is there no room for me?

O'Murphy: Of course, I shall stand up behind, and my servant can go ahead on foot.

Marie: Do you know, your servant bears a strong resemblance to someone I used to know? He wanted to marry me too.

O'Murphy: And you gave him his marching orders?

Marie: He had his own back on me.

O'Murphy: I suppose Desportes was to blame for that as well, was he? Shall we?

[*Offers his arm to her; she bobs and points to her mother. O'MURPHY gives his arm to MADAME WESENER. MARIE follows them out*]

Scene 7

Philippeville

[*DESPORTES, half-undressed, alone in a green room, writing a letter by lamplight, muttering to himself as he writes*]

Desportes: I must try to keep her greased, or there'll be no end to this correspondence, and sooner or later, my father is bound to get hold of one of the letters. [*Reading the letter*] "Your good father is angry with me for making him wait so long for his money. Please pacify him until I can find an opportunity to explain things to my own father, and persuade him to give his consent, my darling, to your being mine for ever. You can imagine I am in the greatest apprehension he may already have intercepted several of your letters, since I see from your last you must have written a good few I have not received. Which could ruin everything for us. So I beg you not to write to me again until I have sent you a new address where I can safely receive your letters." [*Seals the letter*] If only O'Murphy could be made to fall properly in love with her, she might perhaps forget me! If I have to make my adorable Marie a happy woman, he must never stir from my side: he can be her *cavaliere servente*, her *cicisbeo*, her gallant!

[*Walks up and down a few times, lost in thought, then goes out*]

Scene 8

Lille. The house of the COUNTESS de la ROCHE

Countess: [*Looking at her watch; to a LACKEY*] Has my son not come home yet?
Lackey: No, madame.
Countess: Give me the front-door key and go to bed. I shall let him in myself. How is Mademoiselle Catherine?
Lackey: She has had a high fever all evening.
Countess: Go in to her again and find out whether the governess is still awake. Just tell her I shall not be going to bed, but will come and relieve her at one o'clock.

[*The LACKEY goes out*]

Countess: Must a child cause his mother pain and grief till her dying day? If he were not my only son, had he not inherited my sensitive nature..

[*Someone knocks. The COUNTESS goes out, to re-enter with the young COUNT*]

Count: My dear mother, where is the man on duty? Damned fellows, if it wasn't so late, I'd go to the watch this minute and have them thrash the living daylights out of him.

Countess: Calm down, my son. What if I were to be as hasty with you as you are with that perfectly innocent man?

Count: But this is really insufferable!

Countess: I sent him to bed. It's not enough that the poor man has to keep an eye on you the whole day long, must he give up his night's rest on your account as well? I really believe you want to make me think of servants as animals.

Count: [*Kissing her hand*] Dear, dear Mother!

Countess: I must have a serious talk with you, young man! You are starting to cloud my days. You know I have never restricted you, I have always shared in your affairs, as a friend, never as a mother. Why do you now begin to keep your love affairs secret from me? You never made secrets of all your youthful indiscretions, because I was a woman myself, and always knew how to give the best advice. But now... [*Looking at him with severity*] You're becoming something of a rake, my son.

Count: [*In tears, kissing her hand*] Dearest mother, I swear I have no secrets from you. You saw me after supper with Mademoiselle Wesener, and, both from the hour, and the way we were talking together, jumped to conclusions. Marie Wesener is a nice girl and that is that.

Countess: I have no wish to know any more about it. The moment you think you have to conceal things from me... Only remember, from now on the consequences of your actions are your own responsibility. Your fiancée has relatives here, and you must be aware that Mademoiselle Wesener does not enjoy the best of reputations, not her fault, I am given to believe, it would seem the poor child was imposed upon.

Count: [*Kneeling*] That is just it, mother! Her misfortune - if you only knew the circumstances, I must tell you everything, I feel the very liveliest interest in the girl's fate - and yet - how easy it was to impose on her, such an ingenuous, open, innocent heart! - I am appalled, Mama, that she should have fallen into such hands.

Countess: My son, leave compassion to me. Listen to my advice, and follow it. For the sake of your peace of mind, do not see her again, leave the city, go to your fiancée, Mademoiselle Anklam - and rest assured, you are leaving behind the most affectionate friend Marie Wesener possesses – myself. Believe me – [*She embraces him*] – believe me, my heart is no harder than your own, but compassion is less dangerous for me. Will you promise me all that?

Count: [*Looking at her for a long while*] Very well, Mother, I promise – just a word before I leave. She is a very unfortunate girl – that much is certain.

Countess: Calm, calm. [*Patting his cheek*] I believe you, you don't have to convince me.

Count: [*Rising and kissing her hand*] I know you..

[*They go out*]

Scene 9

Lille

Marie: Just leave me alone, Ma! I am going to torment him.

Madame Wesener: Rubbish! Lieutenant O'Murphy has forgotten all about you, not been here for three days, and everybody saying he's fallen for that little Madame Duval, over in the rue de Bruxelles.

Marie: You can't believe how pleasant the young Count is to me.

Madame Wesener: Get along! anyway, *he's* supposed to be promised already. A Mademoiselle Anklam.

Marie: All the same, I can tease O'Murphy about him. The Count's coming here again after supper this evening. If O'Murphy could just see us together when he's out with his Madame Duval!

[*Enter the COUNTESS's SERVANT*]

Servant: Madame la Comtesse de la Roche wishes to inquire whether you are at home.

Marie: [*In the greatest confusion*] Oh, Lord, the Count's mother! – Pray inform her – Ma, tell me, what is he to say to her? [*MADAME WESENER is on the point of leaving*] Tell her it will be a great honour for us – Ma! Mama! Say something.

Madame Wesener: Lost your tongue then – at last? Say it will be a great honour for us – though we are in dreadful disorder here.

Marie: No, no, wait, I will go down to the carriage myself.

[*She goes downstairs with the SERVANT. MADAME WESENER goes out*]

Scene 10

[*MARIE re-enters with the COUNTESS de la ROCHE*]

Marie: You must forgive us, Madame, everything's in such a fankle.

Countess: My dear child, you have no need to stand on the slightest ceremony on my account. [*Takes her by the hand, and sits with her on the sofa*] I want you to regard me as your friend. [*Kisses her*] I assure you, I have the very greatest interest in everything that affects you.

Marie: [*Wiping her eyes*] I do not know what I can have done to deserve such a great favour.

Countess: Don't speak of favours, I beg you. I am delighted we are alone, I have a great, great deal to say to you, which is weighing on my heart, and a number of questions to ask you as well. [*MARIE listens attentively, an expression of joy on her face*] My angel child, I love you – I cannot restrain myself from demonstrating my affection. [*MARIE kisses the COUNTESS's hand ardently*] Your whole air has something so frank, so attractive about it, that makes your misfortune doubly painful to me. You know, do you not, my dear, *new* friend, that there is some – much talk of you in town?

Marie: There are wicked tongues everywhere.

Countess: Virtuous tongues are talking of you as well. You are unfortunate; but you can comfort yourself in the knowledge that your misfortune was not incurred through any vicious fault of yours. Your only fault was that you did not know the world well enough, that you were unaware of the disparity between different classes, and that you had read *Pamela*, the most dangerous book it is possible for a young person of your station to read.

Marie: But I know nothing at all of this book.

Countess: Oh?... well, in that case you have placed far too much trust in the speeches of young gentlemen.

Marie: Only one of them, and I do not know yet know for certain whether he has deserted me or no.

Countess: But pray tell me, my dear, how in all the world did you come to seek a husband so much above your station? Did you think your personal charms could carry you further than other girls of your class? Oh, my dear, but that is just what should have made you act more discreetly. Beauty is never a means to a good marriage. A pretty face must fear a thousand admirers, a thousand flower-strewn dangers, a thousand ruthless seducers, and not one single friend !

Marie: Oh, Madame, I am very well aware how plain I am.

Countess: No false modesty! You are beautiful, Heaven has punished you with that. You saw no necessity to cultivate other more amiable qualities, People above your station in life made promises to you. You could see no obstacles to rising higher, you despised your acquaintance, you shrank from hard work, you behaved with contempt to young men of your own class, and were disliked for it. Poor child! How happy you could have made some honest citizen, if only you had brought to those perfect features, and charming figure, a decent and charitable spirit – you might have been the emulation of your peers and the admiration of your betters! But you wanted to be the envy of your peers and the equal of your betters. Child, what were you thinking of? For what miserable fortune were you prepared to sacrifice all your advantages? To become the wife of a man who would be loathed and despised by his whole family on your account? To hazard all your happiness, all your honour, your life itself on the turn of so wretched a card? What were you thinking of, what were your parents thinking of? Poor misguided child, betrayed by vanity! [*Pressing her to her breast*] I would have given my heart's blood for it not to have happened!

Marie: [*In tears, over the COUNTESS's hand*] But he loved me!

Countess: The love of an officer, Marie! – a man inured to every sort of licentiousness and infidelity, who ceases to be a good soldier the moment he becomes a true lover. He takes an oath to his sovereign not to marry, and accepts money for doing so. Did you think you were the only woman in the world who could keep him faithful – despite the anger of his parents, despite the pride of his family, despite his oath, despite his character, despite the whole world? It is as if you wanted to overturn society; and now in the face of defeat, you imagine you can involve other young men in the same way. You do not understand that what you take for love in them is no more than sympathy, perhaps something worse. [*MARIE falls on her knees, hiding her face in the COUNTESS's lap, sobbing*] Unfortunate girl, make up your mind! There is still time to draw back from the abyss, I will wager my life to keep you from it! Give up your plans for my son, he is engaged; Mademoiselle Anklam is possessor of both his hand and heart. But come under my protection, your honour has suffered a considerable blow, and this is the only way to restore it. You will become my companion, and resolve not to set eyes on any male person for a year. You shall assist me in the upbringing of my daughter - come now, we will go at once to your mother, and ask her permission for you to come with me.

Marie: [*Raising her head pathetically from the COUNTESS's lap*] Madame - it is too late.

Countess: [*Hurriedly*] It is never too late to act sensibly. I shall settle a thousand Thalers on you, as a dowry, I know your parents have debts.

Marie: [*Still on her knees, half falling over backwards, with clasped hands*] Oh, Madame, permit me to think the matter over - to put it all to my mother.

Countess: Very well, dear child, do the best you can - you will find recreation enough with me, I shall have you instructed in drawing, dancing and singing.

Marie: [*Falling forward*] Oh, Madame, you are too good, much too good!

Countess: I must go - I am too deeply affected to meet your mother with any composure. [*She leaves hurriedly, turning at the door, to look at MARIE, who is still lying on her face*] Adieu, child!

□

ACT FOUR

Scene 1

Lille

O'Murphy: To be perfectly candid, Stolzius, if Desportes doesn't marry the girl, I'll have her myself. I am mortally in love with her. I've already had to look for distraction, you know, with La Duval... and then I really do not like that business with the young Count at all, particularly since his mother has taken the girl into her house, but never mind all that - it's no good, I can't rid myself of the infatuation.

Stolzius: Do you not hear from Monsieur Desportes any more then?

O'Murphy: Oh, he writes. His father wanted to force him into a marriage lately - locked him up for a fortnight on bread and water - - [*Rapping his forehead*] And to think, she was walking in the moonlight with me only the other day, complaining of her troubles, how, when her thoughts became too much for her, she would sometimes jump up in the middle of the night, and go looking for a knife. [*STOLZIUS shivers*] I asked her if she loved me too. She said she loved me best of all, including her friends and relations, and pressed my hand to her breast. [*STOLZIUS turns his face away to the wall*] And when I asked her to kiss me, she replied, if it lay in her power to make me happy she would certainly do so. But I would have to have Desportes' permission first. [*Grips STOLZIUS roughly*] If Desportes leaves her stranded, damn me, man, if I don't marry her myself!

Stolzius: [*Very coldly*] She is said to be a great favourite of Madame la Comtesse.

O'Murphy: If only I knew how I might get to speak to her alone. You go and find out.

Scene 2

Armentières

[*DESPORTES in jail. HARDY with him*]

Desportes: I am really delighted to be in prison: no one will find me here.

Hardy: I'll see our friends keep their mouths shut.

Desportes: Above all, see O'Murphy doesn't find out.

Hardy: Or Rammler.

Desportes: Damn fool!

Hardy: Such a good friend of yours, says he was at pains to join the regiment a couple of weeks after you, so as to leave you the seniority. Oh, listen, we played another trick on him the other day, you'll love this. You know Gilbert is quartered on a hunchbacked, cross-eyed old widow, all on account of her pretty niece. Well, every week he gives a musical evening at the house, just to please her. One evening, Rammler gets drunk, and thinking the niece lived in the house, off he creeps off during dinner, and in his usual Machiavellian fashion, snuck into the widow's bedroom, strips off and gets into bed. Meanwhile the widow, who is also not stone-cold sober, takes the lantern and walks her niece home, close by. We all assume Rammler's gone home too. The aunt comes back, goes up to her room, is just getting into bed, when she finds Monsieur in it, in no little confusion. He makes an excuse about not knowing the geography of the house, she packs him off downstairs without more ado, and we laugh ourselves into fits. Rammler implored her – and all of us – not to breathe a word to anyone. But you know Gilbert, he has to go and tell the niece the whole story, and she put it into her old aunt's head that Rammler was mortally in love with her. He actually rented a room in the house, perhaps to try and persuade her not to bruit the thing abroad. So now you have the exquisite spectacle of him and the old trollop keeping company, with her simpering and ogling, twisting her wrinkled, lop-sided old face up at him – it is to die – and him with his great red hawk-nose, and his eyes popping out of his head with terror – a sight not to be contemplated without danger of explosion!

Desportes: When they let me out, Gilbert will be my first port of call. My mother is writing to the Colonel; the regiment can underwrite my debts.

Scene 3

Lille

[*The garden of the COUNTESS de la ROCHE. The COUNTESS walking along an avenue*]

Countess: What's the matter with the girl? Going down into the garden so late? I fear, I very much fear, it is an assignation. She is distracted. She draws distractedly, she plays her harp distractedly, she doesn't listen to a word her tutor says to her, she... wait, did I hear someone? – yes, she is in the summerhouse – someone is answering her from the road. [*Listens at the garden hedge. From offstage come voices*]

O'Murphy: How can you forget all your friends, everything you used to care for?

Marie: Oh, dear Monsieur O'Murphy, I'm sorry and more for it, but it has to be. I assure you, Madame la Comtesse is the sweetest lady to walk God's earth.

O'Murphy: But you might as well be a nun, don't you want to go into the world any more? You know Desportes has written, he's inconsolable, he wants to know where you are and why you don't answer his letters.

Marie: Does he? – Oh, I must forget him, tell him that, and he must forget me too.

O'Murphy: But whyever? – Cruel girl! Is it fair to treat your friends in this way?

Marie: There is no other way – oh, dear Lord, I hear someone down in the garden. Adieu, adieu – just don't deceive yourself..

[*She climbs down*]

Countess: Well, Marie – secret meetings!

Marie: [*Terrified*] Oh, Madame! – a cousin of mine – he has only just discovered where I am –

Countess: [*Grave*] I heard every word.

Marie: [*Half on her knees*] Oh, God, then forgive me, just this once.

Countess: Girl, you are like that sapling in the evening breeze, changing with every breath of wind. Do you imagine you can continue to conduct your affair with Monsieur Desportes under my very nose, by exploiting your acquaintance with his best friend? Had I suspected anything of the kind, I would never have taken you in.

Marie: Forgive me this once!

Countess: I can never forgive you as long as you continue to behave in opposition to your own best interests. Go!

[*MARIE goes out in despair*]

Countess: In all conscience, am I right to rob the girl of her romantic inclinations? What pleasures does life hold if our imagination is not engaged? Eating, drinking, filling one's time with trivialities – without the stimulus of imagination, all these are nothing more than ways of waiting for death. She feels this too, but without education, she can only aspire to a superficial excitement. If I could only find a way to combine what she feels with what I know, so that she might be led by conviction rather than by compulsion, by love of duty and not by fear of censure..

Scene 4

Armentières

[*DESPORTES in prison*]

Desportes: [*Pacing up and down with a letter in his hand*] If she comes to see me here, my whole future will be in ruins - the laughing-stock of all my friends. [*Sits and writes*] - - And God help me if my father ever sees her.

Scene 5

Lille. WESENER's house

Wesener: [*To the COUNTESS's servant*] Marie run away! This will kill me. [*He runs out, followed by the SERVANT*]

Scene 6

O'MURPHY's quarters

O'Murphy: Then let's get after her, God damn it! I'm to blame for the whole thing. Run over and fetch up the horses!

Stolzius: [*Standing there pale and dishevelled*] If only we knew where she..

O'Murphy: To Armentières! To young Desportes! Where else would she go? [*Exeunt*]

Scene 7

WESENER's house

[*Madame WESENER and CHARLOTTE, cloaked*]

Wesener: [*Entering*] It's no good. She is nowhere to be found. [*Beating his hands*] She may have drowned herself - God knows where!

Charlotte: But, Father, who can tell, if..

Wesener: Nowhere. The Countess's people came back, and it's not a half-hour since she was missed. Someone rode after her out of every gate of the town - she can't have vanished off the face of the earth.

Scene 8

Philippeville

Desportes' gamekeeper: [*With a letter from his master*] Well, here's a fine beast headed straight for the snare. She wrote to my master, she was coming direct to him here in Philippeville – [*Looks at the letter*] – on foot. Oh, poor child. I'll have something to cheer you up.

Scene 9

Armentières

[*A musical entertainment in the house of MADAME BISCHOF. Various ladies form a circle around the orchestra, amongthem MADAME and MADEMOISELLE BISCHOF, her aunt. Several OFFICERS, among them HARDY, RAMMLER, O'MURPHY, DESPORTES and GILBERT are standing in conversation with the ladies*]

Mlle Bischof: [*To RAMMLER*] And have you moved in here as well, Monsieur Rammler?

[*RAMMLER bows in silent acknowledgement, and goes scarlet*]

Hardy: He's got lodgings on the second floor, right opposite your aunt's bedroom.

Mlle Bischof: So I had heard. I wish my aunt every good fortune.

Madame Bischof: [*Screwing up her eyes and laughing coquettishly*] Hehehehe... Monsieur Rammler would not have moved in, if Monsieur Gilbert had not recommended my house. Furthermore, I behave to all my gentlemen in such a way they can have nothing to complain of.

Mlle Bischof: That I can well believe; you'll all get on swimmingly.

Gilbert: All the same, there's something going on between them, or Rammler would never have moved in in the first place.

Madame Bischof: Oh, indeed? [*Holds her fan in front of her face*] Teeheehee! Since when then, do you suppose, Monsieur Gilbert, since when?

Hardy: Since your last musical entertainment, if you must know, Madame.

Rammler: [*Pulling at HARDY's sleeve*] Hardy!

Madame Bischof: [*Tapping HARDY with her fan*] Naughty Major! Do you have to blurt out all one's secrets?

Rammler: Madame! I really have no idea how we come to be so familiar, I really must ask you not..

Madame Bischof: [*Angrily*] Indeed, Monsieur? Putting on airs now, are we?

- you should be deeply honoured that a lady of my age and stage should condescend towards you - and in any case, just look at you, who do you think you are, young man?

Officers: Rammler! - Tuts, Rammler! - Not quite the article - treating Madame like that..

Rammler: Madame, hold your tongue, or I'll break both your arms and legs and chuck you out of the window.

Madame Bischof: [*Rising, furious*] Monsieur, come here - [*Grabbing his arm*] - come here this minute! You dare try to lay one single finger on me.

Officers: There's a challenge, Rammler! Up to bed with you!

Madame Bischof: If you get any further above yourself, I shall throw you out of the house, neck and crop, I hope you realise that. Nor is it all that far to your Commanding Officer. [*She begins to weep*] The impertinence of it - in my own house - the insolent lout -

Mlle Bischof: Now, now, aunt, Monsieur Rammler never meant it like that. He was only joking, calm down now.

Gilbert: Rammler, show a bit of sense, really. What sort of honour is it that insults an old woman?

Rammler: The whole pack of you can..!

[*He dashes out*]

O'Murphy: There's a thing now, eh, Desportes? What's the matter? You're not amused?

Desportes: I've got these terrible pains in my chest. This catarrh will kill me.

O'Murphy: It's Rammler who's going to kill me, he's insane! Did you see him? Black with rage? Anyone else would have gone along with the old trout for the joke.

[*STOLZIUS enters and tweaks at O'MURPHY's sleeve*]

O'Murphy: What is it?

Stolzius: I'm sorry to disturb you, Lieutenant, but would you come into the next room for a moment?

O'Murphy: What's the matter? Oh, have you found out something? [*STOLZIUS shakes his head*] Well, then - [*Comes forward a few paces*] - you can tell me here.

Stolzius: Last night the rats got at the lace on your best shirt, and when I opened the wardrobe, two or three jumped out at me.

O'Murphy: What does it matter? - Have some poison put down.

Stolzius: I'd need a sealed chit from you.

O'Murphy: [*With irritation*] Why do you have to come for it just now?

Stolzius: I've no time later, Lieutenant: I must be at the quarter-master's when they're giving out the equipment.

O'Murphy: Oh, very well. Here's my watch, use the seal for the chit.

[*STOLZIUS leaves - O'MURPHY rejoins the company. An overture strikes up*]

Desportes: [*Who has retreated to a corner of the room, aside*] I see her image in front of me incessantly - God damn it, get rid of the thought! What can I do about it, if she turns into a tart? What else did she expect?

[*He returns to the main company, coughing badly. O'MURPHY stuffs a stick of liqourice into his mouth. He gives a start. O'MURPHY laughs*]

Scene 10

Lille. WESENER's house

Madame Wesener: [*To the COUNTESS's SERVANT*] What did you say? Madame la Comtesse has had to take to her bed, she's so affected? Please convey our humble duty to Madame la Comtesse and her daughter. My husband has gone to Armentieres, because they wanted to seal up everything in the house, on account of the bail, and he had heard Monsieur Desportes was supposed to have returned to his regiment. And we're very sorry indeed that Madame la Comtesse should have taken our misfortunes so much to heart.

Scene 11

Armentières

Stolzius: [*Pacing in front of a pharmacy. It is raining*] What are you shivering for? - My tongue is so weak, I know I shan't be able to get a single word out. He'll look at me - but then, those who suffer wrong are always afraid: only wrongdoers show confidence! - - Who knows where she is now, starving under some hedge? Get in with you, Stolzius. If the poison's not for him, then it's for me! And after all, it is the only thing I really want - - [*Goes inside*]

☐

ACT FIVE

Scene 1

On the road to Armentières

Wesener: [*Resting*] No, no, I can't take the stagecoach, even if I have to stay here for life. My poor child had cost me enough, even before she went to the Countess. Always having to be the grand lady; her mother and sister mustn't be allowed to suffer for it. My business has been at a standstill these last two years - who knows what Desportes is doing with her, who knows what he is doing with all of us - she is sure to be with him. We must just trust in God -

[*He remains deep in thought*]

Scene 2

On another road to Armentières

[*MARIE resting under a tree. She takes a piece of dry bread from her pocket*]

Marie: I always thought you could live on bread and water alone. [*Gnaws at the bread*] If only I had a drop of the wine I used to throw out of the window so often - which I used to rinse my hands in for the heat - [*Stomach cramps*] - Oh, the pain - - I've become a beggar - [*Looks at the crust*] I can't eat it, God knows. Better to starve. [*Throws the crust away and drags herself up*] I'll crawl as far as I can, and if I die, so much the better.

Scene 3

O'MURPHY's quarters in Armentières

[*He is sitting with DESPORTES, both of them half-dressed, at a small table, laid for a meal. STOLZIUS is handing out napkins*]

Desportes: I'm telling you, she was a whore from the start - she only made herself agreeable to me because I gave her things. She got me into such debt you wouldn't believe, I'd have been done out of house and home if I'd gone on with the game any longer. Anyway, *mon frère*, before I know where I am, I get a letter from the girl, saying she's coming to see me at home! Imagine the hulaballoo, if my father had got a sight of her!

[*STOLZIUS switches the napkins around, to have an opportunity of remaining in the room*]

Desportes: What to do? I wrote to my gamekeeper, telling him to intercept her and keep her under house arrest in my quarters till I could home myself, and take her back to the regiment in secret. I mean, the moment my father clapped eyes on her, she'd be as good as dead. Well, my man is a strong, well-set-up fellow, and time will be hanging heavy on their hands, alone in that room. What he makes of the situation, we'll have to wait and see. [*Laughs scornfully*] I gave him to understand, discreetly, that it wouldn't be disagreeable to me.

O'Murphy: Really, Desportes, that is hardly honourable.

Desportes: Honourable, what's that got to do with anything? - She's taken care of, isn't she? If the gamekeeper marries her? A girl of that class -

O'Murphy: The Countess had a lot of time for her. And actually, *mon frère*, I might have married her myself if the young Count hadn't put his oar in... - oh, yes, Marie had a lot of time for him as well.

Desportes: Well, you'd have had a fine piece of goods hanging round your neck!

[*STOLZIUS leaves*]

O'Murphy: [*Calling after him*] Bring Monsieur his wine-soup right away - I don't know how the Count got to know her, I think she may even have wanted to make me jealous. I'd been in a vile mood with her for a while. None of which would have mattered a jot, only I called in once, it was in the worst of the hot weather, and she just had on a thin, really thin muslin shift, with those wonderful legs showing through it. Every time she walked across the room, the dress fluttered out behind her - I tell you, I'd have traded my hopes of salvation to have her. Anyway, imagine, that very day ill-luck brings the Count there, and you know the vanity of the girl. She carried on like a lunatic with him, either to vex me, or because girls of that sort never know how to behave when people like us take the trouble to be nice to them.

[*STOLZIUS comes in, places a dish in front of DESPORTES, and, deathly pale, goes to stand behind his chair*]

O'Murphy: I was a red-hot poker plunged into ice-cold water.

[*DESPORTES sets greedily to his soup*]

O'Murhy: I lost every shred of my appetite for her. From that moment, I could never be bothered with her. Particularly when I heard she had run away from the Countess.

Desportes: [*Eating*] Why are we still talking about the little slut? Do me the favour, *mon frère*, never to mention her to me again. Just thinking of her bores the life out of me!

[*Pushes his plate aside*]

Stolzius: [*Behind DESPORTES's chair, his face distorted*] Indeed?

[*O'MURPHY and DESPORTES look at him in astonishment*]

Desportes: [*Clutching at his chest*] I've got cramps - Oooh!

[*O'MURPHY stares grimly at STOLZIUS, saying nothing*]

Desportes: [*Throws himself into an armchair*] Oh!! - [*Twisted in agony*] O'Murphy! -

Stolzius: [*Bounding forward, he seizes DESPORTES by the ear, pulling his face up to his own. In a terrible voice*] Marie! -Marie! - Marie! -

[*O'MURPHY takes his sword, to run him through*]

Stolzius: [*Turning round, completely controlled, and grasping the sword*] Don't trouble yourself. It is too late. I am glad to die if I can take him with me.

O'Murphy: [*Leaving the sword in STOLZIUS' hand, he rushes out*] Help! - Help! - Help!

Desportes: I've been poisoned.

Stolzius: Yes, seducer, you have been - and by me, Stolzius, the man whose bride you whored. She was going to marry me. If you can't live without ruining girls, why must you turn to the ones who can't deal with you, who believe the first word they hear? - Oh, Marie, my angel, you are avenged! For this, God cannot damn me! [*Sinks down dead*]

Desportes: Help!

[*After a few convulsions he also dies*]

Scene 4

WESENER walking by the river Lys at dusk, sunk in thought

[*A cloaked female figure tugs at his sleeve*]

Wesener: Leave me alone - I have no liking for that sort of thing.

Woman: [*Barely audible*] For God's sake, Monsieur, spare me a little.

Wesener: To the workhouse with you. There's whores enough round here, if you were all to get something, there'd be no end to it.

Woman: Monsieur, I've been three days now without a bite to eat; would you be good enough to go with me to an inn where I can get a sip of wine?

Wesener: You filthy little slut! Aren't you ashamed to suggest such a thing to a respectable man? Run after your soldiers.

[*The WOMAN goes out without speaking*]

Wesener: Such a deep sigh, it seemed she gave. My heart misgives me. [*Takes out his purse*] Who knows, my daughter might be begging for charity at this very moment – and where? [*Runs after her, offering her a coin*] There is something for you – but see you turn over a new leaf.

Woman: [*Starting to cry*] Oh, God! [*Taking the money and almost collapsing in a faint*] What good will money be to me!

Wesener: [*Turning round and wiping his eyes, he speaks to her in great agitation*] Where do you come from?

Woman: I mustn't tell you that – but I was the daughter of a respectable man.

Wesener: Was your father a dealer in fancy goods? [*The WOMAN says nothing*] Your father was a respectable man? – Get up, I will take you to my house. [*Tries to help her up*] Does your father live anywhere near Lille – [*At the last word she falls on his neck. WESENER cries out*] My daughter!

Marie: Father!

[*The two of them collapse half-dead on the ground. A crowd collects around them, and takes them out*]

Scene 5

[*Original version*]

Colonel SPANNHEIM's lodging

Countess: Have you set eyes on the unhappy pair? I have not yet plucked up the courage. The mere sight would kill me.

Spannheim: It put ten years on me. And that something of that sort should happen in my corps! But – madame! – what can one do? The hand of Heaven hangs over certain people – I'll pay the man's debts and another thousand Thalers in compensation on top. Then I shall see what I can do through the villain's father for the family he has ruined – morally and financially.

Countess: You are a good man! Accept in these tears my warmest gratitude. I did all I could to save the wretched victim – she did not want to be saved.

Spannheim: The only advice I can think of is for her to enter a convent. Her honour is lost, no man could marry her without shame - even though she maintains she repelled the advances of that damned gamekeeper. Were I the governor, Madame, the fellow would hang -

Countess: The kindest, best of creatures! [*In tears*] I promise you I had begun to entertain the highest hopes of her!

Spannheim: Your tears do you honour, Madame. They affect me as well. Why, indeed, should I not shed tears, I who have to fight and die for my country, having to see a citizen of it and his whole family plunged into irreparable ruin by one of my own subordinates?

Countess: The consequences of enforced celibacy among soldiers.

Spannheim: [*Shrugs*] How can it be helped? You know, of course, Madame, even Homer said a good husband makes a bad soldier.

Countess: A particular thought has always struck me whenever I have read the story of Andromeda. I see the army as the monster to whom from time to time an unfortunate female must be sacrificed so that the other husbands and daughters may be spared.

Spannheim: I have thought the same for a long time, even if I have never expressed it so elegantly. The King should hire people of that sort, who would sacrifice themselves in that manner to the most extreme needs of his servants, for, in brief, the need is common to all Mankind - these people would not be women, who could weaken the resolve of the men, but concubines, who would follow the wars wherever they went, and wherever necessary, like the women of Media under Cyrus the Great, would stiffen up the courage of the troops.

Countess: Oh, if only someone could be found to promote the idea at court! It would benefit the whole nation.

Spannheim: And millions of unfortunates less. A society, shaken by our disorderliness, would flourish anew, and peace, universal prosperity, calm and happiness would join in a single embrace.

Scene 5

[*Second version, prepared by Lenz for publication at the suggestion of Herder, who felt that the COUNTESS's attitude was not correct for a woman of her rank, and that the COLONEL's own reactions could be modified. The versions diverge at the COLONEL's words "How can it be helped?"*]

Spannheim: [*Shrugs*] How can it be helped? Even Homer, as I recall, said that a good husband made a bad soldier. And experience confirms the view. - A particular thought has always struck me whenever I have read the story of Andromeda. I see the army as the monster to whom from time to time an unfortunate female must be sacrificed so that the other husbands and daughters may be spared.

Countess: How do you mean?

Spannheim: The King should endow a nursery of soldiers' women; they would of course have to understand that they must give up all the exalted ideas young women entertain about permanent relationships.

Countess: I doubt whether any woman of honour could agree to that.

Spannheim: They would need to be Amazons. As I see it, one noble idea balances the other. The delicacy of female honour against the thought of martyrdom for the state.

Countess: How little men know of women's hearts and desires!

Spannheim: Of course, the King would have to do his best to make this condition both brilliant and creditable. In exchange, he would economise on the expense of recruiting, and any chidren would belong to him. If only someone could be found to promote the idea at court! I could find sources of support for him. The defenders of the nation would become the good fortune of the nation; the external security of the land would not annihilate the internal; and in a society, until now thrown by us into disorder, peace, prosperity and happiness would join in a single embrace.

THE END

THE NEW MENOZA

OR

HISTORY OF TANDI PRINCE OF QUMBA

A COMEDY

TRANSLATED BY

MEREDITH OAKES

This translation was commissioned by the Gate Theatre, London and first performed at the Edinburgh International Festival, 1993

DRAMATIS PERSONAE

Herr von Biederling, residing in Naumburg
Frau von Biederling
Wilhelmine, their daughter
Prince Tandi
Count Chameleon
Donna Diana, a Spanish countess
Babet, her nurse
Herr von Zopf, a Tyrolean nobleman
Herr Zierau, bachelor of arts
The Mayor, his father
Master Beza, from Schulpforta[1]
Servants, etc.

Scene: here and there

ACKNOWLEDGMENTS
Bettina Munzer, with thanks

---

[1] A famous old school in Saxony

ACT ONE

Scene 1
Naumburg
[FRAU v. BIEDERLING and WILHELMINE. HERR v. BIEDERLING enters with the PRINCE]
Herr v. Biederling: Here, wife! I've brought you a guest. We lodged together at a house in Dresden, and since Naumburg is on his way to France I suggested to him that he put up here with me and take a look at my gardens.
Frau v. Biederling: Delighted I'm sure –
Herr v. Biederling: This isn't one of your everyday birds of passage, wife! he's a prince from another world, wanting to acquaint himself with our world here in Europe and see if it deserves its fame. So we for our part must do our best to give a good impression of ourselves. Think of it, to be known as far afield as Qumba, a land not even on the map.
Frau v. Biederling: What unexpected good fortune for this house, a traveller of such exalted birth –
Prince: Enough, friends, if you please [*Sits*], my birth is not exalted. If you desire to make my stay agreeable, treat me as you would your son.
Herr v. Biederling: We should like that as well [*Sits near him*]. Sit down, wife! Mina! you may sit with us. What was I about to say, since you have desired us to be plain with you – Peter! are the bags in? – yes, will you but tell me something of your journey, Prince, and your adventures, you've come a good long way for your purpose, you must assuredly have a tale to tell. And pray how did you fall into the notion of travelling?
Prince: It would be as well to rule a land and its inhabitants and not know human nature, as for a master of arithmetic to turn horse trainer.
Herr v. Biederling: Or our Master Beza at the college, ha ha ha. But tell me, who was it told you of Europe, when egad! we who are so clever here in Europe know not a single thing concerning the kingdom of Qumba.
Prince: I was born in Europe. A company of Jesuit missionaries took me to Asia.
Herr v. Biederling: But hey! hey! how did you become prince, then, if I may ask?

Prince: In the way of the world, where luck dances uphill and down, I became a page, and then a royal page, was adopted, was made heir to the throne, then down I fell again, and rolled right down the mountainside and all the way to hell! ha! ha! ha!

Herr v. Biederling: Mercy upon us! how? how?

Prince: The story is wearisome and vile. A woman, the queen –

Herr v. Biederling: What is it with women, it's what I always say, women are the cause of all the world's misfortune. Oh I beg you, go on.

Prince: She'd have had me defile her husband's marriage bed, a man who loved me more than he loved himself, and his wife more than both of us. When I refused, I was placed in the Pyramid Tower, where all who attack the person of the king or queen die a lingering death. The fear that I would reveal the truth made her more cruel with every day that passed. Each day they took me one floor higher, to a narrower place of confinement, until upon the thirtieth day I stood at a giddy vertiginous height, within walls so close they scarce offered a foothold to a statue. But after one night in that dreadful abode, I resolved to throw myself down –

Frau v. Biederling: Throw yourself down – oh dear!

Prince: Imagine an abyss shrouded in a clammy mist that hid all living things from sight. In that fearsome blue emptiness I could see nothing but myself, and the movement I made in jumping. I jumped –

Frau v. Biederling: Daughter!

Herr v. Biederling: [*Jumps up*] What is it, addlehead! Mina! What is it?

[*They try to revive WILHELMINE, who lies fainting*]

Prince: Perhaps I am to blame – oh my ill-timed stupid tale!

Herr v. Biederling: To bed, to bed with her. Oh gemini, women are such creatures! Creatures of paper, that's what you are!

Scene 2

Dresden

[*COUNT CHAMELEON. His STEWARD*]

Count: Within four months you must hand over the buildings ready and in good order, never mind the expense, so that Captain Biederling can take up his lease before the planting season.

Steward: And is it not permitted to ask what he will pay?

Count: You need not concern yourself with that, he and I have agreed, there's no going back on it.

Steward: But if I were to bring you one who'd pay more than the Captain will pay: forgive me, sir! I'll speak plainly, I know what's to be made of the property by a person who understands what he's about, and the proof of it is, I have a public house in Naumburg and the wine-growing and the thingummy, everything - no man can pay you what I can, sir. It's no object.

Count: Once and for all.

Steward: And if I were to bid you twice as much.

Count: He's bid me nothing, just so you may know it and leave me in peace. He is my good friend, and I have had him choose from among my estates the one most fit for his agricultural schemes.

Steward: Agricultural schemes indeed, he'll ruin himself, the honest Captain, he'll need a purse of quite a different length -

Count: Keep silence and obey.

Steward: Oh heavens! the Countess.

[*DONNA DIANA enters, dishevelled. The COUNT leaps up*]

Count: Lady, what is it?

Donna Diana: It's my life, it isn't safe.

Count: What do you want? Where have you come from?

Donna Diana: [*Throws herself into a chair*] Gustav! Curse you Count! what sort of men are your servants?

Count: Gustav - attacked your life?

Donna Diana: If I'd not had the antidote about me, it would have been over by this time.

Count: Where is he?

Donna Diana: In the world. Gone with coach and horses. We were two hours from Dresden, he made me chocolate, and when I proved too slow in dying, he seized me by the throat and -

Count: Poison -

Donna Diana: I screamed. The landlord came. He said he was trying to make me spit it up. And when the landlord went to summon help, he leaped away and was gone-

Count: People, after him at once - [*He exits with STEWARD*]

Donna Diana: If I'd once in my life harmed the fellow! Nothing could vex me more than his desiring to kill me with no reason. If I'd but known it, I'd have put out his eyes in his sleep, or given him arsenic, that he might have held it against me. But not to have deserved it - I think I shall go mad.

Scene 3

Naumburg

[*HERR v. BIEDERLING. FRAU v. BIEDERLING*]

Frau v. Biederling: What then? when you take up your lease? Are you unhinged? what are we to do with a strange man?

Herr v. Biederling: But he's married, what do you mean? And sick, he desires to take the waters here; may we not concede him that small favour, when he offers me up his house and home for eighteen years?

Frau v. Biederling: Offers you up a rope to hang yourself. The last remains of what we've carried off from the shipwreck of the war and of your schemes will be consumed, we shall sink, I see it all in advance.

Herr v. Biederling: You're forever seeing it all, seeing – the bright side. You madam wives should keep indoors with what you see. See to it that there's something on the table we can eat, me and my dear Kalmuck prince, and leave the rest to God and your husband. But observe, a few weeks hence I shall have another guest whom I'm sure you're not expecting – and you'd better receive him properly, so prepare – from Trieste.

Frau v. Biederling: Herr von Zopf?

Herr v. Biederling: You've hit the nail on the head. – Now why this amazement, why those staring eyes? He's an honest man, I've talked with him concerning the whole matter –

Frau v. Biederling: Unnatural father!

Herr v. Biederling: He but waits in Dresden for the silkworm eggs that he will bring for me, and then –

Frau v. Biederling: Yes, if it's silkworms, but no, it's only your children. Oh heaven! would you punish me so highly, that not until now do I see what manner of a man I have in my husband.

Herr v. Biederling: Will you hold your tongue, fool! Not another word concerning that affair, I insist upon it. It is all past and gone, and none of women's business.

Frau v. Biederling: So I'm not to trouble myself concerning my own son?

Herr v. Biederling: Mercy now, your son, can you bring him back to life with your trouble? Since it has pleased God to afflict us with misfortune –

Frau v. Biederling: Since it has pleased Herr von Biederling, child –murderer! What did I say, when you entrusted him to Zopf, what did I say? But you were resolved to cast him upon the waters, you were resolved to be rid of him – Out of my sight, villain! You are my husband no more –

Herr v. Biederling: What? Tarantara, thunder and lightning, 'sdeath, what do you want from me? have you gone mad? Yes, that was the question indeed, whom to entrust our son to, if it had been a very gypsy I'd have thanked him. Called to the field, and not a crust to eat, it does you much honour to scold about it, when we were crying ourselves half blind with hunger - yes now she howls when you tread on her toe; now that she sits in the lap of plenty she'd far rather forget where the shoe pinched.

Frau v. Biederling: Is there an unhappier woman under the sun than I?

[*She exits*]

Herr v. Biederling: Under the moon, you mean.

[*He exits*]

Scene 4

[*WILHELMINE sits on a sofa, deep in thought. The PRINCE enters; some moments pass before she becomes aware of his presence and stands up, a little alarmed*]

Prince: [*After greeting her respectfully*] Pardon me - I thought your parents were with you.

[*Exit. WILHELMINE, having made him a deep curtsey, resumes her former attitude*]

Scene 5

[*COUNT CHAMELEON, HERR v. BIEDERLING, FRAU v. BIEDERLING*]

Herr v. Biederling: But why have you not brought your wife with you?

Count: My wife? - Who has said to you that I am married?

Herr v. Biederling: All Dresden - forgive me, but the Spanish countess who came back with you -

Count: Is the wife of my brother.

Herr v. Biederling: The wife of your brother, who remains in Spain... oh! oh! oh! but think of that, think of that! and I was entirely certain that - but please don't take it amiss -

Count: He too will return to this country at the earliest opportunity -

Frau v. Biederling: And how comes it that we so unexpectedly have the pleasure -

Count: I have had to alter my plans, madam! I've not come here to take the waters, an unforeseen blow of fate has forced me to seek out this place of sanctuary.

Herr v. Biederling: Not a duel, is it - God forbid.

Count: It is. I am pursued by the law, and my poor health prevents me from leaving the country. I have shot Count Erzleben.

Frau v. Biederling: Mercy on us!

Herr v. Biederling: So no one must discover he is here, do you understand! not even our daughter, not a human soul, I think we shall lodge him in the summerhouse, there's a stove in it after all, he can make himself up a little fire, seeing that the nights are still cold, and I myself shall take all his meals to him - no, confound it, that will be observed, I shall sup with him in the summerhouse at all times, as if doing it for my own pleasure, and you must always bring the food to me there, dear Susy, will you?

Count: What sort of people are in the house?

Herr v. Biederling: None, but for an Indian prince, the charmingest politest man in the world, he means to be in Paris this summer.

Count: Surely he'd not give me away.

Herr v. Biederling: No, assuredly not. Should I tell him? But then I'm expecting another good friend, likewise my good friend to be sure, though I wish he - he's a great admirer of the Jesuits do you see, devil knows what he sees in them - no, no, as I have said, you will stay in the summerhouse and that is what we shall do, otherwise Zopf may surprise us.

Count: Your leasehold will be ready at the soonest, I have letters from my steward, the buildings will soon have a roof on. Several enclosures have already been fenced about to serve as nurseries, should you desire to try out your mulberry trees.

Herr v. Biederling: Oh your humble servant, your humble servant! Zopf is to bring me several hundred. But wife, see to it that the summerhouse is clean - shall we go and view it? our bedroom opens directly upon the garden, do you see, and it isn't five steps away - You couldn't be safer in Abraham's bosom.

Scene 6

Garden

[*The PRINCE carves a name upon a tree*]

Prince: Now grow - [*He kisses it*] grow - but enough [*Is about to leave, looks around*], the tree gives me thanks. You have good reason. [*He exits*]

Scene 7

The PRINCE's room

[*He sits at a table covered in books, with a map in front of him. ZIERAU, bachelor of arts, enters*]

Zierau: Your most obedient servant, Your Highness!

Prince: And yours, sir. Who are you?

Zierau: A bachelor of arts from Wittenberg, although for the last three years I have offered up to the muses and graces in Leipzig.

Prince: What brings you to me?

Zierau: Curiosity and esteem at once. I have heard of the noble intention with which you undertook your journey, desiring to acquaint yourself with the customs of Europe's most enlightened nations, and to transplant them to your native soil.

Prince: That is not my intention. By all means, if the customs be good – do sit down –

Zierau: Forgive me! The improvement of every art, every discipline and every condition has been for several thousand years the united endeavour of all our best minds, it seems that now we draw near to the moment when we shall at last gather the fruits of those Herculean labours, and it is much to be hoped that the world's most remote nations should come and share in our harvest.

Prince: Indeed!

Zierau: Especially since now in Germany the light of *belles lettres* has dawned, holding up a torch to the profound and fundamental sciences where our forefathers made their discoveries, and only now, so to speak, acquainting us with all our riches, so that we may stand amazed at the splendid mines and lodes which they have hollowed out, and forge into coin the gold which they have dug.

Prince: Indeed!

Zierau: For almost a century now, we have been able to point to names that we may boldly set against the greatest geniuses from among our neighbours, and all of them writing to procure the improvement and refinement of our nation, a Besser, a Gellert, a Rabner, Dusch, Schlegel, Uz, Weisse, Jacobi, but chief among them the immortal Wieland who towers, so to speak, above them all, *ut inter ignes luna minores*, most particularly in the latest treatise which he has written and with which he seems likely to have crowned all his works, *The Golden Mirror*, I don't know if you've heard of it, in my view he should have called it *The Diamond Mirror*.

Prince: What is the book about?

Zierau: What is it about? Indeed it is most comprehensive, it is about the improvement of the state, it is about the establishment of a perfect state whose citizens, if I may express it so, surpass in their grace all our extremest fictions concerning the angels.

Prince: So, and where are these people to be found?

Zierau: Where? aha, in Hofrat Wieland's book. If you like, I shall instantly bring you a copy.

Prince: Please don't put yourself to any inconvenience, I prefer to take people as they are, without the grace, rather than proceeding from the point of some well-sharpened quill. - Do you have something else there?

Zierau: In deepest humility I desired Your Highness to - Herr Wieland dedicated his *Golden Mirror* to the Emperor of Cochin China and I, emboldened by so eminent an example [*Takes out a manuscript*], I have a work in hand which I hope will contribute no less to the common good, the title is quite modest, but I intend to exceed the expectations of my readers: *True Alchemy, or, Disinterested Suggestions Concerning the Bringing Back of the Golden Age, or The Golden Age, an Attempt to...* I'm not yet of one mind with myself.

[*He hands the PRINCE the manuscript, smiling*]

Prince: And in what do your suggestions consist, if I may ask? will you give me a glimpse of your secrets!

Zierau: What they consist in? - I shall tell you. After all, if it's to be dedicated to you, well then. [*Looks about. Then, rather quietly*] If, first of all, education is put upon a different footing, with worthy and learned men in the schools and academies, if the clergy are selected from among none but deserving, discerning people, neither bigots nor fanatics, nor mere gluttons and sluggards, if courts of justice are experienced, skilled at law, old, venerable, if the difference in condition is not birth nor money, but only merit, if the sovereign, if his counsellors -

Prince: Enough, enough, with all these ifs of yours the world will not get better nor worse by so much as a hair, dear respected Herr Author. Forgive me if I recall to your mind that pope who also, with a book of alchemy by another of your persuasion [*Gives him back the manuscript*] – and good day to you.

Zierau: Either he's bereft of culture, or the poor Prince is overwrought and belongs *aux petites maisons*[2].

[*He exits*]

☐

---

[2]*Les petites-maisons* was the name of a lunatic asylum in Paris

ACT TWO

Scene 1

Night, moonlight in the garden

[*WILHELMINE carves at the tree with a pen-knife*]

Wilhelmine: How do I dare. Whoever carved my name [*Stands looking at it*] – I shall remove it all, but no, if it is the Prince's hand – yes it is his, certainly it is his, no other hand could form such bold, noble characters. [*She binds ivy around the tree*] So! grow now and flourish together, and if he should return to see – oh I shall die of shame. I must – [*Falls upon the tree and tries to peel away the bark*] Oh heaven preserve me! who comes there! [*Runs off*]

[*The PRINCE enters*]

Prince: You stars! dancing in your joyful course over my torment! only you, kind moon – but don't pity me. I suffer willingly. Never have I been so happy as now in this agony. Infinite vault of the heavens! you must be my roof tonight. And still too confining for my restless heart.[*He throws himself down in the shrubbery*]

[*COUNT CHAMELEON enters with WILHELMINE, who resists him*]

Count: Whither away? – Now you know all my story. But come into the summerhouse if still you will not believe me.

Wilhelmine: I believe you.

Count: So please allow us to enjoy the evening here in the garden, sweet girl, it is excessively inviting.

Wilhelmine: I must go –

Count: Captivating shyness! do you hold it so dangerous to walk in the garden with a sick man? all I desire is to restore my health. You can restore it, a word from you, a breath.

Wilhelmine: My mother –

Count: Let her come out here and look for you, I spurn your mistrust, do you see.

Wilhelmine: Will you let me go?

Count: No I shan't let you go, my goddess, until you've allowed me to worship you. [*Kneels*]

Wilhelmine: Help!

Count: Cruel one! will you not even permit me this rapture – [*Puts his arms* *around her knees and presses his face to them*] I'd not take a kingdom for this moment, I am happy, I am a god –

[*PRINCE enters with drawn sword*]

Prince: Villain! [*COUNT runs away*] Fräulein! I must not leave you, or I'd after the knave and spill that hot blood of his. But first I'll take you to your door. [*Both leave in silence*]

Scene 2

The summerhouse

[*The PRINCE. The COUNT sitting by the stove*]

Prince: Here – I know you – but be you who you are, I demand a reckoning – if you listen to your conscience you should welcome death. Where is your sword?

Count: [*Stands*] What do you want with me?

Prince: A reckoning, a reckoning, a bloody reckoning. Take up your sword. Perhaps you'll have the same good fortune with that as formerly with pistols.

Count: What have I done?

Prince: Blasphemously defiled a beauty from which even dragons and monsters would reverently keep apart. You are worse than a beast of prey, let's see if you'll also have their courage in standing over your kill.

Count: Am I supposed to fight you, I don't know you.

Prince: Do you need to know names in order to fight? [*Breaks off a branch*] Then I'll christen you a rogue with this. You scum! you're not fit to stain my sword.

Scene 3

Immenhof

[*DONNA DIANA. BABET, her nurse, has a letter in her hand*]

Donna Diana: Read it out, I say.

Babet: I beg you on my knees, allow me to burn it unread.

Donna Diana: I shall hear it at once, even if I should die on the spot.

Babet: If you were a woman like any other, but with your great heart, with your noble blood, nobler than your origins.

Donna Diana: What mean you, nobler than my origins - witch! will you speak with disrespect of my father.

Babet: He's dead.

Donna Diana: Dead - silence! - is he dead? - hold your tongue, don't say another word. [*Pause*] By what means did he die?

Babet: May I?

Donna Diana: Say by what means.

Babet: Alas!

Donna Diana: [*Hits her*] What means? or I'll stab you through the heart! What means?

[*DONNA DIANA looks for a dagger*]

Babet: Poison.

Donna Diana: Poison? That is sad - that is wicked - abominable. Indeed, poison - well then, read me the letter.

Babet: How you abuse me. But if I read it, it will be the end of me.

Donna Diana: Fool! Damned witch!

Babet: You'll kill me.

Donna Diana: What difference does it make, if another such bag should die? One pair of bellows more or less in the world - for what more are we, nurse? I hold myself no better than my dog, so long as I'm a woman. We should put breeches on, and drag men by the hair through their own blood.

Babet: Oh heavens! What makes your animal spirits so keen? Though I've seen you more docile.

Donna Diana: We leave everything to men, those dogs that lick our hands and bite our throats out as we sleep. A woman must not be docile, or she's a whore who'll be stretched over a barrel. Read, witch! or I'll tear off your skin, the only possession that still remains to you, and sell it to be made into a drum.

Babet: [*Reads*] "If your heart, vile creature, is still capable of fear, for all other sentiments have long since departed from it - Your father has died of poison. If your husband is still with you, tell him that I shall cause the law to require from him my jewellery which you stole from me. As for you, I hereby tear the veil from your eyes and inform you of who you are. Not my daughter, I could not bear a parricide - you were - exchanged -"

Donna Diana: No more - no more - merciful God and saints of heaven! Let one catch one's breath. [*Throws herself down on a chair. BABET tries to creep away, but she jumps up and pulls her to the ground*] Damned hobgoblin! Will you read?
Babet: [*Reads*] "Your mother is.."
Donna Diana: Read.
Babet: Alas.
Donna Diana: If you faint, I'll stab you, I'll carve up the pair of us.
Babet: Alas.
Donna Diana: Who is she?
Babet: Me.
Donna Diana: So die! for then I'll be a matricide as well. No. [*Lifts her*] Come! [*Flings herself upon her and weeps loudly*] No, mother! Mother! [*Kisses her hand*] Forgive me God, as I forgive you for being my mother. [*Falls to her knees before her*] Here I kneel and pay you homage, yes I am your daughter, and if you desire to beat me with rods, speak, and I shall cut thorns for you to do it. Scourge me, I poisoned my father, I must do penance.
Babet: The future will reveal all. Let me go to bed, I can't endure any more.

Scene 4
Naumburg. The PRINCE's room
[*HERR v. BIEDERLING. PRINCE TANDI*]
Prince: I shall travel, but not onward, back! I have seen and heard enough. It repels me.
Herr v. Biederling: To Qumba?
Prince: To Qumba, so I may breathe again. I believed myself to be in a world where I should meet finer people than at home, great, all-encompassing, active in many spheres - I shall suffocate.
Herr v. Biederling: Would you like to have a vein opened?
Prince: Do you jest?
Herr v. Biederling: No truly - your blood is so full, I thought that in this passionate speech you might have done yourself a mischief -
Prince: It's in your mire that I shall suffocate - I'll continue no longer - upon my soul I shan't. This, the enlightened world! Wherever one sniffs, indolence, vile impotent greed, babbling death where there should be fire

and life, empty prattle where there should be action - this, the pinnacle of the world! Fie, for shame!

Herr v. Biederling: Oh permit me - you are still young, and then you're foreign, and assuredly you'll settle and fit yourself to our customs. It's of no consequence.

Prince: [*Seizes him by the hand*] Without prejudice, my friend! in cold blood - I fear to continue lest my discontent should well up as before - but do you know the cause, why your customs make foreigners so amazed? - Oh I'd rather not speak, I know not where to start, I'll leave you in peace and travel home, innocently to enjoy my patrimonial possessions, rule my country and surround it with walls so that any man who comes there from Europe may first be quarantined, before he spreads his plague-blisters among my subjects.

Herr v. Biederling: [*Pulling back his shoulders*] That is astonishingly harsh, dearest Prince! I so much desired that you should take home a good opinion of us. You have not yet concerned yourself with our farming and horticulture. But there it is, you are young still, you should stay with us ten or twenty years at least, until you learn how we have excelled all other nations in the whole world.

Prince: In deception, in roguery.

Herr v. Biederling: Hey what? what? I was speaking of agriculture and you -

Prince: [*Seizes his hand*] All granted - but I shall cultivate my heart first, then my surroundings - all granted, you know an astonishing amount, but you do nothing - I don't speak of you, you are the hardest-working European that I know.

Herr v. Biederling: Yes I should think so, I'm busy all day.

Prince: I meant that you know nothing; all the knowledge which you have patched together remains on the surface of your understanding and becomes artifice, not feeling, you don't know the meaning of the word; what you call feeling is hidden lust, what you call virtue is face-painting that you smear over your brutality. You are wonderfully beautiful masks, stuffed with vices and basenesses like a fox's pelt with straw, heart and stomach one seeks in vain, by the twelfth year of age they're gone to the devil.

Herr v. Biederling: [*Very hotly*] Farewell - [*Comes back*] If you'd like to take a walk with me out beyond the gate, on my land - but if you have things to do, then don't discommode yourself on my account -

Prince: I shall leave tonight.

Herr v. Biederling: So may God protect and keep - but what have we done to harm you?

Prince: Would you give me your daughter to take with me? As I go back to Qumba.

Herr v. Biederling: To take with you? My daughter? What do you mean?

Prince: I wish to make your daughter my wife.

Herr v. Biederling: Tra la la, one two three and it's done. No, sir, with us it's not so quick!

Prince: Offer her the kingdom of Qumba as wedding gift, my mother the queen is dead, here is the letter, and my father, who has learned of my innocence through my friend Alkaln, will resign throne and realm to me as soon as I return.

Herr v. Biederling: I should heartily like to believe it all, but –

Prince: I shall swear an oath by almighty God.

Herr v. Biederling: Yes an oath – what sort of oath –

Prince: Truly you're a European!

Herr v. Biederling: And even if all this were agreeable to – but to let my daughter travel so far away?

Prince: Is it the father that speaks in you?

Herr v. Biederling: Ah sir! it's – call it what you will.

Prince: To spare the father, then, I'll stay five years in Europe. Your daughter may accompany me wherever she desires to go, I'll no longer travel far, but only choose a few more viewing points from which to gaze upon the nations through the spying glass of reason.

Herr v. Biederling: Certainly! which can't be done in Naumburg. So what you'll need to do, is to go about the region hereabouts, informing yourself somewhat concerning the management of the land; would you like to come to Rosenheim tomorrow, that's the name of the leasehold which his lordship the Count has made me a present of, as good as made me a present anyhow –

Prince: The Count should not make you a present of anything, I'll buy it as your property.

Herr v. Biederling: Buy it – my dear Prince –

Prince: And let it be an early wedding gift.

Herr v. Biederling: But by offering I'll offend him.

Prince: You'd do well to offend him, he has offended you, he has abused the laws of hospitality, which should be holier to us than sacred worship.

Herr v. Biederling: How so? how so? that's only as it seems to you, he intended nothing ill towards my daughter.

Prince: Europeans, you are not fathers! when you wilfully make children of yourselves. He who besmirches a father's child attacks his very life.

Herr v. Biederling: Devil take him, if he should make me angry.

Prince: Speak of my proposal with your daughter, then say if you'd be strong enough to have your child leave your arms forever after five years. If not, I shall envelop myself in my sorrow and travel home without complaint.

Scene 5

[*COUNT CHAMELEON, FRAU v. BIEDERLING*]

Count: So you see, madam! how matters stand. My entire peace of mind, my entire happiness in your hands. – Oh fate, why was I not struck down by my enemy's bullet!

Frau v. Biederling: Indeed I shan't pretend, Count! that I don't foresee endless difficulties in it, not only on my side, I assure you, for as to what I can do in this affair –

Count: Oh dear, dear madam! [*Kisses her hand*] not half as many as you imagine, pardon me if I speak boldly. All, all depends merely upon your consent. The young lady your daughter is the very picture of yourself, all that I may obtain from you I am assured of from her. One kiss upon your lovely cheeks, where the sun shines in his midday [*Kisses her*], is every bit as much to me as a kiss upon the dawning Wilhelmine's –

Frau v. Biederling: You're very galant, you won't be expecting me to reply to that. In Naumburg our relations are not pitched at so high a tone.

Count: But madam! what answer will you give me then? am I to live or die, despair or hope?

Frau v. Biederling: You should seek an answer from my daughter, or my husband –

Count: You are your daughter, you are your husband. I possess means, madam! but they are a burden to me, if I do not share them with a person in whose society I shall at last begin to be alive. Before, I was no more than a machine, in Wilhelmine you have bestowed a divine being upon the world, and she alone is capable of instilling a soul in me. [*Kneels*] Oh see me at your feet, see me praying, languishing, weeping, despairing.

Frau v. Biederling: You're excessively persuasive – but think what you have asked! a secret wedding, with no witnesses, no proclamation, forgive me,

I know what you'll say in objection, that I speak in a provincial fashion, not in the manner of the great world - but those unlucky enough to have once burned their fingers, my husband and I have enough with which to reproach ourselves by way of carelessness with our children - my elder son fell victim to it - forgive me, at the memory - I can't prevent myself [*Weeps*], he is no more.

Count: [*Kisses her knee*] But you won't mistrust me [*Kisses it again*], dear adorable lady! If you do, I am the most unfortunate creature under the sun, the only counsel remaining is the first bullet that comes, straight through my head. I should needs be the blackest villain, the most worthless, the most depraved, the vilest deceiver –

Frau v. Biederling: Oh Count! I implore you, don't construe me in that fashion, mistrust in the honorable nature of your intentions is the furthest thing from my mind. But as you yourself are a fugitive, as you are obliged to remain hidden and afterwards to flee the country - ah that is precisely what happened with my son, and yet we could not have given him into safer hands.

Count: Madam! You will witness a misfortune if you refuse to hear me with favour. I am capable of anything, a life that is wretched can only be dear to a rogue.

Frau v. Biederling: Oh merciful heaven, what am I to do with you? I'll speak of it with my husband, I'll put it to my daughter.

Count: I have every reason to believe she loves me.

Frau v. Biederling: Still, you might be mistaken.

Count: Mistaken - you'd slay me.

Frau v. Biederling: I can promise you nothing, I must speak with both of them first.

Count: My whole fortune is hers.

Frau v. Biederling: That I don't require - and besides you cannot give it. You have a father, you have brothers and sisters.

Count: I have no father except your husband, no brothers and sisters but yourself. I shall liquidate it all, and when I arrive in Holland, into the bank with it, then I can make it over, if I wish.

Frau v. Biederling: That would be an injustice to which I could never be party, and which I can only excuse by your passion.

Count: Oh if you could see my heart [*Kisses her hand and mouth*], adorable mother! pity me! If you could see my heart! Wilhelmine - or I shall go mad.

Scene 6

The PRINCE's room

[*The BACHELOR OF ARTS. MASTER BEZA. PRINCE TANDI*]

Zierau: I have the honour of presenting to Your Highness a scholar with whom you will probably be better contented, Master Beza, who has translated Thomas à Kempis into Arabic, so proficient in the philosophy and languages of the Levant that he might have been born for Qumba not for Saxony.

Prince: [*Motions them to the canapé*] So then we shall agree.

Beza: [*Stands up*] Oh your devoted servant!

Zierau: In any event Master Beza is even less satisfied with our ways than is Your Highness. He claims we cannot go on as we are much longer, we shall be consumed in fire and brimstone, as was Sodom.

Prince: Don't scoff; little wit is needed for that.

Beza: Ah!

Prince: What makes you sigh?

Beza: Nothing.

Zierau: No need to dissemble, Master, the Prince will undoubtedly be of your opinion.

Beza: The world goes ill – its end is near.

Prince: That would be sad. Our friend would have us believe it was different before. I think the world no worse than it has been at any other time.

Beza: No worse? no worse? At what other time was such an abomination ever heard of, as has now become not just the fashion but the necessity? Truly *dura necessitas, durissima necessitas*. Drunkenness, dancing, skipping about and all the sensual pleasures of life have taken such hold that he who refuses to take part in them and fears God goes every day in danger of starving to death.

Prince: Why do you speak of that in particular?

Zierau: But I must explain to you that the Master is a sworn enemy to all the joys of life.

Prince: Perhaps not without cause. Mere enjoyment seems to me to be the very sickness from which Europe suffers.

Zierau: What's life without happiness?

Prince: Action makes us happier than enjoyment. Animals enjoy.

Zierau: Men act, to gain enjoyment and secure it.

Prince: Excellent! if it is distributed! – and we also care for others.

Beza: Indeed that is the freethinkers' philosophy, worldly philosophy, but every man who is in earnest with his soul will shake his head at it. It is all vanity. Oh vanity, vanity, how it can fetter luckless mankind, so that heaven is forgotten for its sake, and yet it is only ordure, dust, nothing!

Prince: We have a mind that can make this nothing into something.

Zierau: You won't bring him to think differently. I know him, he has the infirmity all Germans have, he builds up a system for himself, and all that will not fit with it belongs in hell.

Beza: While you fops and Frenchmen, with respect, live on, having neither system, goal nor purpose until the devil carries you off, and then you are lost, here to the world, there to eternity.

Prince: Don't be so stern, sir! Granted, one thing is quite as bad as the other; he who lives with no goal soon lives himself to death, while he who frames a system all alone in his study, and will not accommodate it to the world, either lives each moment directly at odds with his system, or does not live at all.

Zierau: It seems to me that to live reasonably is the best system.

Beza: Yes, that is truly the summit.

Prince: Truly – but it is never reached. Reason without faith is short of sight and weak, besides I know animals that are reasonable as well as ones that are not. Faith is to true reason the only weight that will set its wheels in motion, else they stand idle and rust, and then woe to the machine!

Zierau: True reason teaches us to be happy, and to strew our path with flowers.

Prince: But flowers fade and die.

Beza: Indeed, indeed.

Zierau: Why then, pick more.

Prince: What if the ground were not to put forth any more. Everything would fall.

Zierau: We shall lose ourselves in allegories.

Prince: They are easy to decipher. Mind and heart must expand, sir –

Zierau: Therefore they must not love, nor enjoy.

Prince: Pleasure and love are the only happiness in the world, and yet our inner state must set its tone.

Beza: Ha, love, a pretty religion that crams our brothels even fuller.

Zierau: I would we could but teach our youth to love, then the brothels would soon be empty.

Prince: But then the world might fare even worse. For love is fire, better burn straw with it than a field of corn. Unless other ways were to be found –

Zierau: When the Golden Age returns.

Prince: But it only exists in the heads of poets, thank God. I can't tell how I should feel about it. Perhaps we'd sit there like Midas, staring at everything but able to enjoy nothing. So long as we're not made of gold ourselves, the Golden Age is of no use to us, but if we are, then we can just as well make our peace with the Brazen Age or the Leaden Age.

Scene 7

[*HERR v. BIEDERLING. FRAU v. BIEDERLING*]

Herr v. Biederling: I find nothing unreasonable in it, wife, supposing the girl will have him, and already I've often caught her casting timid looks at him, when his eyes answered hers in such a way that I thought he'd set light to her, therefore if heaven has decreed it, and who knows what changes five years might still bring.

Frau v. Biederling: You always have a faith that would move mountains, it's the very same story as with our son, the very same.

Herr v. Biederling: Don't speak of it, I pray you. We shall still have the honour and joy of our son, unless he's dead. If Zopf would but come quickly, then you'd be obliged to play me a different tune.

Frau v. Biederling: When I see him again, the infamous fellow – I'll scratch his eyes out, I tell you.

Herr v. Biederling: Zopf is an honest fellow, what do you mean? To have travelled to Rome on our account, who else would do the like? And I am assured he only stays so long because he waits upon the answer of the Pater General, who has written to Pater Mons in Smyrna, so what do you mean? Why the devil does the man inflict all that trouble upon himself, all those cares and journeyings, you should be ashamed, ready at once to wag your tongue and blacken his name, and the man is doing more for your child than you yourself.

Frau v. Biederling: You are right, you're always right, do as you please with

your daughter and son, sell them into the galleys, I shall knit your
stockings and sing songs of penance, as a housewife should.

Herr v. Biederling: Well well, when she detects she's in the wrong, it makes
her angry. Who can help you?

Frau v. Biederling: Death. I'll make you a present of our daughter, do with
her what you will, good sir, I shall patiently await my end.

[*PRINCE TANDI joins them*]

Prince: What's the matter? I'd hate to be the reason for your quarrel –

[*Exit FRAU v. BIEDERLING*]

Herr v. Biederling: Nothing, Prince, nothing, a little wrangle, a tiny doubt,
I mean to say, an excessively large doubt on the part of my wife – only,
she is of the opinion that to give our child to a foreign gentleman to take
away with him to another world – is as if she were journeying off into
blessed eternity –

Prince: Does Wilhelmine say so too?

Herr v. Biederling: Well now, you know how women are, we shall hear
her, her mother's gone to fetch her. And the more I think upon the
thing, the tighter it feels about my heart as well, turning her back in such
a way upon father and mother and all forever, as if it had been a dream,
and so goodnight. [*He weeps*]

Prince: She'd find all again, in me.

Herr v. Biederling: But not us, Prince, not us. Oh you don't know,
Kalmuck, all that you rob us of in her! I consent to it with all my heart,
but God in heaven alone knows what my suffering is.

Prince: [*Embraces him*] Father – I shall stay in Europe seven years.

Herr v. Biederling: Done – perhaps in that time I shall die, perhaps we'll
both die. – Young man! It is all in the hands of my maiden. If she can
resolve herself – well then, though it cost me my life.

Prince: When you go to graft a cherry shoot on to a plum, must you not cut
it from the old tree? There it might never perhaps have borne a single
cherry, give it a new tree to bless and make fruitful, on the other it was
but dead and barren.

Herr v. Biederling: [*Jumps up*] Charmant, charmant – hey! tell me that again, tell
it to my wife and daughter too. 'Slife, it is also true that I am bringing
mulberry trees from Smyrna and shall plant them here to cover all the land,
and so my daughter will make all of Qumba happy. – You must tell her that.

Prince: Though now I woo your child from you - hereafter Wilhelmine's heart alone must speak, free and absolute like a divinity dealing life or death. No persuasions, no fatherly admonitions, no advice, or I'll jump straight into my carriage and away.

[*Enter FRAU v. BIEDERLING with WILHELMINE*]

Wilhelmine: What would you have me do?

Herr v. Biederling: Child! - [*Coughs and wipes his eyes. Long ilence*]

Prince: Fräulein! the time has come, the silence must be - my tongue can't utter it - look into my eyes and see in these tears, which I can no longer restrain, all my dreams, my shining hopes for the future. - Will you make me happy? - If this sudden white then red, this wonderful play over the sweet lines of your face, this weeping and laughing of your eyes tells me you will listen - oh my heart strikes its poor translator dumb [*Presses her hand to his heart*], you must hear it speak like this - I shall die of rapture.

Herr v. Biederling: Answer! what says your heart?

Frau v. Biederling: We have given the Prince our word neither to persuade nor discourage you, but first you should know this, that the Count has here formally asked for your hand and desires to make you the beneficiary of all his worldly goods.

Herr v. Biederling: And first you should know this as well, that the Prince offers you a whole kingdom, and that for my sake he and you are to stay on seven years here with us in the country.

Wilhelmine: Do with me as you will.

Herr v. Biederling: Now it isn't a case of that, my child! Be quiet, wife! did you speak? I say: daughter! we quit you here of all obedience towards us, here you are father and mother to yourself; what says your heart? That is the question. Both of the gentlemen are rich, both have behaved generously towards me, both can make you happy, it is for you alone to decide.

Frau v. Biederling: Consult your heart! Now you know the conditions on both sides.

Herr v. Biederling: But know this as well, that the Count cannot nest here permanently with us in Naumburg, indeed he too must leave and part you from us.

Frau v. Biederling: But he'll take you no further than Amsterdam, and come over every year to visit us.

Herr v. Biederling: So quick and make up your mind, it is all in your hands.

Prince! Why so disconsolate then? Now if heaven has decreed it so, and her heart does not speak to her of you - after all it's no small matter, think upon it yourself, to be fair, taking a young half-grown child two thousand miles - oh daughter, I cannot - my heart is breaking. [*Falls upon her*]

Wilhelmine: [*In their embrace*] I shall live single.

Herr v. Biederling: [*Tears himself away*] Odds life no [*Stamps*], I won't have that. If I'm of no use in the world except to stand in the way of your happiness - better to cut down the old unfruitful tree! don't you think, Prince? what do you say?

Prince: You are cruel to force me to speak. Such pain as mine can find no relief except in silence [*In a weak voice*], silent, secret forever. [*About to leave*]

Wilhelmine: [*Quickly pulls him back*] I love you.

Prince: You love me. [*Swoons at her feet*]

Wilhelmine: [*Falls upon him*] Oh I know it, I cannot live without him.

Herr v. Biederling: Hola! Give him a kiss to wake him up.

[*They carry the PRINCE to the canapé, where WILHELMINE sits beside him and sprinkles him with sal volatile*]

Prince: [*Opening his eyes*] Oh from such a hand..

Herr v. Biederling: There it is, then. Yes, Mina, that look you gave him. You and he agree, then. Now may God bless you. [*Puts his hands to their brows*] Prince! As with you, so with me, the devil's got my tongue and it won't be long before that damned swooning takes me too... [*In a weak voice*] Wife will you wake me? [*Falls*]

Frau v. Biederling: Mercy, what... [*Goes to him*]

Herr v. Biederling: [*Jumps up*] Nothing, only a joke. Ha ha ha, we can bamboozle you women just as we please. Now be merry as a cricket, little wife [*Takes her by the chin*], and put that Count of yours right out of your head, I shall have him out of the house, just wait and see, I never could abide him for all that.

Prince: [*To WILHELMINE*] So am I - [*Stammers*] can I hope that I -

Wilhelmine: Did the tree not tell you?

Prince: That was the only thing that gave me courage to ask for your hand. Oh when the moon showed me with her silver light what you had carved, when I read what my heart in its wildest imaginings had never dared to hope... ah I thought that heaven had come down to earth and poured itself in blissful dreams around me.

Herr v. Biederling: Well wife? Why do you stand there? do not you love to see the young people chattering and preening and making eyes at one another... why do you screw up your brow like an old wrinkled glove, quick, give them your blessing, wish them all the pleasures we have known, then it will be well with them, won't it, Prince?

Frau v. Biederling: That remains to be seen.

[*She exits*]

Herr v. Biederling: [*Looks after her*] Addlehead! - she's fallen in love with the Count, that's the thing - but let me speak with her... [*Calls after her*] Wait.

□

ACT THREE

Scene 1

In the summerhouse

[*The COUNT in a dressing gown drinks tea. HERR v. BIEDERLING with a big bag of money under his arm*]

Herr v. Biederling: You won't take it ill, Count, if I descend on you so early. I've been reflecting, your leasehold suits me so exceedingly well, you've said to my wife that you desire to sell your possessions and go to Amsterdam, how much do you want for it?

Count: I – from you? nothing – I shall make you a present of the property, upon one condition.

Herr v. Biederling: No, no, nothing can come of that, that way we shan't see daylight. I'll pay you its value in KronenThaler[3].

Count: But I'll take nothing.

Herr v. Biederling: You must take it, Count, I tell you once and for all, I am no beggar.

Count: Then pay what you will.

Herr v. Biederling: No, for I will pay what you will. Nothing again, is it. What the devil do you take me for?

Count: Ten thousand Thaler.

Herr v. Biederling: So here are [*Takes out a purse*] ten thousand Thaler in banknotes and here are [*Puts several bags in the corner*] five thousand Thaler in gold and silver coin... but now I intend to profit by it. I have the honour of bidding you farewell.

Count: One word more. [*Seizes his hand*]

Herr v. Biederling: That's settled then, is it not?

Count: You can make me the happiest of mortals.

Herr v. Biederling: How?

Count: You have a daughter.

Herr v. Biederling: What do you mean?

Count: I shall marry her.

Herr v. Biederling: God forbid. She's been a wife these last three days.

Count: A wife!

[3]Gold coins

Herr v. Biederling: Do you not know? Hey hey hey, well it's true, we carried out the matter quietly. Prince Tandi, my honest travelling companion, has married her, and funny enough this, not a soul to witness it, yet they were married with due observance before our pastor Straube, and yesterday what's more was a great celebration – how fares it with you, Count! you roll your eyes about in your head, as if –

Count: Do you jest with me?

Herr v. Biederling: Certainly not, sir – yet it's all the same to me what you take it for. And so adieu.

Count: [*Seizes him by the throat*] Die, wretch, before –

Herr v. Biederling: [*Wrestles with him*] Deuce take it... I'll... [*Throws him to the ground and tramples him*] you rogue!

Count: [*Lying there*] Harder! harder, Herr von Biederling.

Herr v. Biederling: [*Picks him up*] What do you intend with me?

Count: [*Putting his arms around his knees*] Can you forgive me?

Herr v. Biederling: Well, but pray you get up! The devil alone would endure it, having one's throat squeezed in – and sir, the sooner you go from my house the better, I'll suffer you no longer.

Count: Tell me again, are they married? how? where? when?

Herr v. Biederling: How? That I cannot tell you, but they were married at Rosenheim, and yesterday the Prince gave a banquet attended by every creature that can eat: the table was laden from morning till late in the night, the doors were open, and everyone who would, came in, was served and was merry. I've never seen the like in all my life, all the people were as if in heaven, every kind mixed up together, beggars, students, old women and Jews and plenty of respectable burghers too, at times I laughed fit to burst. That's the custom in Qumba, do you see, they know nothing at all of the needless foolery at our weddings, they say the only witnesses you need, in order to be wed, are your next of kin and a priest to ask God's blessing.

Count: No proclamation! so it seems you'd pull the wool over my eyes, but I can see through it. I'm not to hinder this marriage, is that so? But what if the Prince were already to have a wife?

Herr v. Biederling: Now Count! Don't take that tone with me. Mistrust is found only among Europeans. The Prince and I have spoken of it at length.

Count: Have the Qumbanians no passions?

Herr v. Biederling: No.

Count: You say so.

Herr v. Biederling: No, I tell you. It's on account of, how should I know, on account of their upbringing which causes the Qumbanians to fear God, which means they find satisfaction in their work, with head or hands, it's all the same, and after their work they come together to make merry, young and old, great and obscure, all mixed up together, and whichever one makes the most entertainment for the others, he is the most admired, which means, do you see, that they have no need to be enslaved to fantasies, for fantasy, do you see, is a thing that... wait, but how did he express it?... in company it's quite splendid, but at home it doesn't do at all, it's like some shining haze, a varnish that we paint on all things that come in our way, and use to render them charming and pleasant.

Count: [*Strikes himself on the forehead*] Oh!

Herr v. Biederling: But wait, hear me out! For when we take this varnish home with us we stick to it, do you see, and then it becomes the devil's daub to delude us.

Count: By all means listen to his prattle... is it not the very same with us? must we not work? do we not come together to amuse ourselves?

Herr v. Biederling: Yes and no, we desire nothing but to amuse ourselves perpetually, and in the end not one pleasure keeps its savour, and our very pleasure becomes a pain to us, that's the difference. And because we don't labour with understanding, we labour instead with fantasy and I don't know what, he explained it all, speak with him yourself of it, he'll be a joy to you.

Count: Make us good friends, Herr von Biederling. Indeed I long to know him better.

Herr v. Biederling: Yes, but in God's name, just now I thought you were still off to Amsterdam. - You can't be so very safe with me for long.

Count: And where should I go? Leaving all my possessions to be confiscated?

Herr v. Biederling: Yes I see... but mark, what if the Elector were to make some future claim even upon my Rosenheim? What news have you from your lawyer?

Count: For that very reason, take back your money until I hear for certain from my lawyer how the matter stands at court. In the meantime you can still take up the lease.

Herr v. Biederling: Yes, but then I must pay you the rent.

Count: If you desire to injure me at my sore point.

Herr v. Biederling: Well then - I have the honour to thank you most exceedingly, if you will absolutely have it so. And I shall see to it that you become more closely acquainted with the Prince, he's a very gallant man, though I shouldn't say so as he's now my son-in-law, and as for what happened between the two of you a week ago, he's long since forgotten it, assuredly! It was a sort of Qumbanian thing that, for there in fact, do you see, it's considered a sin to speak to a young girl in the absence of her parents regarding love and so on, they punish it as fornication in the same way as if I were to seize someone by the throat and he were fortunately to remain alive. I have the honour to bid you farewell.

Count: Oh first - do you forgive me?

Herr v. Biederling: Now now, *il n'y a pas du mal* as the Frenchman says. - Will you dine with us today? and with my new son-in-law, you can become better acquainted.

Scene 2

Immenhof

[*DONNA DIANA. BABET*]

Babet: [*A letter in her hand*] Both of your parents are still alive. My good friend writes to tell me so, she's informed of it now, a certain gentleman from Trieste is in communication with her, it seems he corresponds with your father.

Donna Diana: The Polish woman?

Babet: The same.

Donna Diana: Oh what do I care for my parents? Does she not write of the Count? does he still visit her?

Babet: He has unexpectedly disappeared from Dresden.

Donna Diana: And I am left sitting in Immenhof! Have you money?

Babet: The little sum remaining that you gave me before we came here at Shrovetide.

Donna Diana: Give it here, we shall after him even if he were hidden in the inmost hollow of the earth. I'll haul him out, and woe to the Io[4] that I find him with!

Babet: But where first?

[4]Nymph loved by Zeus, who changed her into a heifer to conceal her from his wife.

Donna Diana: Leave it to me, I can't tell until we're on our way. My heart will guide me, it's like a compass, it can't fail.

Babet: In Dresden for certain we shall find out where he's hidden.

Donna Diana: I'll - don't speak! come! The ground's burning under my feet - I wish I'd never seen a man, or that I could wring the necks of all of them.

Scene 3

Naumburg

[*PRINCE TANDI, WILHELMINE, sitting together on a canapé*]

Prince: Won't you tell me who it is that you've dressed yourself up for today?

Wilhelmine: But I told you, for my father.

Prince: Rascal! You know full well, your father won't so much as cast an eye on you. Since you're not a baby silkworm.

Wihelmine: But think! Do you not hold it worth the trouble of casting an eye on me?

Prince: No.

Wilhelmine: I thank you.

Prince: A man must cast his whole self on you.

Wilhelmine: [*Stopping his mouth*] Should you speak to me once more in that fashion, I'll say - that you're in love with me, and yet you've told me so often that people in love are not clever.

Prince: But I'm clever. For I've never yet told you that I was in love with you.

Wilhelmine: Never told me? - Ha ha ha! poor pitiful man! never told me? and wouldn't it half kill you to say it? oh my brave knight.

Prince: Never told you, little Mina! Unless it was last night.

Wilhelmine: [*Crossly*] If you speak to me so once more - I shall be angry.

Prince: And what then? Only the inconvenience of making it up again.

Wilhelmine: Give me a divorce.

Prince: Why not? A divorce - little fool! it would be the death of you.

Wilhelmine: You have a high opinion of yourself I must say. And if I did it you'd hang yourself.

Prince: Fie, for shame! Enough of such stuff. I'd rather confess I'm in love with you.

Wilhelmine: You simpleton, that little shiny drop there on your eyelid confessed it long ago.

Prince: It's said, then. [*Presses her hand to his eyes*]

Wilhelmine: It's answered, then. [*Kisses him*]

[*HERR von ZOPF enters. They stand*]

Herr v. Zopf: [*In travelling clothes*] Your obedient servant, Miss Mina! oh how fine and big you've grown since the last time I saw you. You won't know me I'm sure, my name is Zopf.

Wilhelmine: [*Makes him a deep curtsey*] We're very pleased - my parents have often said to me -

Herr v. Zopf: Is your good father not at home? Your parents will not have been content with me, but they no longer have cause. I bring good news for your parents, and for yourself. [*To TANDI*] Is it not true that you are Prince Tandi of Qumba? at least that's what I was told in Dresden, that you'd travelled here with Herr von Biederling. It could not have worked out more splendidly, rejoice together with us all, you are in your father's house.

Prince: What?

Wilhelmine: What?

Herr v. Zopf: Embrace one another. You are brother and sister. [*WILHELMINE falls back on the sofa. TANDI stands pale, hanging his head*] How's this? Will you not thank me? Are you not happy? Depend upon it, I tell you, I have just had the letter from the Pater General of the Jesuits and I straight away mounted my horse to bring you the good news. You are brother and sister, it's certain. [*TANDI is about to leave. WILHELMINE jumps up, flings her arms around his neck*]

Wilhelmine: Where are you going?

Prince: Let go!

Wilhelmine: No never, not until death. [*TANDI breaks away from her. She falls fainting*]

Herr v. Zopf: [*Reviving her*] I can well see, Fräulein! that something has happened here -

Wilhelmine: [*Waking*] Where is he, I shall die with him -

Herr v. Zopf: Have you taken a little liking to him? It's but an exchange. Now you may love him as your brother.

Wilhelmine: [*Kicks him*] Away! hateful to my sight! away! We are man and wife. You must give me death or him.

Herr v. Zopf: Merciful heaven, what do I hear!

Wilhelmine: [*Snatches his dagger from his side and puts it to his chest*] Give me back my husband. [*Throws the dagger aside*] Keep your accursed exchange – [*Picks it up*] Oh, or run me through. You have plunged a knife into my heart already, inhuman man! you'll not find it difficult.

Herr v. Zopf: Under what ill-fated planets was I born, that all my services turn only to disaster. I'd like to forswear and confound this helping of my fellow men; not once in my whole life have I yet succeeded in doing good for my good friend, every time I've been struck by some idea and believed I could make him happy, the outcome has been poisoned, and I have made him sad. I'm heartily sorry for it, God knows –

Scene 4

Dresden

[*DONNA DIANA. BABET*]

Donna Diana: Have you heard? Gustav went with him to Naumburg.

Babet: I've not yet recovered my senses.

Donna Diana: What's to astonish you, fool! what better can you expect of a man? Poisoners, assassins all of them –

Babet: He'd have you poisoned? Gracious heavens, why?

Donna Diana: Why? foolish question! because I loved him, is not that reason enough? – Ah hold my head! Unlace me! There's a brightness before my eyes – so – wait – no spirits [*Shrieks*], no spirits!

Babet: God have mercy! But you're fainting.

Donna Diana: [*In a weak voice*] What's it to you if I faint. [*Straightens herself*] So! Now it's over. [*Walks about*] Now I'm Diana once more. [*Clasps her hands together*] We shall catch you again, just wait! just wait! What he did, dear Babet, you could never imagine all that he undertook, in order to seduce me. Vows that moved heaven, sighs, howls, despair. [*Falls into her arms*] Babet, I could not hold out! pity me. If the devil were prowling here in human form he'd have thought of no more cunning ways to win a young girl's heart. And now he wants me poisoned, because I poisoned my father to oblige him, and robbed my mother, and am dishonoured, accursed, pursued by the law, oh! – perhaps my mother has already written to the court, to have me arrested as a criminal.

Babet: Calm yourself, dear madam! She has not done that, certainly not, that she will not do, well she knows that she herself shares the blame for this misfortune, she stole you from your parents.

Donna Diana: [*Stands up*] Silence! I have forbidden you once and for all to speak of it. Better to have murdered my father than be the daughter of an old retired army officer, the tenant of my husband. Wilhelmine, what does she look like? Heaven erred in making her a Velas, I deserved to be one, and you did right in arranging the matter.

Babet: Oh my conscience!

Donna Diana: What does she look like, quick! a pretty farm girl? –

Babet: Pretty enough to capture a heart, a pair of eyes like the heavens opening.

Donna Diana: That's but justice: if he'd preferred a hideous ape to me, it could not have been forgiven. But has she breeding in her face, Donna Velas in her eyes?

Babet: Would the parents then have exchanged her? A snub nose – for three days his lordship could not eat a single morsel. But when I obtained you from my friend he shouted, that is a Velas face, that aquiline nose will cut me a path to the throne, and with the two eyes I shall strike down the King of Portugal.

Donna Diana: But silence, that I am adopted, or it will cost your life. I shall tear your heart from your mouth along with your tongue if you speak. I must retrieve the Count, then back to Madrid. Luckless papa whom I poisoned, I'll bear out your prophecy! and so in the grave at least I'll bring you joy. The jewels back to my mother so she will keep silence and then – is there fire enough in you still?

Babet: Enough to consume the world. But will you bring back the Count?

Donna Diana: The Count? Wretched woman! Oh fie, I'll beckon him back, the butterfly, and if he won't come, I'll snatch him and crush him in my hand. His goods are mine after all, he is my lawful husband, I can show the contract and the seal.

Babet: But spare poor Wilhemine.

Donna Diana: Foolishness [*Hits her*], witch! What are you dreaming of? That I'd vent my power on a farm girl? Dungheap of a woman! What do you take me for?

Babet: But if the Count –

Donna Diana: What? if the Count - go on, if the Count - if he loves her, if he marries her - by my presence I shall bring down confusion, despair and destruction upon him. Like a god I shall appear, my glances will be lightning, my voice will be thunder - let's speak of it as we go along, it's bliss to me if I can speak of it. In all his life he never will have trembled so before any person, no, not before God almighty - the contemptible brute! If I were but in Madrid, I'd have him locked in my zoo!

Scene 5

Rosenheim. A garden

[*HERR v. BIEDERLING in linen smock, a spade in his hand. HERR v. ZOPF*]

Herr v. Biederling: [*Looks up*] Is that you, Zopf? - I'm just planting one of your trees. Well how are you? [*Stretches out his hand to him*] have you come from Dresden?

Herr v. Zopf: I've come - yes I've come from Dresden. I'm glad I find you here alone. Freudendahl was with me as you know, I've left him in Naumburg.

Herr v. Biederling: Why should that coxcomb meddle in our affairs? Do you know, I've powder and shot right here, we can settle our business on the spot.

Herr v. Zopf: Forgive me! but he was witness to the fact that you impugned my honour.

Herr v. Biederling: But think of it, you can very well say to that meddling little Leipzig student that I've given it back to you, and if he refuses to believe it, then I for my part shall call him a scoundrel. But think of it, am I expected to ride back there for the sake of that fool? Why didn't the lout come with you? - Do you like my nursery?

Herr v. Zopf: Very nice, God grant you it thrives. - But what possessed you to accuse me in Freudendahl's presence - the whole thing could be settled in a few words.

Herr v. Biederling: You desire me to apologize? - No, brother! it will not be [*Carries on digging*], I'll not go back on my word, do what you will.

Herr v. Zopf: And have you not wronged me? In a public house, upon the very first greeting, forthwith insulting me and beating me with sticks -

Herr v. Biederling: You had wronged me also.

Herr v. Zopf: When I am doing everything in the world to serve you? That is atrocious.

Herr v. Biederling: If my head had been clearer, perhaps it wouldn't have gone so far, but - in short, let's not go over the whole thing again. As to your services, what in God's name are such services to me, my child left unprotected, when I relied on you.

Herr v. Zopf: I have only one thing with which to reproach myself: that I took him with me to Smyrna.

Herr v. Biederling: Not so, brother monsieur, wherever you were, there my son was sure to be well raised, but that you gave him to be taken by the Jesuits, in order to be rid of him, hey! Jesuit yourself, that's where it rubs. [*Throws the spade away*] Come, come draw, I'm just in the right humour now to exchange a few bullets with you.

Herr v. Zopf: Look, I've brought silkworm eggs.

Herr v. Biederling: Show me [*Wipes his hands on his breeches*], show them here! [*Opens them*] that's good, that is most civil; now my silk farm can go roaring on like a storm; only - but how by all the devils have they not got damp? *a propos*! have you heard - do you not know, listen to this! about the oven that must be built for the purpose, how do they do it? I think I must write to Leipzig for an expert opinion.

Herr v. Zopf: I thought you might prefer to travel there yourself.

Herr v. Biederling: Or young Zierau in Naumburg, that will be a farmer besides - what wonderful creatures of God there are in the world, look at that tiny little black egg! who would have thought a thing could come out of there and spin such astonishing stuff? *A propos*! have you no news from Rome?

Herr v. Zopf: Yes I do, and much desired.

Herr v. Biederling: Oh dearest Zopf, [*Falls on his neck*] I nearly upset all the eggs - what is it? what has happened? is he still alive? is there any trace of hope?

Herr v. Zopf: Not only does he live, he is found, you shall see him.

Herr v. Biederling: Oh you're an angel, we'll not shoot one another then, all is forgiven and forgotten. Only forgive me, I'll publicly ask your forgiveness in Dresden town hall.

Herr v. Zopf: Come back with me to Naumburg, I'll read my letter to you there, but only when you've asked for my forgiveness in Freudendahl's presence. Then we'll go together to your house, and tell your family the rest.

Scene 6

Naumburg

[*WILHELMINE lies on a bed. FRAU v. BIEDERLING and COUNT CHAMELEON
stand before her*]

Wilhelmine: I'll not hear of comfort, leave me, leave me, I wish to die.

Frau v. Biederling: Just to please your mother, your father - just a little little
spoonful of hot soup - you'll kill us with your desperate affliction.

Wilhelmine: How should I eat, he's gone, how can I eat? And not said
goodbye to me. He's shot; he's drowned! oh dear Mama! why do you
desire to be more cruel to your child than any thing that should be cruel?
why will you not let me die?

Frau v. Biederling: He is inhuman! not to see his mother.

Count: If only it could be discovered where he is. Even if I had to go to the
King.

Frau v. Biederling: Oh Count! what have we done to deserve the kindness
that you show towards this house?

Count: I shall instantly dispatch my man Gustav to Dresden, perhaps he can
get news of him there. I know to whom I shall send him.

Frau v. Biederling: When I reflect upon the thing I would I were struck
down dead. My only son - there before my eyes then - gone -

Wilhelmine: Alas! alas!

Frau v. Biederling: Must we fetch a doctor? Merciless child!

Wilhelmine: Yes if he can kill you'd better fetch him.

Count: For the sake of your health, which is beyond price -

Frau v. Biederling: Count, your entreaties are vain! God has chosen to put
an end to us. Oh unhappy woman that I am! [*Weeps*]

[*Enter HERR v. BIEDERLING*]

Herr v. Biederling: Hola, victory, hurrah! What is it, wife! Girl! where's he
hiding? where's our son? bring him out, quick, where is he? - Well what
is the meaning of this?

Frau v. Biederling: For whom do you inquire?

Herr v. Biederling: Is this joy or sorrow? - Ha ha, I observe you mean to
surprise me. Out with him now, I know all, Zopf has told me all -

Frau v. Biederling: You know all, and can be merry? Then God curse the
hour in which -

Herr v. Biederling: Now what is this, in God's name! are you at your
prophesying again? - where is he?

Frau v. Biederling: Go after him, monster! He's the image of his father!

Count: The Prince has disappeared.

Herr v. Biederling: 'Sblood, what's the Prince to me? it's my son I'm asking for.

Frau v. Biederling: Has the man gone mad?

Herr v. Biederling: My son! out with him, or I will go mad, what's this foolery, I shall see him. Mina, where's your brother, I command you to inform me.

Wilhelmine: [*Sobbing*] The Prince?

Herr v. Biederling: The Prince your – [*Sinks down on a chair*] God, almighty father –

Frau v. Biederling: Did Zopf not tell you?

Herr v. Biederling: [*Staring at the ground*] He told me nothing – nothing –

Count: He's vanished, none can get word of him, but I shall instantly – [*He exits*]

Frau v. Biederling: The Count has the soul of an angel.

Herr v. Biederling: It – it – [*Stands up and walks about*] Almighty God! what have I done to deserve your anger?

[*Enter MASTER BEZA*]

Master Beza: I come to offer you at once my heartiest good wishes and sincere condolences –

Herr v. Biederling: Here, Master! talk to my wife, I can't reply to you. There's nought but lamentation in this house. [*Sits on the bed*] Mina! Mina! what shall we do?

Master Beza: Permit me to say to you – that I've heard all about it, the news of this wonderfully strange circumstance has already spread through all of Naumburg, but permit me to demonstrate to you for your comfort according to God's word that there is not the slightest danger in the whole affair, thanks be to God.

Herr v. Biederling: How's that? Master! how's that?

Master Beza: Yes it is too complex for me to expound upon it here, but I can tell you this much, that the greatest theologians are unanimous on this very point –

Herr v. Biederling: Then I'll make a trip to Leipzig, perhaps I can have them ratify the marriage. Master, you must accompany me – Mina, be of good cheer.

Wilhelmine: Never in all eternity.

Master Beza: Yes, if I can but absent myself from my school – besides I desired to show you clearly and plainly from the customs and usages of Arabia that –

Herr v. Biederling: Nonsense, I shall be answerable to your school, only come, you may much enlighten the scholars of Leipzig in these matters, I'm convinced of it, Master, you're a learned man as the whole world knows.

Master Beza: Oh! – ah! –

Herr v. Biederling: Mina! dear Mina! so do be of good cheer! We shall go instantly in the carriage, sir! he won't have unharnessed yet, and the very first thing we shall do is to seek out the Prince – Mina, I beg you, courage for God's sake.

[*He exits*]

Scene 7

On the road from Dresden

[*DONNA DIANA, BABET, travelling in a carriage. GUSTAV, riding, encounters them*]

Donna Diana: [*From the carriage*] Halt, where are you going?

Gustav: [*Falls off his horse*] Madam!

Donna Diana: Now I'm revenged. The boy has a conscience. [*Jumps out of the carriage*] Where? [*Seizes him*] tell me this instant.

Gustav: [*Trembling*] To Dresden.

Donna Diana: Into the carriage with you, your horse can go to Dresden. What business had you there?

Gustav: I've forgotten.

Donna Diana: Speak!

Gustav: To see if Prince Tandi was there.

Donna Diana: Your horse can go and see. [*Seizes his elbow*] Into the carriage with you! be comforted boy! no harm will come to you. You're too much beneath me, creature! for me to take revenge on you. But tell me on the spot, did your master have a part in my murder?

Gustav: Madam!

Donna Diana: Don't coil up, you worm, or I shall tread on you, did your master have a part in my murder?

Gustav: I'll tell you everything.

Donna Diana: Up then, into the carriage, and you shall have the pleasure of travelling with me. Be without fear, we shall be the best friends in the world, because what the Count gave you, I can give you too. [*They climb into the carriage*] Drive on!

Scene 8

Naumburg

[*FRAU v. BIEDERLING, WILHELMINE, each with a letter in her hand*]

Frau v. Biederling: So he's in Leipzig - [*Reads*]

Wilhelmine: Not till five years have passed - pitiless man! [*Reads*]

Frau v. Biederling: I'm done.

Wilhelmine: [*Kisses her letter*] Never! [*Passes it to her mother*] My death sentence. - He wishes me to learn to hate him before I may see him.

Frau v. Biederling: There you see how he turns against you in his thoughts. I'd not desire your father to bring him back, he has no feeling for you, he has never loved you.

Wilhelmine: If you but knew him.

Frau v. Biederling: Is this tenderness? Then the goings on within a tender heart must be most strange. The Count has more feeling, and he's not even a member of the family. I'm sure he slept not a wink last night, the poor man's quite wasting away.

Wilhelmine: Mama - you're unjust to him, God knows you're unjust.

Frau v. Biederling: I forbid you to speak of him ever again to me.

Wilhelmine: But he's your son.

Frau v. Biederling: He requests me in three words, quite coldly, to come to Leipzig, but to say nothing of it to you. - You must forget him.

Wilhelmine: Forget?

Frau v. Biederling: What then? Fret yourself to death for him? - In order to forget him, you must divert yourself and accustom your heart to dwell upon other objects, until you're the master of it. You were as good as blind, indeed, so long as he was about you. I'll not go to Leipzig, you're too much on my mind.

Wilhelmine: Ah my kind mother!

Frau v. Biederling: If only you'd obey me.

Wilhelmine: Not for five years?

Frau v. Biederling: Forget him.

Wilhelmine: He thinks it a sin to see me before?

Frau v. Biederling: He's never loved you. Forget him.

Wilhelmine: If only I could.

Frau v. Biederling: You must - or make us all unhappy.

Wilhelmine: Yes I wish I may hate him, that I may forget him.

Scene 9

A coffee house in Leipzig

[*HERR v. BIEDERLING and MASTER BEZA are smoking, the LANDLORD stands before them and pours coffee*]

Landlord: Yes he's a queer fish, we've had a lot here, but never one of his *espèce*[5]. He was a gentleman that would go through a thousand Gulden a year, sitting all day long in Keinerts, not that he got up to anything, God forbid! he sat with his book in his hand and studied there, the late Professor Gellert himself gave him the character of being the aptest man of all his students.

Herr v. Biederling: And you don't know where he's lodging now?

Landlord: The Arabian prince? well now, that we soon shall know. You've but to ask after him as you go past the Blue Angel, you'll hear wonders of him there. Every day, I tell you, the blind, the lame and the hunchbacked are gathered where he is, to eat and drink at his expense, as if they were in a fairy castle, for none may see him. I said the other day to my cousin in the Angel: didn't he know then, there are many Brahmins in Arabia, or whatever they call the monks there, who frequently take such vows and wander about the world.

Master Beza: Oh ignorance!

Landlord: Hey hey hey, Master! You're not to laugh at me because I speak of things as best I understand them. Others say he was in a duel and that in order to ease his conscience a little he – it's true he must have something that weighs heavy on him, for I saw him once and he looked, God forgive me, like an *Ecce-homo*[6].

Herr v. Biederling: [*Startled while drinking, drops his cup*] Lord! Why does he tell me this?

Landlord: Yes I see – I didn't know you were acquainted with the gentleman, I beg your pardon. – *Marqueur*[7], run to the Angel straight away, inquire where the foreign prince is lodged that arrived last week.

---

[5]French in the original text; meaning species

[6]A Christ crowned with thorns

[7]Waiter keeping the tally

Scene 10

A hall. Table laden

[*SERVANTS. A company of BEGGARS and POOR PEOPLE feast around the table*]

A Hunchback: The Prince's health, gentlemen!

A Lame Man: A fine man! God comfort him!

A Blind Man: Would that God would grant me the gift of seeing his face.

Another Blind Man: I wouldn't desire to see him, they say he always looks so sad and that would break my heart.

Lame Man: They say he lost a woman, a great beauty. Yes, yes, death too likes a nice thing for himself, lame dogs like us he leaves alive. [*Pours for himself*] Her health good people, drink her health. [*They knock glasses with each other*]

Blind Man: Where are your glasses, where are you?

Lame Man: Not you, you'll spill it on our breeches.

[*Enter PRINCE TANDI*]

Prince: What are you doing? For whom do you intend it?

Lame Man: [*Stands up*] Sir, you've come at the right time. [*Pours for himself*] I've something to say in your ear, noble sir. [*Hobbles over to him on his crutch*]

Prince: [*Goes towards him*] Pray stay where you are, I'll come to you. [*Both stand in the middle of the room*]

Lame Man: [*Raises his glass high*] Prince! God hearken to me, I drink a health which must be nameless, but God knows it comes from my heart!

Prince: Whose then? Out with it.

Lame Man: Yes but you don't mean it, you know very well of whom I speak. Long live - are your esteemed parents still of this world? Well then, they must lead the way [*Empties his glass*], but that was not yet the one. [*Goes back to the table and pours for himself*]

Prince: I wish I could give you back your feet.

Lame Man: Not needed - [*Hobbles back to the PRINCE, his glass raised*] To - to - to [*Beside the PRINCE*] her serene highness your beloved. [*Drinks. PRINCE leaves rapidly*]

ALL: The Prince's beloved! [*They throw their glasses through the window*]

[*Enter HERR v. BIEDERLING and MASTER BEZA*]

Herr v. Biederling: Ow, a hailstorm! what's this? It's enough to make you laugh.

Master Beza: Oriental! oriental!

Lame Man: Come, you must drink with us. [*Brings BIEDERLING a glass*] At once, no ceremony! and you Mr Blackcoat, hunchback! bring a glass here quick.

Herr v. Biederling: But you're a bad waiter, you've knocked half of it out of my glass.

Lame Man: And you'd throw your glass down your neck like that, without once saying: to the Prince's good health? Say it this instant or I'll - [*Raises his stick and falls full length*]

Herr v. Biederling: Ha ha ha, to the Prince's good health. [*To MASTER BEZA*] Do you hear, the thing pierces me to the heart, it's enough to make you weep.

Master Beza: [*Drinks*] To the Prince's good health.

Herr v. Biederling: [*To a SERVANT*] Go and say to my son that I desire to speak with him.

Lame Man: What's this? Your son? well then [*Throws his crutch in the air, falls to the ground again*], well then - Is it true? You're his papa? This will make him happy, this will make him happy, this very moment I drank your health and God has heard my prayer. - Drink brothers, drink! I couldn't be better pleased if I'd just been given a hundred Thaler.

Scene 11

A little garden at the inn

[*PRINCE TANDI. MASTER BEZA. SERVANT*]

Prince: I cannot see him, not yet. Do you not feel why it must be so? And you'd condole with me, condole, with such a heart as yours? Cold comforter, leave me!

Master Beza: But how have I deserved that you should speak to me so unjustly? When I, from the best designs, and on account of duty and conscience, so to speak -

Prince: I hate friends in need, they are crueller than the fiercest enemies, far crueller. You come to rub caustic in my open wound, away with you.

Master Beza: I cannot and must not leave you. Christian love -

Prince: Ha, Christian love! Do not dishonour the words! if you could feel as I do, then you would understand that that which you wish to remove from an unfortunate, I mean his pain, is his only and greatest good; you'd snatch away the last thing that remains to him, barbarians!

Master Beza: Now that is very perversely said.

Prince: It is truly said! You have never yet lost all, all, all that can bring peace to the soul and bliss after striving: now I must seek my bliss in tears and sighs, and if you take them from me, what is left but cold despair.

Master Beza: Now if I can but make you comprehend that all your scruples are of no account, that God has not forbidden close marriages –

Prince: Not forbidden?

Master Beza: That it had its basis in the particularities of the Jewish constitution, in customs and usages arising from the fact that you were bound to see your closest relatives unveiled, so in order to guard against precocious fornication –

Prince: Who has told you that? It was because marriages with relatives were forbidden that it was permitted to see them unveiled, just as in Rome they were permitted to kiss. If God had had no other reason for the prohibition, he had only to forbid unveiling.

Master Beza: But you must read Michaelis. It was a mere political provision made by God, which was not intended for us, if it had been a general natural law, God would have laid the cause of the prohibition there.

Prince: But is it not there? Is it not written in giant letters there? Must I cut the scales from your eyes?

Master Beza: Why what, what? thou shalt not marry thy sister, because she is thy sister.

Prince: Do you fail to understand it? Woe to you, that you fail to understand it. You should fall to the ground and give thanks that the lawgiver saw things otherwise than through your spectacles. He ordered the eternal relations which alone can bring joy and rapture to your life, and you would destroy them? Oh you giants, beware the mountain does not fall on you, if you would storm against the thunderer. What makes the happiness of the world, if not the harmonious God-pleasing play of sentiments which from the lowest creature up to God himself are tuned to each other in eternal proportion? Would you remove the difference that stands between the names of father, son, sister, wife, mother, and beloved? do you wish to think no differently, or to feel no different emotion, with the one from with the other? well then, do not seek to rise above the animals which among themselves, without order or distinction, mate with whichever one comes near them, and let the whole wide world be a pigsty for my sake.

Master Beza: How sad. You are set upon weighing down your conscience in an unnecessary manner, making yourself and your sister unhappy –

Prince: What torture. Should you not rather have wished to efface this picture from my mind? I see her lying at war with herself, fighting in a noble fight, filled with hate and love, indicting against the gods and silently struggling before God himself - [*Falls on a grassy bank*] Ah tormentor!

Master Beza: [*Draws near to him*] All this you could spare yourself.

Prince: And fill my conscience with poison? Away, traitor! The knowledge of having done right can never make us unhappy. Grief and pain are no misfortune, they are better than a dubious happiness whose deepest foundation is an unquiet conscience. Wilhelmine will not be wretched forever: uncorrupted beauty has help in heaven and needs no treacherous consolation.

Master Beza: May I summon your father?

Prince: To make her picture still more vivid to me? Behind me, Satan! [*Pushes him out of the garden*]

Scene 12

A street in Leipzig

[*HERR v. BIEDERLING. MASTER BEZA*]

Herr v. Biederling: No matter. I shall travel to court, and if the Consistory approves the marriage, he'll oblige me by taking back his wife again, even if I have to force him to it with bread and water. If the churl is unwilling - very well then, he'll not see me but he'll feel the effect of me. And you must stay here incognito, Master! and don't take your eyes off him for a moment, I think he'll not leave Leipzig at once, and in case of need you have only to cause his effects to be seized on my behalf, he may not depart if he is involved in a matter that waits upon the decision of the court.

Scene 13

Naumburg

[*COUNT CHAMELEON. ZIERAU*]

Count: I'd so much like to dance the sweet young woman out of her melancholy. Your father must possess some pleasant villa hereabouts, could we find room for twenty or thirty people -

Zierau: Leave it to me. Though my father is not at home - I shall be answerable to him for it.

Count: How much is this amusement likely to cost?

Zierau: Give me twenty or thirty ducats into my hand to begin with, I shall see how far I shall go with them. Often much depends upon the manner of the commencement –

Count: The chief requirement here is taste, and I know you have it. As for the cost, you need spare nothing. How far is it from here?

Zierau: A good hour.

Count: All the better. I should like to see us remain there several days. Would there be beds, in case of need?

Zierau: Certainly I can have some held in readiness.

Count: I should like above all things to view the place. Shall we ride out to it? Gustav! – I mean Johann! is Gustav still not returned? Harness the cabriolet, I wish to take it out with this gentleman.

Zierau: I shall go on ahead at once, and make arrangements so that suitable provision of fine wines and punch, arak, lemons – the ladies love that, when they've been dancing.

Count: Can you make a good punch? and strong, otherwise it's not worth it.

Zierau: I know of nothing more charming than a lady who's a little drunk. Are masks to be distributed also?

Count: Why yes, whoever desires – that was well thought of – I myself shall appear *en masque* – quite so, let no-one come up without a mask – but do you have a comfortable room in which to change? we must inspect it all.

☐

ACT FOUR

Scene 1

Naumburg
[*FRAU v. BIEDERLING lays two dominos over a chair. WILHELMINE is sewing on a frame*]
Wilhelmine: To be honest –
Frau v. Biederling: Come, what is it?
Wilhelmine: Truth to tell, mama –
Frau v. Biederling: Have I not said it? as often as you sit with that frame, it's as if an evil spirit – for do you not know it's a sin to think of him? what's the purpose of the stupid thing, I swear that before you know it I shall cut it out, and into the fire with it.
Wilhelmine: You'd only make matters worse.
Frau v. Biederling: Will you dress or will you not? The company has quite certainly been waiting several hours for us already.
Wilhelmine: [*Sighs*] You'll be angry.
Frau v. Biederling: What is it then? Have you already changed your mind again? Absurd creature. No, God knows it is not to be borne. Yesterday you solemnly promised the Count –
Wilhelmine: To please you.
Frau v. Biederling: Me? will you cower at home forever weeping for the fool? What will come of that? Quick put on your clothes, you'll not regret it, you'll be in a mask besides, you can dance or look on, whatever you like, so you but divert yourself.
Wilhelmine: Ah! in such company! Merry company is the very rack to an unfortunate.
Frau v. Biederling: What then? Stay at home and make verses? – To be sure, here's someone been sent for us.
Zierau: [*Elaborately dressed*] Forgive me, madam!... Fräulein! if I descend upon you too soon perhaps. I have come in the carriage to fetch you. [*To WILHELMINE*] It is a little divertissement that you can give to your sorrow.
Wilhelmine: My divertissement is here.
Zierau: How? What? Ah, you'd mimic Penelope, withholding your charms from your admirers until – is it not so, not until you've finished the work, and then – What pattern is it, with your gracious permission [*Stands*

looking at the frame], well, that is really excellent, excellent - but too sad, dear lady, far too serious, too dark - despite all the cupids and graces! and this must be Hymen himself, extinguishing his torch. But from what old funeral speech did you take the idea? Excellently drawn, it is true, the embroidery is admirable! see how his disconsolate eye peeps through the hand which he holds to his brow! it sets all my blood stirring.

Wilhelmine: It is from a vignette on Haller's Ode to his Marianne.

Zierau: Why, but let Haller be Haller, besides he married again.

Wilhelmine: I could wish that I had a corpse to weep over. But now that Hymen has put out our torch before it had burned down, now - [*Weeps*] Do not insist, Herr Baccalaureus, the Count will not blame me.

Zierau: No, me. The whole celebration will lose its lustre if you do not appear. You need only show yourself, you do not need to dance: reflect that the world needs its heaven, which your charms must provide.

Wilhelmine: The only reply I can make to your flattery now is to scorn it. Pray don't blame me. What would happen if I were there, and some stranger were to start tinkling with such bells about my ears.

Frau v. Biederling: She's on her way to losing her wits I tell you.

[*DONNA DIANA enters with BABET*]

Donna Diana: I come unannounced, madam! Count Chameleon, who is said to be lodging in your house, is giving a *festin*, as I hear. I am his good friend whom he will not be expecting to see again.

Frau v. Biederling: Surely not the Spanish countess, his sister-in-law.

Donna Diana: His sister-in-law? Yes, his sister-in-law. I should very much like to profit by this occasion to give him a pleasant surprise.

Frau v. Biederling: Has your esteemed husband perhaps arrived? This is an unexpected pleasure -

Donna Diana: No compliments, Frau Captain! Is there room for me in your carriage? He'd recognize mine.

Wilhelmine: Oh if your ladyship would take my place -

Donna Diana: Your place, child? Oh how kind you are. Ha ha ha, forgive me, a strange idea was passing through my mind. But I should be most sorry, sweet child! to deprive you of your place.

Zierau: [*Softly, to WILHELMINE*] But what will the Count say, madam, if you -

Wilhelmine: Your ladyship would be doing me an inestimable favour. I could almost not withstand the earnest solicitations of the Count and his messenger.

Donna Diana: Indeed? is his messenger so earnest? I know my brother-in-law, he is very galant, but not very earnest, probably his messenger was wishing to make good the deficiency. So you'd like to stay at home, Fräulein? and lend me your mask, that is splendid, ha ha ha, the notion is most timely, it could not be better if I'd planned it [*Puts on the domino*] so we're ready, come, Frau Captain, let's waste no time here. And you sir, you look like the king in a game of chess whose queen has been taken. But rest content, it's not for you that we shall play. - Your hand, if I may. Adieu, Fräulein, and if ever I can return the favour - my dame d'honneur will stay with you.

Scene 2

Outside ZIERAU's villa. An alley of trees. Twilight
[*The COUNT, masked, walks up and down*]

Count: Devil take the fellow, what's keeping him, what's keeping him, what's keeping him! He said he'd be back straight away, he said he was ready to fly like Phaeton with the horses of the sun - poetical booby! If I can but prevail upon her to dance! The music, the excited enjoyment all around her, the tumult of her animal spirits, the punch, my little powder - damn me! [*Striking his forehead*] why does my head ache so! If he'd but come, if he'd but come, by all the devils! if he'd but come. [*Stamps*]. But what's keeping him? I shall likely go mad before all this is over, and then so much for my game. Perhaps he's enjoying her himself - Satan prince of hell! I've never believed in hell and all such stuff [*Strikes his head and his breast*] except in here - and here - I shall have to go into the town myself - she must have changed her mind, she's not coming - perhaps the Prince has returned - perhaps - I must go into the town myself, even if the devil were to swallow me up at her feet. -

Scene 3

Naumburg
[*WILHELMINE and BABET walk in the garden*]

Wilhelmine: Oh don't go yet, dear, dear Frau Wändeln! If you knew how much comfort your presence bestows on me. I can't account for it, I feel an unknown bond - I cannot conceal it, the hidden powers of sympathy sometimes play on us so strangely, so strangely. [*Kisses her*]

Babet: [*Falls weeping on her neck*] Oh my peerless Mina.

Wilhelmine: What's the matter?

Babet: I can suppress it no longer, even if the Donna were at my back with a dagger in her hand. It's mortal danger, Mina! but to see you suffer longer is impossible to me, you are not Prince Tandi's sister.

Wilhelmine: How can that be? My dear! how? At your knees I embrace you.

Babet: The Donna is his sister, I was your nurse, I exchanged you.

Wilhelmine: Oh nurse! [*Flinging her arms around her neck*] oh more than my mother! oh you give me a thousand lives. Come, come, tell me, relate it, I can't comprehend this miracle, I can but believe it and be happy. Take the last doubt from me, if this joy were in vain, it would be more than cruel.

Babet: [*Sobbing*] Rejoice - it is not in vain. Your father is the Spanish Count Aranda Velas, who was at the court in Dresden just at the time the Captain went to Silesia to the war. His wife followed him, and left her newborn child with a Polish woman to await her return, and I was likewise obliged to entrust you a few days to her, because my milk had dried up. Your mother once visited you there, and because at first it seemed you would suffer from rickets, I myself helped to persuade your parents to this godless exchange. I have had to endure enough from this Donna because of it, but you, dear one [*Kneeling*], you, who must ascribe all your ill fortune to me alone, you have not yet punished me for it.

Wilhelmine: With a thousand kisses I shall punish you. You've made me now unspeakably happy. Up, my dear, let's into the carriage and go seek him, who was everything to me, and who now will again be everything to me, the only one. Oh! oh! oh! the power that is in words, what heaven! in three words you've lifted me to heaven up from hell. Away now! let's fly like a pair of seraphim until we find him, until we - away! away! [*Runs off with outstretched arms*]

Scene 4

Outside ZIERAU's villa, which is seen brightly illuminated. It is pitch dark
[*GUSTAV enters*]

Gustav: It's like the sulphur pits of hell. She's here, yes she's here, I saw her in the carriage quite clearly. Knows that he'd have had her poisoned, and were he the devil himself and bearing her off alive, she loves him. [*Strikes his forehead*] Almighty God and all the elements! Ah you great soul abandoning heaven, you living angel. [*Falls*] I can no longer stand on my feet, it's fiercer than drink, it's fiercer than poison - I'll go in and see if he takes her for Wilhelmine, and if he touches her - I'll tear his guts out of his body, the soul-murderer, the dog -

Scene 5

[*GUSTAV comes out again, masked*]

Gustav: In there is hell itself - they're dancing around like furies. He offered her punch, I think it was a love potion. The glass was there, ready poured, she wouldn't take off her mask. If you'd wanted to know who she was, idiot Satan, you'd have made her take the mask off. I'll go in and stab him through with my pocket-knife, to teach him to be cleverer. - Ah Donna! Donna! Donna! if I could be damned with you, hell would be sweet.

[*He goes in*]

Scene 6

The ballroom

[*A crowd. At a pause in the dancing, ZIERAU leads FRAU v. BIEDERLING to the punch table*]

Frau v. Biederling: She's gone off with him.

Zierau: Would you not like a biscuit, madam, to go with that? - No doubt he recognized her - I assure you, he recognized her as soon as she entered the room.

Frau v. Biederling: But then he'd not have shown himself so besotted with her. Upon my word, it was provoking. The company holds her to be my daughter, she has precisely her gait, her figure - and he conducted himself most stupidly.

Zierau: He most certainly recognized her. He never would have allowed himself to take liberties with your daughter.

Frau v. Biederling: I'd not have wished her brother to be present. Herr Baccalaureus, if it goes on like this -

Zierau: I but regret I was unable to achieve my objective of offering your daughter a little harmless distraction. She'll be at home now, brooding on her sorrow, and for that gibbering confused Don Quixote of a knight, truly it's not worth the trouble.

[*Noises. The whole company springs up*]

A Lady: In the room over here.

A Cavalier: The door's locked.

Donna Diana: [*Screaming offstage*] Help! he's strangling me.

Lady: They must bring a locksmith.

A Hefty Lad: I'll take a run at it.

Zierau: What is it, what is it?

Mask: A dreadful noise here in this room.

Another Mask: Listen to the shrieking!

Zierau: Devil take it, is there no means? Servants, an axe. [*The HEFTY LAD runs at the door. A pitch dark room is seen*] Light here! Light here! they're on the floor. [*Lights are brought. DONNA DIANA springs up*]

Count: [*Pulling a knife from his wound*] I've been murdered. [*They stanch his wound*]

Donna Diana: [*Dishevelled, trying to rearrange her hair*] The dog tried to strangle me. – Why do you stand there? what are you gaping at, what's to astonish you? That out of hand I've stabbed a dog who attacked my throat, and all because he would have raped me but found I was not the right one.

Zierau: For heaven's sake.

Donna Diana: What, you pimp – where's my knife. [*Grabs his hair and throws him to the ground beside the COUNT*] Now let the Count give you your pay. He's a whoremaster, you must know, you must post it at every corner of the city, and publish it in all the European papers. I shall straight away set about destroying the dragon's nest that is here, only wait, there must be a sheriff somewhere close by.

[*She exits*]

Zierau: She's a fury.

Count: She has stabbed me to the heart – help me to bed. [*Turns his head painfully to one side*] Oh! – [*Stares*] you gods, what do I see? Put out the lights! The sight is too dreadful. [*One of the company lifts up a light. GUSTAV is seen in a corner, having hanged himself*] My servant oh! [*Falls unconscious*]

☐

ACT FIVE

Scene 1

A staging post on the road from Leipzig to Dresden

[*HERR v. BIEDERLING, PRINCE TANDI, rushing to embrace each other*]

Herr v. Biederling: My son!

Prince: Father!

Herr v. Biederling: Where have you come from? Where are you going? Has that damned schoolmaster let you run off? Don't I always say? might as well write down a nought as set one of the men in black coats in a place, as God's my judge, those people behave as if there were no head on their shoulders.

Prince: I'm on my way to Dresden.

Herr v. Biederling: Why I'll – you must come straight back to Naumburg, your poor sister will be all but dead of your keeping away. It is all valid and made right, the Consistory has not a word to say against the marriage.

Prince: [*Lifting his eyes to heaven*] Oh help me now!

Herr v. Biederling: Now turn about! who's the horse been saddled for? ha ha, did you have to leave your equipage in Leipzig? Well, well, I've done him an injustice, our Master Beza. – Quick, I command you! on with your travelling cloak. Why did you refuse to see me, monsieur! after I'd been travelling eight hours on your account. You have bees in your bonnet like the alchemists, and for their sake father and mother and sister and all must be laid waste.

Prince: [*Wraps his arms around his father's knees*] Father! The bees are sacred, more sacred than everything.

Herr v. Biederling: She's dying, devil take me, she'll needs die of grief, the girl won't be comforted. Have you lost your reason then, or would you be cleverer than the whole theological faculty? I command you as your father, on with your coat and back with me, or nothing will ever be well.

Prince: I shall obey you.

Herr v. Biederling: Will you? that's good. So come, let me embrace you once more and press you to my heart, [*Putting his arms around him*] prodigal son! I thought from the start, if one could but speak reason to him, you're not in Qumba here, my son, we're in Saxony here, and what's good for all the others must also be good for us. Go, make ready, you'll give your sister back her life - meanwhile I shall eat breakfast, I've not touched a thing, God help me, since four o'clock this morning. [*He exits*]

Prince: This was the moment I feared. I have seen him, Wilhelmine, seen your father, I am too weak to resist. If you still love me, angel from heaven - oh if you but hated me! if you but hated me! What if I were instantly to mount upon my horse and ride away in secret - but she's my flesh! God help me! she's my flesh and blood. Let me go, beloved woman, sacred phantom! heaven requires it, your soul's peace requires it - triumph -

[*He is about to leave through the door. WILHELMINE and BABET collide with him*]

Wilhelmine: You here!

Prince: [*At her feet*] Your suffering husband!

Wilhelmine: Is this a dream? [*Puts her arms around him*] Is it really you?

Prince: Spare me! Spare yourself! Oh sin! who could resist you, when you take Wilhelmine's form?

Wilhelmine: I'm not your sister.

Babet: I protest by all that's holy, she's not your sister. I was her nurse, I exchanged her.

Prince: Oh that healing balm! More of that balm! Heaven-sent relief!

Wilhelmine: [*Throws herself into his arms again*] I'm not your sister.

Prince: This my sorrow never dared to hope, never wished! I was dead, now I wake. Tell me again, a hundred times.

Wilhelmine: I wish I could dissolve in your arms, my husband! brother no more! my husband! I'm all rapture, I'm all yours.

Prince: Mine forever, my newfound life.

Wilhelmine: My newfound soul!

[*Enter HERR v. BIEDERLING, with table napkin*]

Herr v. Biederling: What's the matter here? - Well holy wonder! where have you come from? Didn't I say, if one just talked sense to him, and there they are, man and wife together, and this moment half an hour ago, for your sake he was ready to castrate himself.

Babet: We have wonders to tell you, sir.

Herr v. Biederling: Then come in here, come in here, aren't you ashamed to be playing at Rebecca[8] with your wife while the whole world's watching, they do that kind of thing in Qumba I dare say, dear man! but not in Saxony, not in Saxony. [*They go in*]

[8]Biblical reference: Moses XXVI, 8

Scene 2

Naumburg

[*ZIERAU sits playing the violin. His father, the MAYOR, enters in a roquelaure[9], hat on*]

Mayor: Pretty stories! pretty stories! I'll teach you to put on parties - Hey! Come with me, the weather's so bad, I must have entertainment tonight.

Zierau: Where will you go then, Papa? I'm half undressed.

Mayor: Put your fiddle away! We'll to the puppets. I've been at my desk all day, writing myself blind and lame, I must laugh again.

Zierau: Fie on it, papa! Night after night! You demean yourself.

Mayor: But see, what's this again, what have you got against the puppets? Are they not every bit as good as those things of yours in Leipzig, what are they called? So long as I can laugh my heart out, I do love that rascal Punch, I shall certainly give him a present at New Year[10].

Zierau: Pleasure without taste is no pleasure at all.

Mayor: Indeed I can't fathom it, whatever it is he means by this taste of his. Are you simple in the head? Boy! why should the puppets not be a pleasure to the taste?

Zierau: That which does not imitate the Beautiful in Nature, Papa! cannot possibly please.

Mayor: But the puppets please me, boy! what's your Beautiful in Nature to do with me? Isn't it good enough for you there where it is, booby? would you presume to teach God to do better? I don't know, I always get pains in my ears when I hear the brat with his reasoning.

Zierau: But for all the world, what pleasure can you find in a performance lacking the slightest illusion.

Mayor: Illusion? and what sort of a thing is that?

Zierau: It is one thing instead of another.

Mayor: You mean barter.

Zierau: Oh Papa! You look at it like a shopkeeper, that's why I don't like to discuss it with you. There are specific rules for illusion, that is, for the deception of the senses which makes me believe that I truly see what is merely being represented to me.

Mayor: Well? and what sort of rules are those? That's true, I always think when I'm there that it's only a performance.

[9]A coat buttoned all the way down, as worn by the Prussian military

[10]It was a German tradition to give Punch a New Year's present

Zierau: Yes, but you should think it no more, if the play were even tolerable. To this end particular rules have been established, without which this deception of the senses cannot take place, among them especially the much disputed three unities, if in other words the whole action does not occur within a space of four and twenty hours at most, and in a particular place, then I cannot imagine it well, and there's an end to all the pleasure of the play.

Mayor: Wait! hm! then today I shall examine this, I fathom, I begin to fathom, three unities, that's the same as three times one. And secondly four and twenty hours is all that the whole thing may last? but how? hey? in all its days it's never gone on as long as that.

Zierau: But father, that's another matter altogether, I'm to imagine, do you see, that it's only gone on four and twenty hours.

Mayor: Why good, good, that's the way I shall imagine it - won't you come? I'll just give the thing a try tonight, shall I, and if it seems to me they don't understand what they're about, it's straight out of town with the fellows.

[*He exits*]

Scene 3

[*ZIERAU in a dressing gown throws his violin on the table*]

Zierau: I'm bored! Bored! - Oh Naumburg, what sort of place are you? For there's not a single intelligent way to amuse oneself, it's impossible, downright impossible. If it were enough to smoke and drink beer - fie, disgusting! and I'm weary of girls as well - I've lived too much - have I? I've lived too little - and now I'm nothing. If only I'd finished my book, my *Golden Age*, truly, I'd do as the Englishman did and shoot myself through the forehead. That's what I call a resounding conclusion - and it would also attract more attention to my book - Hm! if I - but I've never fired a shot - and what if I were to start shaking and miss like young Brandrecht - Oh if it goes on long like this, Desperation! I'm yours. [*Throws himself on the bed*]

[*The MAYOR enters with stick held high*]

Mayor: Still idling here? Wait, I'll give you your three unities and your four and thirty hours [*Hits him*], devil take you. I believe you suffer from ennui, I'll pass the time for you. [*Dances with him around the room*]

Zierau: Papa, what's wrong, Papa?

Mayor: You dog! will you ruin honest people's pleasure? My whole night poisoned, and I'd crippled myself at my counting desk, then along comes a dog's hind leg of a good-for-nothing like yourself and talks to me about three times one and the Beautiful in Nature, and so I spent the whole night sitting there like a fool who doesn't know what God created him for. Counting and calculating and looking at the time [*Hits him*], I'll teach you to write rules for me as to how I'm to enjoy myself.

Zierau: Papa, how can I help it?

Mayor: Of course you can help it, stop your reasoning. I see the boy grow idle, I see he stinks, in times gone by he would be reading at least, he'd be doing, but now - and he didn't deign to take up his place at Schulpforta, did he, was the young gentleman too fine, or too distinguished, how should I know? or perhaps it was because the three times three is not observed there, wait, I'll three times three you. You'll go into my counting house, you huckster of taste! to write until you're crippled and lame, and after that the puppets will quite delight you. I've never heard the like in all my life, I think the youth of the world has at last been stood on its head, and all for the Beautiful in Nature. I'll counsel you, I'll read you a lecture on the Beautiful in Nature, just wait!

THE END

THE TUTOR

OR THE ADVANTAGES OF PRIVATE EDUCATION

TRANSLATED BY

ANTHONY MEECH

This translation was commissioned by the Gate Theatre, London, and first performed at the Edinburgh International Festival, 1993

DRAMATIS PERSONAE

Herr von Berg, Privy Councillor
The Major, his brother
The Major's Wife
Gustchen, their daughter
Fritz von Berg
Count Wermuth
Läuffer, a tutor
Pätus, a student
Bollwerk, a student
Herr von Seiffenblase
His **Tutor**
Frau Hamster, a councillor's wife
Mistress Hamster
Mistress Knicks
Frau Blitzer
Wenzeslaus, a schoolmaster
Marthe, an old woman
Lise
Old Pätus
Old Läuffer, a city preacher
Leopold, squire to the Major, a child
Herr Rehaar, a lutanist
Mistress Rehaar, his daughter

Translator's note: None of the above names have been translated [except in the case of Läuffer's assumed name in Act Three, Scene 2, where not to translate *Mandel* as Almond would negate Wenzeslaus' pun], nor the more common titles such as *Herr* and *Frau*. However *Jungfer* is translated as Mistress and *Graf* as Count.

ACT ONE

Scene 1

Insterburg, Prussia

Läuffer: My father says: I'm not suitable to be his a lecturer. But I believe the fault lies in his purse. He's not prepared to pay for me. I'm too young to be a pastor, too well educated, and I've seen too much of the world, and the Privy Councillor wasn't prepared to take me on at the municipal school. So be it! The man's a pedant. I've no doubt the Devil himself wouldn't be sufficiently qualified for him. In six months I could brush up on what I learnt in school. That would certainly more than qualify me to be a class teacher; but the Privy Councillor knows best. He keeps calling me Monsieur Läuffer, and whenever we talk about Leipzig he asks after Händel's beer garden and Richter's coffee house; I don't know if he's trying to be satirical or – I've heard him deep in erudite discussion with the deputy headmaster often enough. I suppose he doesn't take me seriously. – Here he comes with the Major; I don't know why, but he scares me more than the Devil himself. There's something about the man's face that I just can't abide.

[*He passes the PRIVY COUNCILLOR and the MAJOR and bows in a friendly and obsequious manner*]

Scene 2

[*The PRIVY COUNCILLOR, the MAJOR*]

Major: Well, what do you want? Isn't he a nice enough young fellow?

Privy Councillor: Nice enough, too nice in fact. But what's he supposed to teach your son?

Major: I don't know, Berg. You do ask such strange questions.

Privy Councillor: No honestly! You must have some aim in mind when you take on a private tutor, and open your purse wide enough to let three hundred ducats fall out. Tell me, what do you hope to get for your money; what are you going to expect from your tutor?

Major: I want him – well – I want him to instruct my son in all the branches of knowledge, as well as courtesy and good manners – oh, I don't know what you're after with all your questions. It'll all sort itself out. I'll tell him all in good time.

Privy Councillor: You mean you're going to be tutor to your tutor. Have you considered what you're taking on – Tell me: what do you want your son to be, anyway?

Major: What's he...he's going to be a soldier; a fine fellow like I was.

Privy Councillor: Forget that idea, my dear Brother. Our children shouldn't, mustn't become what we were. Times change, customs, circumstances, everything. What if you'd been nothing more nor less than a faithful copy of your father –

Major: Hell's teeth! To rise to major, to be a fine fellow and to serve the king as honourably as I have!

Privy Councillor: That's all very well, but in fifty years time there may well be a different king, and a different way to serve him. But I can see that I mustn't get involved in all this, the more I quizz you, the less I'll get out of you. You're just following the line your wife's laid down for you.

Major: What do you mean by that, Berg? I'll thank you not to meddle in my domestic arrangements, as I don't in yours – Oh but look! There's that young gentleman your son with two of his schoolmates. – What a splendid education, Herr Philosophus! He's sure to turn out well. Who in the world would believe that street urchin was the only son of His Excellency Privy Councillor –

Privy Councillor: Let him be – Those high-spirited friends of his will do him less harm than some braided layabout, the protégé of a vain patroness.

Major: Now you're going too far. – Adieu.

Privy Councillor: I feel sorry for you.

Scene 3

The MAJOR'S WIFE's drawing room

[*The MAJOR'S WIFE on a sofa. LÄUFFER sitting very humbly beside her. LEOPOLD standing*]

Major's Wife: I have spoken with your father, and instead of the three hundred ducats salary you receive at present, we have agreed on one hundred and fifty. And for that I also require that you, Herr – what's your name? – Herr Läuffer, that you appear in clean clothes and that you do nothing to bring discredit on this house. I know you are a man of taste; I have already heard reports of your time in Leipzig. You understand that what people nowadays take notice of above everything else in the world is whether a man knows how to comport himself.

Läuffer: I hope, Your Grace, that you will be satisfied with me. At least in Leipzig I never missed a ball, and I must have had more than fifteen dancing masters in my life.

Major's Wife: Really? Let me see then. [*LÄUFFER stands*] Don't be bashful, Herr... Läuffer! not bashful! My son's shy enough as it is; if his tutor's timid too, he'll be done for. Try doing a minuet bow for me, as a test, so I can see. - Good, good, that's fine! Well, my son won't need a dancing master for the present! And now a few steps please, if you wouldn't mind. - That's most satisfactory. I'm sure that, were you to be present at one of our soirées, you would fit in very well... Are you musical?

Läuffer: I play the violin, and the piano at a pinch.

Major's Wife: All the better. When we go to the country we are sometimes visited by Fräulein Milchzahn. Up 'till now I've had to sing something when the dear children felt like dancing. This will be much better.

Läuffer: Your Grace, I am at a loss. Where in the world is one to find a virtuoso who on his instrument might hope to match your voice.

Major's Wife: Ha ha ha. You haven't heard me yet, have you... Wait. Do you know this minuet? [*Sings*]

Läuffer: Oh... oh... forgive in me this rapture, this enthusiasm which quite transports me. [*Kisses her hand*]

Major's Wife: And me with a cold as well. I must be croaking like a raven. *Vous parlez français, sans doute?*

Läuffer: *Un peu, Madame.*

Major's Wife: *Avez-vous déjà fait votre tour de France?*

Läuffer: *Non Madame... Oui Madame.*

Major's Wife: *Vous devez donc savoir, qu'en France on ne baise pas les mains, mon cher!*[1]..

Servant: [*Entering*] Count Wermuth..

[*Enter COUNT WERMUTH who, after a silent bow, sits next to the major's wife on the sofa. LÄUFFER remains standing in embarrassment*]

[1]**Major's Wife**: You speak French, of course?
Läuffer: A little, Madam.
Major's Wife: Have you made your tour of France yet?
Läuffer: No, Madam... Yes, Madam.
Major's Wife: You should know then, that in France one does not kiss hands, my dear!

Count: Has Your Grace seen the new dancing master yet, the one who's come from Dresden? He's a marchese from Florence, called... honestly, in all my travels I've only met with two one would prefer to him.

Major's Wife: Well, I confess, only two! Indeed you're making me curious; I know what refined taste Count Wermuth has.

Läuffer: Pintinello... isn't it? I saw him dance at the theatre in Leipzig; there's nothing remarkable about his dancing..

Count: He dances – *on ne peut pas mieux*[2] – When I say to you, Madam, that in Petersburg I saw one Beluzzi who was preferable; but this one has a lightness in his feet, a certain freedom, a heavenly nonchalance in his carriage, in his arms, his turns –

Läuffer: At Koch's Theatre he was booed off the stage the last time he appeared there.

Major's Wife: Now look, son, domestics don't engage in conversation with people of quality. Go up to your room. Who asked you to speak?

[*LÄUFFER steps back several paces*]

Count: Presumably the tutor you've engaged for the young gentleman?..

Major's Wife: He's fresh from the university. Just go, will you! You can see that we're talking about you, so it's all the less correct for you to stay.

[*Exit LÄUFFER with a stiff bow*]

Major's Wife: It's quite insupportable that you can't find anyone decent for your money nowadays. My husband wrote three times to his former professor and this is the one who's meant to have the best manners in the whole academy. But it's obvious from his clothes – trimmed on the left. Just imagine, two hundred ducats travelling expenses from Leipzig to Insterburg, and an annual salary of five hundred ducats, isn't that frightful?

Count: I believe his father is the parson here..

Major's Wife: I don't know – he may be – I haven't enquired, yes, I believe you're right; his name's Läuffer too. Well then he should certainly be well enough behaved. His father's an absolute bear of a man, at least his growling's driven me out of the church once and for all.

Count: Is he a Catholic?

Major's Wife: Good Lord, no. You know there's no Catholic church in Insterburg. He's Lutheran, or should I say Protestant; he's Protestant.

Count: Pintinello can dance...It's true my dancing has cost me all of thirty thousand guilders, but I would give as much again if..

[2]One could not do better

Scene 4

LÄUFFER's room

[LÄUFFER. LEOPOLD. The MAJOR. The MAJOR surprises LÄUFFER and LEOPOLD sitting at a table with a book]

Major: Good, good; that's the way I like it; a hive of activity - and if the reprobate won't take it in, Herr Läuffer, then hit him round the head with the book, until he can't stand up, or should I say, you have only to come to me with your complaint. I'll make you see reason, you little heathen! Look at him sulking again. So it upsets you when your father speaks to you like this does it? Who else is going to, then? You'd better change your attitude towards me, you spiteful little beast, or I'll flog you 'till your innards burst! And you, Sir, be zealous with him, I insist on that, and no holidays, no breaks, no recreation, that I will not tolerate. Nonsense, no-one ever caught *malum hydropisiacum*[3] from hard work. That's just an excuse dreamed up by intellectuals like you, Sir. - How's he getting on? Does he know his Cornelius? Idiot! I've told you a thousand times: in God's name, hold your head up! Keep your head high, boy! *[Straightens him up]* or I'll break your backbone in a thousand million pieces for you.

Läuffer: I'm sorry, Herr Major, but he can barely read Latin.

Major: What? So the wretch has forgotten, has he. And his former tutor told me his Latin was perfect, perfect... hammered into him - but I don't want you to - I don't want to have to answer to God for not having kept you under my thumb, when you end up a gaol bird like young Hufeise or your uncle Friedrich. Before I let you become a worthless street urchin like them - I'll beat you to death - *[Boxes his ears]* Like a question mark again, are we? He won't listen. - Out of my sight! - Get out! Do I have to help you? I said, get out.

[Stamps his foot. Exit LEOPOLD. The MAJOR sits on his chair. To LÄUFFER]

Major: Stay there, Herr Läuffer; I wanted to have a word with you alone, that's why I sent the young gentleman away. Stay there; you may always remain seated, always, always. Hang me, but you'll break the chair if you insist on sitting on one corner... That's what chairs are for, to sit on. You're so widely travelled, and haven't learned that yet? - Listen, you seem to me to be a nice, pleasant sort of fellow, God-fearing and

---

[3] The dropsy

obedient, otherwise I would never be doing what I am for you. I
promised you a hundred and forty ducats a year. That makes three - wait
- three times one hundred and forty: how much is that?

Läuffer: Four hundred and twenty.

Major: Right! Is it really that much? Now, to give us a nice round figure,
I've decided to make your salary four hundred Prussian Thalers, and that's
more than my income from the whole of the estate.

Läuffer: But if Your Grace will permit me, your lady wife told me one
hundred and fifty ducats; that makes four hundred and fifty Thalers, and
it was to those terms that I agreed.

Major: What do women know, eh? - Four hundred Thalers, Monsieur; you
can't in all conscience demand any more. Your predecessor received two
hundred and fifty and was as pleased as Punch. And yet, my word, he was
a learned man and a courtier too; the whole world could testify to that.
There'll have to be some changes in you, Sir, before you can compare to
him. I'm only doing what I am for you out of friendship for your father,
and for your own sake too. While you stay nice and obedient, I'll know
how to look after you, you can be sure of that. - Now listen here: I have
a daughter, who's the image of me, and the whole world can testify
there's none to match her for beauty anywhere in Prussia. The girl's
nature is quite different from that wretched son of mine. She needs quite
different handling! She knows her catechism through and through, but
even so, as she's going to make her first communion soon, and I know
what priests are like, I would like you to take her every morning for
classes in her catechism. An hour a day in the morning, you're to go up
to her room; properly dressed, of course. God forbid that you should be
like one filthy swine we had who had every intention of coming to the
breakfast table in his nightshirt. - Can you draw too?

Läuffer: A little, Sir. - I could show you some of my sketches.

Major: [*Examining them*] These are charming! - Very good. Right, you can
teach my daughter to draw too. - But listen, my dear Herr Läuffer, for
God's sake don't be strict with her; the girl's nature is quite different from
the boy's. God knows! it's as if they weren't brother and sister. She's there
day and night with her books, her precious tragedies, and if anyone so
much as says a word to her, particularly me, she can't bear comments
from me, her cheeks flare up and tears stream down them like pearls. I
just want to say: the girl is my only consolation. My wife makes my life
miserable. She always has to have the upper hand, and she can because

she's cleverer and more cunning than me. And our son is her favourite. She wants to bring him up according to her methods, all nice and gentle like Absalom, and we'll end up with some sort of gallows bird who's no use to God nor man. Well, I won't have it. - As soon as he does anything wrong or makes a mistake or hasn't learnt his law, just tell me and I'll beat the hell out of him. - But you take care with my daughter. My wife will no doubt encourage you to be strict with her. She can't abide her, I'm aware of that; but that is of no account. I'm telling you: I am the master in this house, and if anyone gets too near my daughter - she's my one treasure, and even if the king offered me his kingdom for her, I'd send him packing. Every day she's in my evening and morning prayers, my grace at table; she's everything to me, and if God would be gracious enough to grant that before I die I might see her settled down with a general or a top ranking minister - because no one else would be worthy to share her life - I'd happily die ten years before my time. - Mark my words - anyone who gets too near my daughter, or harms her at all - I'll blow his brains out. Mark my words.

[*He exits*]

Scene 5

[*FRITZ VON BERG. GUSTCHEN*]

Fritz: You won't keep your word, Gustchen, you won't write to me when you're in Heidelbrunn, and I'll die of a broken heart.

Gustchen: Do you think your Juliet could be so inconstant, then? Oh no; I'm a woman; it's men who are inconstant.

Fritz: No, Gustchen, it's only women. If only you were all like Juliet! I know. When you write to me call me your Romeo; grant me that favour. I assure you I will play Romeo in every respect. I'll even carry a dagger! I could even stab myself, if it came to that.

Gustchen: Go on with you! Yes, you'd do it like in the Gellert poem: he looked on the blade's point and edge, and plunged it slowly in once more.

Fritz: You'll see. [*Grasps her hand*] Gustchen - Gustchen! If I should lose you, or my uncle were to give you to another. - That godless Count Wermuth! I can't speak my thoughts, Gustchen, but you may read them in my eyes. He will be our Count Paris.

Gustchen: Fritzchen - Then I will act as Juliet did.

Fritz: What? - How, then? - It's all just make-believe; there are no such sleeping draughts.

Gustchen: No, but there are draughts to grant eternal sleep.

Fritz: [*Embraces her*] How cruel!

Gustchen: I can hear my father in the corridor. Let's run into the garden! No, he's gone. - We're leaving straight after coffee, and as our carriage disappears from your sight, so will I too fade from your thoughts.

Fritz: May God never remember me, if I were to forget you. But beware of the Count, your mother thinks so highly of him, and you must know that she just wants you out of her sight, and 'till I've finished school and three years at the university, that's such a long time.

Gustchen: What can we do, Fritzchen! I'm still a child; I haven't made my first communion yet. But tell me - Oh, who knows how soon I'll speak to you again! - Wait; come into the garden.

Fritz: No, no, your papa has just passed. - What did you want to say to me?

Gustchen: Nothing...

Fritz: Dear Gustchen..

Gustchen: You must - No, I cannot ask that of you.

Fritz: Ask my life, my last drop of blood!

Gustchen: We should swear an oath together.

Fritz: Why yes! Splendid! Let us kneel here by the sofa, and you raise your fingers like so, and I'll raise mine. Now tell me, what should I swear?

Gustchen: That in three year's time you will return from the university and make Gustchen your wife, no matter what your father might say.

Fritz: And what will you swear in return, my angel... [*Kisses her*]

Gustchen: I'll swear that in all my life I will be no man's wife but yours, even if I was asked by the Tsar of Russia himself.

Fritz: I swear a hundred thousand vows -

[*Enter the PRIVY COUNCILLOR. GUSTCHEN and FRITZ leap up with a loud cry*]

Scene 6

[*PRIVY COUNCILLOR. FRITZ VON BERG. GUSTCHEN*]

Privy Councillor: What are you doing, you foolish children? Why are you trembling? - Tell me everything, at once. What have you been doing? You were both on your knees - Master Fritz I would like an answer at once - What were you doing?

Fritz: I, Sir?

Privy Councillor: I? and in a tone of such hurt innocence? Look, nothing escapes me. No doubt you'd like to lie to me, but you're either too much of a fool or too much of a coward, and you're hoping to extricate yourself with this "I?"...And you, little lady? - I know Gustchen would never keep anything from me.

Gustchen: [*Falls at his feet*] Oh, Father -

Privy Councillor: [*Raises her up and kisses her*] Would you like me as a father? Too soon, my child, too soon Gustchen, my child. You haven't yet made your communion. - Why should I hide the fact that I was listening to you. - That play-acting was very naïve of you; especially you, sensible, grown-up Master Fritz, who'll soon have a beard like me, wear a wig and carry a sword. Hm, I would have thought my son had more sense. This shows you must be younger than I thought, and will therefore have to stay on longer in school. And I'm bound to say to you too, Gustchen, that at your age it's not right to behave in such a childish fashion. What novels were they that you were acting out? What vows were they that you swore to each other, and which you will break as surely as I am speaking to you now. Do you really believe you are old enough to swear a vow, or do you think that a vow is some childish game like hide-and-seek or blind-man's-buff? First find out what vows mean, learn to tremble before them, and only then venture to swear. Believe me, perjurers are the most despicable and miserable creatures under the sun. Such a one may neither look to the Heaven which he has denied, nor at his fellow men who will forever shun him and avoid his company more assiduously than that of a snake or a vicious dog.

Fritz: But I intend to keep my vow.

Privy Councillor: Is that so, Romeo? Ha! You could even stab yourself, were it to come that. Your vows make my hair stand on end. So, do you really intend to keep your vow?

Fritz: Yes, Sir, by God, I intend to keep it.

Privy Councillor: One vow reinforced with another! - I must bring this to the attention of your headmaster. Let him put you back for a fortnight into the second year, Master Fritz; and in future learn to swear with greater circumspection. And what was the vow? Is it in your power to fulfil what you've sworn? You want to marry Gustchen! Just think, will you! Do you have any idea what marriage means? Go on then, marry her;

take her back with you to the Academy. No? I have no objection to your seeing each other, or your liking each other, or against your saying that you like each other; but you must abandon this folly; no aping of us adults until you're as mature as us. No more play-acting at novels; they're simply products of the overheated imaginations of poets, and bear no resemblance to the world as we know it. Go on! I won't tell anyone, so you won't need to blush when you see me. - But from now on you are not to see each other alone. Do you understand me? And you are not to correspond with each other except by open letter and that only once a month, or at most every three weeks. And the moment a secret note to Master Fritz or Fräulein Gustchen is discovered - he'll be sent for a soldier and she'll be sent to a convent, until they become more reasonable. Do you understand me? - And now - say goodbye, here in my presence. - The carriage is ready, the Major is keen to get started, my sister-in-law has finished her coffee. Say goodbye. There's no need to be shy in front of me. Come on, embrace. [*FRITZ and GUSTCHEN embrace*] And now, Gustchen, my daughter, as you like the word so much, [*Lifts her up and kisses her*] a thousand times farewell, and treat your mother with respect; no matter what she says to you - Go on now, go! - [*GUSTCHEN takes a few paces, looks round. FRITZ flies weeping to her embrace her*] These little fools will break my heart! If only the Major were more reasonable, or his wife less domineering!

☐

ACT TWO

Scene 1

[*PASTOR LÄUFFER. The PRIVY COUNCILLOR*]

Privy Councillor: I feel sorry for him - and all the more for you, Herr Pastor, that you have a son like him.

Pastor: Forgive me, Your Grace, but my son gives me no cause to complain; he is a modest and gifted young man. The whole world as well as your brother and sister-in-law would vouch for him.

Privy Councillor: I don't deny him any of that, but he's a fool, and has no-one to blame but himself for any dissatisfaction, he ought to thank heaven that my brother is beginning to find the money he pays his tutor too dear.

Pastor: But think a moment: only a hundred ducats, a hundred measly ducats; he'd promised him three hundred for the first year alone, but by the year's end he'd only paid him one hundred and forty. At the end of the second year, with my son's work steadily increasing, he's paid him a hundred, and now at the start of the third even that's too much for him. That's an offence against justice! Forgive me.

Privy Councillor: There's no need - I could have told you this would happen. And yet your son should thank God if the Major were to take him by the scruff of the neck and throw him out of his house. Tell me, man: What's he doing there? You want to be a good father to your child and yet you close your eyes, your ears and your mouth when his happiness is at stake? Idling his time away and receiving payment for it? Spending the noblest hours in the day sitting with a young gentleman, who has no desire to learn but with whom he may not fall out. And the hours that remain, which should be kept sacred to eating and sleeping - to the preservation of life - he sighs away chained like a slave, hanging on Madame's every whim or learning to read the Major's every expression; eating when he's full, and fasting when he's hungry, drinking punch when he'd like to piss, and playing cards when his luck's out. Without freedom a man's life deteriorates sharply. Freedom is Man's element, as water is for fish, and a man who surrenders his freedom poisons the noblest spirit in his blood, nips the sweetest joy in life in the bud, and destroys himself.

Pastor: But - Oh! forgive me, but that's something every tutor has to endure.

No-one can expect their own way all the time, and my son would be quite happy to put up with that, except –

Privy Councillor: So much the worse for him, if he's prepared to put up with it, so much the worse. He will have forfeited the prerogatives of a man, who must either live by his principles or cease to be a man. Let those miserable creatures whose aspirations to happiness reach no higher than food and drink remain in their cages 'till they die, but an educated man, someone who is aware of the nobility of his soul, should be less afraid of death than of acting against his principles..

Pastor: But what on earth can be done? What is my son supposed to do if your brother revokes his position?

Privy Councillor: Let the lad learn something which might be of use to the state. Hell's teeth, Pastor, you surely didn't bring him up to be a servant, but what else is he but a servant when he'll sell his freedom as an individual for a handful of ducats? He's a slave, over whom his masters have unlimited power. Only he has learned enough at the academy to be able to anticipate their capricious demands, and thereby to apply a fine veneer to his servitude. What a nice, polite fellow, an incomparable fellow; what an incomparable scoundrel, who, instead of employing his physical and mental powers for the good of everyone, prefers instead to pander to the aberrations of an oppressive woman and a repressed officer, whose influence expands daily like a cancer and will end up by being incurable. And what will he gain from it all? A roast at lunchtime and punch each evening, and a large dose of bile rising into his mouth every day to be swallowed down each night as he lies in bed. That makes for healthy blood, upon my honour! and for a first-rate heart too in the long run. You complain so bitterly about the gentry and their pride, and that everybody regards tutors as domestics. You fool! What else are they? Aren't they employed in just the same way as servants? But who is it asks you to encourage pride in them? And who asks you, when you've acquired some learning, to revert to a domestic servant, to make yourself dependant on some mulish nobleman, who's never known anything but slavish subservience from his household?

Pastor: But Herr Privy Councillor – Merciful God! There is no other way. You must have a position from which to look around for a public appointment after coming down from the university. You must then await the divine call, and a patron is very often the means to your advancement; at least that's how it was in my case.

Privy Councillor: Hold your tongue, Herr Pastor, I beg you. Speaking like that does you no credit. We are, of course, all aware that it was your late wife who acted as your divine call. Otherwise you'd still be muckspreading for Herr von Tiesen now. You reverend gentlemen are forever talking humbug. No nobleman has ever taken a tutor into his employment without painting for him a seductive prospect of advancement after his eight or nine years of slavery. And when those eight years are over, he'll follow Laban and simply start the process all over again! It's all a trick! Learn something and stay an honest man. The state will not leave you standing in the market for long. There's a demand for honest men everywhere, but scoundrels, scholars only on paper, whose heads are full of nothing..

Pastor: That view may be widely held, Herr Councillor! - But, God knows, there is a place in the world for private tutors. Not everyone can hope to become a Privy Councillor straight away - even if he were a Hugo Grotius. Nowadays there's more to it than simply scholarship.

Privy Councillor: You're getting excited, Herr Pastor! - My dear and esteemed Herr Pastor, let us not lose the thread of our argument. I maintain: there should be no more private tutors in the world! The scum aren't worth a devil's curse.

Pastor: I didn't come here to listen to such rudeness from you. I was myself a private tutor once. I have the honour -

Privy Councillor: Wait a moment; stay, my dear Herr Pastor! I had no intention of insulting you. Heaven forbid! And if I have unintentionally, I offer you a thousand apologies. It's simply a wretched habit of mine to get excited when I find a conversation interesting. I lose sight of everything but the matter in hand.

Pastor: But you're throwing - forgive me, I too am choleric and like to speak my mind - you're throwing the baby out with the bath water. "Private tutors are good for nothing". How can you prove that? Who else is there to instil reason and good manners into your young gentlemen! What would have become of you, Herr Privy Councillor, if you hadn't had a private tutor?

Privy Councillor: My father sent me to public schools and I bless his memory for it, as I hope my son will one day bless mine.

Pastor: Well, there's a good deal more to be said on this matter, Sir! For my part, I can't agree with you. Of course, if the public schools were all they ought to be - But the stale approach to subjects which so often predominates in the classes, the pedantic methods they employ and the appalling manners which are the norm among the young people there.

Privy Councillor: Who's fault is that? Who's to blame if not you venomous private tutors? If noblemen were not encouraged by you in the folly of establishing their own petty courts where they can sit enthroned like monarchs, receiving the homage of their private tutor, their Mamselle, and a whole host of other good-for-nothings, they would have to put their sons into public schools. They would then devote the money which at present they waste on raising their sons to be aristocratic idiots to funding those public schools. That would allow for the payment of intelligent people to teach in them, and all would be well. The young students would have to learn something in order to be of any use at such an establishment, and the young milords, instead of artfully and oh-so-politely concealing their indolence from Papa and their aunties (who anyway are no hundred-eyed Arguses) would have to exercise their brains to keep ahead of the bourgeois boys, if indeed they wanted to be distinguished from them. - And as for manners, they really will come of their own accord, as soon as they are not taught from infancy like their noble cousins to stick their noses in the air, and nonchalantly to utter nonsense from a great height while staring people straight in the face when they doff their hats to them to make it obvious that they have no intention of returning the courtesy. The devil take good manners! Engage a dancing master at home for the boy if you like and introduce him to polite society, but don't remove him from the circle of his school friends or encourage in him the belief that he is a creature in some way superior to others.

Pastor: I haven't the time, [*Pulls out his watch*] my dear Sir, to engage any further in this argument, but something I do know is that the aristocracy is not universally of your opinion.

Privy Councillor: Then the bourgeoisie should be. Necessity will soon force the aristocracy into changing their minds, and we could look forward to better times to come. Upon my soul, what's to become of the nobility when one person has to be factotum to their children? In the unlikely event that he is indeed a polymath, where will one man find the fire, the vigour, the energy he'll need when he is forced to devote himself to a single numbskull, especially when father and mother insist on meddling time and again in his teaching, and forever knocking the bottom out of the barrel he is trying to fill?

Pastor: I have to be at a sick bed at ten. Please excuse me - [*In leaving turns*] But would it not be possible, my dear Sir, for you to board out your second son with the Major for half a year? I'm sure my son would be happy with eighty ducats, but he just can't make do on the sixty your brother intends giving him.

Privy Councillor: Let him quit! I won't do it, Herr Pastor! You won't persuade me. I'd sooner send your son the thirty ducats. No. I won't hand my son over to any tutor. [*The Pastor gives him a letter*] What am I to do with this? There's no point.

Pastor: Read it - just read it -

Privy Councillor: Yes but, he's not - [*Reads*] - "Do everything in your power to convince the Herr Privy Councillor to - you cannot imagine how miserable I am here; they have not fulfilled any of their promises to me. I only eat with the adults if they have no visitors. - - but the worst thing of all is that I cannot get away from here. I haven't set foot out of Heidelbrunn in six months - I was promised a horse, so I could visit Königsberg every three months, but when I demanded it the Frau Major asked if I wouldn't prefer to go the carnival in Venice instead -" [*Throws the letter down*] Well then, let him quit; why is he such a fool as to stay?

Pastor: That's just the point. [*Picks up the letter*] Please be so good as to read it to the end.

Privy Councillor: What more can there be? - [*Reads*] "Nonetheless I cannot leave this house even if it were to cost my life and health. I can say this much, that the prospect of blessings in the future, when put against my present toils and tribulations" - Perhaps he sees blessings in eternity. I can't imagine any other prospects my brother could offer him. He's deceiving himself, believe me. Write back to him and tell him he's a fool. I'll give him thirty ducats from my private purse this year, on the understanding that he abandons any further approaches to my son Karl. I will not allow my son to suffer simply to please yours.

Scene 2

Heidelbrunn

[*GUSTCHEN. LÄUFFER*]

Gustchen: What's the matter?

Läuffer: How's my portrait coming on? So, it's true. You haven't given it a thought. If I had been as dilatory as you - If I had known, I would have withheld your letter, but I was a fool.

Gustchen: Ha, ha, ha, my dear Herr Tutor! It's true I haven't found the time yet.

Läuffer: You cruel girl!

Gustchen: But what is the matter, please tell me. You've never been this preoccupied before. Your eyes are forever filling with tears, and I've noticed you're not eating.

Läuffer: Have you? Really? You're the very model of sympathy.

Gustchen: Oh, Herr Tutor - -

Läuffer: Would you like a drawing lesson this afternoon?

Gustchen: [*Grasps his hand*] My dearest Herr Tutor! Forgive me for abandoning you yesterday. It really was impossible for me to draw. I had the most amazing attack of the sniffles.

Läuffer: As no doubt you will again today. I think we should stop drawing altogether. It no longer gives you any pleasure.

Gustchen: [*Half crying*] How can you say such a thing, Herr Läuffer? It's the only thing I do enjoy doing.

Läuffer: Or you could leave it until you're in town this winter where you could have a drawing master. Anyway I am going to ask your father to remove the object of your revulsion, your hatred and your cruelty. I can see that in the long run it will become quite intolerable for you to receive instruction from me.

Gustchen: Herr Läuffer -

Läuffer: Let me be - I must find a way to put an end to this wretched existence of mine as it appears that death is denied me -

Gustchen: Herr Läuffer -

Läuffer: You're torturing me - [*Tears himself away and exit*]

Gustchen: How I pity him!

Scene 3

Halle in Saxony. PÄTUS's Room

[*FRITZ VON BERG. Pätus, in a dressing gown sitting at a table*]

Pätus: Well now, Berg! You're not a child any more to go running to Mama and Papa - Damnation! I always took you to be a decent sort of fellow, but if you weren't an old schoolfriend of mine, I'd be ashamed to be seen around with you.

Fritz: On my honour, Pätus, it's not homesickness. I find it embarrassing that you should suspect me of such stupidity. I would like to have word from home, that I will confess, but I have my own reasons for that.

Pätus: Gustchen - Right? Just think, you poor soul! A hundred and eighty hours from her side - and what forests and rivers lie between you? But wait a moment, there are girls here too. If my wardrobe was in better shape I'd take you to a party this very day. I don't know how you do it; a year in Halle and you haven't spoken to a girl. That's enough to make you depressed in itself, it must be. Wait a moment, you must move in here with me. That will cheer you up. What are you doing with that clergyman anyway? That's no place for you -

Fritz: What do you pay here?

Pätus: I pay - I really don't know, Brother. I'm lodging with a good honest Philistine. I grant you his wife's a bit odd now and then, but why not. What's it to me? We row from time to time. I put up with that. They put everything on a slate, my rent, coffee and tobacco, everything I ask for and then I settle up each year, when my allowance arrives.

Fritz: Do you owe them much now?

Pätus: I paid last week. It's true that this time they've really annoyed me. They've kept my whole allowance down to the last Pfennig, so my coat which, being on my uppers, I pawned a few days ago, remains at the hock shop. Heaven alone knows when I'll be able to redeem it again.

Fritz: How are you coping now?

Pätus: Me? - I'm ill. This morning Frau Hamster sent me an invitation, so straightaway I crawled into bed..

Fritz: But staying indoors all the time when the weather's so good.

Pätus: It doesn't worry me. In the evening I go for walks in my dressing gown. If I didn't do that I wouldn't be able to bear the heat in here during the day. - But good God! Where's my coffee got to? [*Stamps his foot*] Frau Blitzer! - now you'll see how I deal with these people - Frau Blitzer! Where on earth - Frau Blitzer. [*Rings and stamps*] - I've only just paid her. That means I can be a little more outspoken - Frau..

[*Enter FRAU BLITZER with coffee*]

Pätus: Where were you, Mother, where on earth were you? Are you governed by the weather? I've been waiting here for over an hour now -

Frau Blitzer: What? You good-for-nothing lout. What are you moaning about? You're no use to anyone, you penniless louse. In a minute I'll take the coffee back downstairs -

Pätus: [*Pours himself coffee*] Now, now, don't be so cross, Mother! but where are my biscuits, my biscuits!

Frau Blitzer: Yes, those precious stones of yours! There are no more biscuits in the house. Do you really think that whether a miserable, threadbare lout spends his afternoons eating biscuits or not –

Pätus: Damnation! [*Stamps his foot*] You know I can't take a mouthful of coffee without a biscuit – What am I paying for anyway –

Frau Blitzer: [*Gives him a biscuit from her apron and pulls his hair*] Look, there's a biscuit, my little chubby cheeks. He's got a voice like a whole regiment of soldiers. Well, is the coffee nice? Is it? Tell me, or I'll tear every last hair out of your head for you.

Pätus: [*Drinking*] Incomparable – Ah – I've never tasted better in my life.

Frau Blitzer: Do you see, scamp! If you didn't have me to mother you, to take you under my wing and give you food and drink, you'd starve on the street. Just look at him, Herr von Berg, how he goes about with no coat on his back, and that dressing gown looks as if he'd been hanged and dropped off the gallows in it. Now you're a good-looking gentleman, I just don't know how you can bear to have anything to do with this creature. I suppose there's always some slight blood relationship somewhere among fellow countrymen. But then I'm always saying, if only that Herr von Berg would come and lodge with us. I know you have a lot of influence over him; perhaps something decent could be made of him, but otherwise, really –

[*She exits*]

Pätus: Do you see that? Isn't she a cheery, genial woman. I let her get away with it, but damn me, if ever I get serious, she soon knuckles under – Won't you join me in a cup? [*Pours for him*] You see, I'm well looked after here; I pay a good deal, I grant you, but for that I do get..

Fritz: [*Drinking*] This coffee tastes of barley.

Pätus: What did you say? – [*Tastes his as well*] Yes, you're right. What with the biscuit I couldn't – [*Looks in the pot*] Damn it [*Throws the coffee pot out of the window*] Barley coffee and five hundred guilders a year! –

Frau Blitzer: [*Rushing in*] Hey! What the devil's going on? Are you mad, Sir, or has the Devil got hold of you? –

Pätus: Be quiet, Mother!

Frau Blitzer: [*With a frightful cry*] But where's my coffee pot? What! Damn you! Out of the window – I'll scratch your eyes out for that.

Pätus: There was a spider in it, I was afraid and I threw it. Is it my fault if the window was open?

Frau Blitzer: If only the spider had finished you off! If I were to sell you body and soul, it wouldn't pay for my coffee pot, you useless dog. You bring me nothing but misfortune and unhappiness. I'll sue you; I'll have you thrown into gaol. [*She runs out*]

Pätus: [*Laughing*] What can I do, Brother! You have to let her rant and rave after all.

Fritz: But what about your money?

Pätus: So what! - If I have to wait until Christmas, who else is there who will give me credit that long? And then she's only a woman, and a stupid woman at that; she doesn't mean it. If her husband had talked to me like that, that would have been different, I would have given him a beating. Do you see!

Fritz: Do you have a pen and ink?

Pätus: There on the window-sill.

Fritz: I don't know. My heart is so heavy. I've never attached much importance to reprisals.

Pätus: Neither have I - The Döbblin Company is here. I'd love to see them play, but I have no coat to wear. My mean-spirited landlord won't lend me one, and I'm such a great fat beast that none of yours would fit me.

Fritz: I must write home at once. [*Sits by the window and writes*]

Pätus: [*Sits opposite a wolf's skin coat hanging on the wall*] Hm! Nothing but this fur coat left of all the clothes I have and those I wanted to have made. Just this fur, which I really can't wear in summer, and which even the Jew wouldn't let me pawn, because it had a touch of worm in it. Hanke, Hanke! It's quite inexcusable that you won't make me a coat on tick. [*Stands up and walks around*] What have I done to you that you won't make a coat for me of all people? Me of all people whose need is so desperate because I don't have a single one, me of all people! You must have the Devil in you. He gives credit to every Tom, Dick and Harry, only not to me! [*Puts his head in his hands and stamps his foot*] Just not to me, just not me! -

Bollwerk: [*Who has slipped in and been listening, grasps him. Pätus turns round and stands silently in front of Bollwerk*] Ha ha ha...Well poor old Pätus - ha ha ha! Yes indeed, the ungodly Hanke, and you of all people - But where's your red suit with the gold, which you ordered from him, and the blue silk with the silver buttons on the waistcoat, and the red velvet with the black velvet lining, that would be just the thing at this time of year. Tell me! Answer me! Damn Hanke! Shall we go and tan his hide? Why's he taking so long over his work for you? Shall we go?

Pätus [*Throwing himself on a chair*] : Leave me alone.

Bollwerk: But listen Pätus, Pätus, Pä Pä Pä Pätus [*Sits beside him*] Döbblin's here. Listen Pä Pä Pä Pä Pätus, what are we going to do? I think you should put on your wolfskin coat and come to the play tonight. What does it matter, you're a stranger here and everyone knows that you've ordered four suits from Hanke. Whether he'll make them for you or not is another matter! Damn the fellow! Let's break his windows for him if he doesn't make them for you!

Pätus: [*Vehemently*] Leave me in peace, I said.

Bollwerk: But listen... but... but... listen listen listen Pätus; take care Pätus not to run about the streets at night in your dressing gown. I know you're afraid of dogs, well word is that there ten rabid dogs on the loose in the town. They have already bitten several children; two survived, but four died on the spot. That's the dog days for you! Right, Pätus? It's good that you can't go out now, isn't it? You'll take care not to go out now? Right, Pä Pä Pätus?

Pätus: Leave me in peace... or we'll fall out.

Bollwerk: Don't be such a child - Berg, are you coming to the play?

Fritz: [*Distracted*] What? - What kind of play?

Bollwerk: There's a company here - put your scribbling aside. You can do your writing this evening. They're playing "Minna von Barnhelm" today.

Fritz: That I must see - [*Puts letter away*] Poor Pätus, what a shame you've no coat -

Bollwerk: I'd gladly lend him one but, Devil take me, this is the only one I have myself.

[*Exeunt*]

Pätus: [*Alone*] To hell with your sympathy! It's worse than a slap in the face -Well now, what am I going to do? [*Takes off his dressing gown*] Let people think I'm mad! I must see Minna von Barnhelm, even if I have to go naked! [*Puts on his wolf-skin coat*] Hanke! Hanke! You'll pay for this! [*Stamps his foot*] You'll pay for this!

[*He exits*]

Scene 4

[*FRAU HAMSTER. MISTRESS HAMSTER. MISTRESS KNICKS*]

Mistress Knicks: I can't tell you for laughing, Frau Hamster, I'm going to be ill with laughing. Just imagine; we were walking with Mistress Hamster in the alleyway when a man ran past us in a wolf skin coat, just as if he was running the gauntlet, with three huge dogs after him. Mistress Hamster was pushed against the wall. She hit her head and she was crying so loudly.

Frau Hamster: But who was it?

Mistress Knicks: Just imagine, when we had a look at him, it was Herr Pätus - He must have taken leave of his senses.

Frau Hamster: In a wolf skin coat in this heat!

Mistress Hamster: [*Holding her head*] I'm sure he must have got out of bed in a high fever. He sent word this morning to say he was ill.

Mistress Knicks: The three dogs running after him, that was the funniest thing. I'd made my mind up to go to the comedy today, but I don't think I will now, it couldn't make me laugh any more than this. I'll never forget it as long as I live. His hair was flying out behind him like the tail on a comet, and the faster he ran, the faster the dogs chased him, and he didn't dare to look round... It was priceless!

Frau Hamster: Wasn't he screaming? He must have thought the dogs were rabid.

Mistress Knicks: I don't think he had time to scream, but he was as red as a lobster and had his mouth open like the dogs after him - Oh it was priceless! I would have given my string of real pearls not to have missed it.

Scene 5

Heidelbrunn. GUSTCHEN's Room

[*Gustchen lying on the bed. Läuffer sitting on the bed*]

Läuffer: Try to understand, Gustchen, the Privy Councillor won't do it. You see that your father is making life more and more unpleasant for me. Now he intends giving me only forty ducats next year. How can I tolerate that? I'll have to resign.

Gustchen: How cruel, and what will I do then? [*After they look at one another for a while*] You see, I'm frail and sickly; here in isolation subject to a barbaric mother – Nobody asks after me; nobody cares about me; none of my family can abide me any longer; not even my father. I don't know why.

Läuffer: Have them send you to take your instruction in the catechism with my Father in Insterburg.

Gustchen: Then we'd never see each other. My uncle would never let my father send me to lodge with your father.

Läuffer: Damn his aristocratic sensibilities!

Gustchen: [*Taking his hand*] Don't you be disagreeable too, my Hermann! [*Kisses his hand*] Oh Death! Death! Why do you not take pity on me!

Läuffer: Tell me too – Your brother is the worst mannered boy I know. recently he boxed my ears, but I couldn't punish him for it, I couldn't even complain about it. Your father would have broken his arms and legs for him, while your gracious mama would have laid all the blame on me.

Gustchen: But for my sake – I thought you loved me.

Läuffer: [*Plunges his free hand into the bed, while she continues from time to time to bring his other to her lips*] Let me think.. [*Remains sitting lost in thought*]

Gustchen: [*During the above*] O Romeo! If this were but your hand – And yet you leave me, ignoble Romeo! See you not your Juliet dies for you – by all the world, her family too, hated, despised cast out. [*Presses his hand to her eyes*] Oh, inhuman Romeo!

Läuffer: [*Looking up*] Are you maundering again?

Gustchen: It's a monolgue from a tragedy which I like to recite when I'm troubled. [*Läuffer falls again into a reverie, after a pause she continues*] Perhaps you're not wholly to blame. Your father did forbid you to exchange letters with me; but love transcends seas and rivers, and prohibitions, even the fear of death itself – You have forgotten me... Perhaps you were concerned for me – Yes, yes, your tender heart could see that which threatened me was worse than that I suffer now. [*Ardently kissing Läuffer's hand*] Oh, divine Romeo!

Läuffer: [*Kisses her hand for a long time, then looking at her in silence for a while*] What happened to Abelard could happen to me too –

Gustchen: [*Sitting up*] You're mistaken – my sickness lies in my soul – no-one would suspect you – [*Falls back*] Have you read La Nouvelle Heloïse?

Läuffer: I can hear someone on the way to the schoolroom. –

Gustchen: My father – Oh, my God! – You been here three quarters of an hour too long! [*Läuffer rushes out*]

Scene 6

[*The MAJOR'S WIFE. COUNT WERMUTH*]

Count: But, Madam, is one never to see Fräulein Gustchen? How did she fare on the hunt the day before yesterday?

Major's Wife: With respect, she was suffering with a tooth ache during the night. That is why she will not be seen today. How is your stomach, Count, after the oysters?

Count: Oh, I'm used to them. Just recently my Brother and I on our own and at our own expense ate six hundred and drank twenty bottles of Champagne to go with them.

Major: Don't you mean Rhine wine?

Count: Champagne - It was a whim but it agreed with us both very well. The same evening there was a ball in Königsberg; my Brother danced 'till noon while I lost some money.

Major's Wife: Shall we play a hand of Piquet?

Count: If Fräulein Gustchen were here, I would like to take a turn in the garden with her. I would not presume to suggest that to you, madam, not with that ulcer on your foot.

Major's Wife: I don't know where the Major is hiding himself either. He's never in his life before been so passionate about the estate. The whole blessed day he's in the fields, and when he comes home he sits there as silent as the grave. You can imagine I'm beginning to worry about him.

Count: He seems melancholy.

Major's Wife: Heaven knows - Just recently he took it into his head to sleep with me again, but then, in the middle of the night, he sprang out of bed and he - ha ha, I shouldn't be telling you this, but you are already acquainted with my husband's ridiculous side.

Count: And he..

Major's Wife: Threw himself down on his knees and beat his breast and sobbed and howled so much that I began to be alarmed. I haven't liked to ask him in what way this tomfoolery of his is likely to affect me. If he wants to become a Pietist or a Quaker, it's all one to me! It will render him neither more hateful nor more endearing to me. [*Gives the Count a mischievous look*]

Count: [*Touching her on the chin*] You wicked women! But where is Gustchen? I would dearly love to walk with her.

Major's Wife: Hush, here comes the Major...You can go walking with him, Count.

Count: But - it's your daughter I wish to go with.

Major's Wife: She still won't be dressed. It's quite insupportable how lazy the girl is-

[*Enter MAJOR VON BERG in a nightshirt and straw hat*]

Major's Wife: Now how are you, Husband? Where are you gadding off too now? We never see you from one day's end to the next. Just take a look at him, Count, doesn't he resemble the *Heautontimorumenos*[4] in my big edition of Madame Dacier - I believe you've been ploughing, Herr Major. We are still in the dog days.

Count: Indeed, Herr Major, you've never looked so unwell, so pale and haggered; you must have something weighing on your mind. What are we to make of those tears which start in your eyes as soon as one observes you closely? I've known you for ten years now, and I've never seen you look like this, not even on the death of your Brother.

Major's Wife: Meanness, nothing but exasperating meanness, he thinks we'll starve if he doesn't root about all day in the fields like some mole. He digs, he ploughs, he harrows. You don't intend becoming a peasant do you? If so, you must allow me another servant to keep an eye on you.

Major: I must keep producing and scrimping and saving in order to provide for a place in the hospital for my daughter.

Major's Wife: What kind of nonsense is that? - I really must send for Dr Würz from Königsberg.

Major: My genteel wife never notices anything, do you! Not that your child is wasting away day by day, that she's losing her beauty her health and everything about her, as if poor Lazarus - God forgive me my sin in saying this - had hold of her - it's eating my heart away -

Major's Wife: Just listen to him! How he raves at me! Am I to blame for this? Have you gone mad?

Major: Most certainly you are to blame. Who else could it be? May lightning strike me but I don't understand it. I always thought to find a match for her from one of the finest famlies in the land; for there's no-one anywhere on earth to match her for beauty. And now she looks like a cow-herd -

[4]Self-tormentor

yes most certainly you're to blame, what with your severity, your cruelty and your envy. She's taken it all to heart, and now its showing itself in her face. But all this should bring you joy, Madam, as you've long been jealous of her. You can't deny that, can you? You should be ashamed, truly you should!

[*He exits*]

Major's Wife: But... what have you to say to that, Count! Have you ever heard such a maddening collection of sottises in all your life?

Count: Come; we shall play Piquet until Fräulein Gustchen is dressed..

Scene 7

Halle

[*FRITZ VON BERG in prison. BOLLWERK, VON SEIFFENBLASE and his TUTOR surround him*]

Bollwerk: If only I had the young man here, I'd skin him alive. It's an infamous business to land an honest young man like Berg in prison because no-one would come to his aid. It's the truth; not one of his fellow countryman would lift a finger to help him. If Berg hadn't stood surety for him, he'd be languishing in prison now. And the money should be here in a fortnight. To leave Berg in a predicament like this, the man must be an out-and-out swine. Damn you Pä Pä Pä Pä Pätus! Just you wait, hang you Pätus, just you wait! –

Tutor: I cannot adequately express, my dear Herr von Berg, how much it grieves me, especially for your father's and your family's sake, to see you in such a condition, when it is none of your fault but the simply the result of the rashness of youth. It was one of the seven Greek sages who said: Beware of standing surety, and truly nothing could be more shameless than a young degenerate, whose dissolute life has plunged him into misery, trying to drag others down with him. No doubt he had some such thing in mind when he first sought you out as a friend at the Academy.

Seiffenblase: Yes, yes, my dear Brother Berg! Don't take this amiss, but you have made a terrible mess of things. It's all your own fault; you should have seen from the first that the fellow was going to betray you. He came to me and gave me the story that he was on his uppers, and his creditors were all for putting him away somewhere where neither the sun nor moon would reach him. Let them, I thought, it would serve you right. Most of the time you'll barely even look down your nose at us, but when you're in trouble, an aristocrat is good enough for you as a surety. He spun me a yarn about how he had his pistols loaded and ready in case his creditors were to attack him - and now the dissolute swine has prostituted you in his stead. Truly, if this had happened to me, I wouldn't be able to take it all so calmly. Herr von Berg locked up, and all on account of some dissolute student.

Fritz: He was a schoolfriend -- let him be. If I'm not complaining about him, what business is it of yours to? I've known him longer than you. I know that he's not leaving me here deliberately.

Tutor: But Herr von Berg, in this world we must be reasonable. It doesn't worry him that you're sitting here; as far as he's concerned you can stay sitting here for the next century -

Fritz: I've know him since we were young. We've never refused each other anything. He's loved me like a brother, as I have him. When he was to travel to Halle he wept for the first time in his life, because he could not travel with me. He could have gone to the Academy a whole year earlier, but in order to be able to go with me, he made himself out before the preceptors to be more stupid than he was, and yet fate and our fathers did not wish us to travel together, and that was his undoing. He never learned how to handle money, and would give anybody anything they asked for. If a beggar had ripped his last shirt off his back and said: "By your leave, my dear Herr Pätus", he'd have let him have it. His creditors have behaved like highwaymen towards him. His father never deserved this prodigal son, who despite all his misery was always so good-hearted when he came home.

Tutor: Oh, forgive me, you're still young and see everything from the most favourable point of view. One must live for a while among men before one is able to judge character. Herr Pätus, or whatever he calls himself, has worn a mask with you, and only now is his true face seeing the light of day. He must have been one of the finest and most cunning of swindlers, because a simple cheat..

Pätus [*In travelling clothes embraces Berg*]: Brother Berg -

Fritz: Brother Pätus -

Pätus: No - stop - I must throw myself at your feet - You here - on my account. [*Tears his hair with both hands and stamps his feet*] Oh fate! Fate! Fate!

Fritz: Well, what news? Have you brought the money? Are you reconciled with your father? What does your return mean?

Pätus: Nothing, nothing - He wouldn't see me - a hundred miles and all in vain. Your servant, Gentlemen. Don't weep, Bollwerk it would humiliate me too much to know you still thought well of me. - Oh Heaven, Heaven!

Fritz: You must be the most inveterate idiot ever to walk on the earth. Why did you come back? Are you insane? Have you quite taken leave your senses? Do you want your creditors to find out your whereabouts - Away with him! Bollwerk, take him away; see to it that you get him safely out of the city - I can hear the gaoler - Pätus, you'll be my enemy forever if you don't this instant -

[*Pätus throws himself at his feet*]

Fritz: I could go mad -

Bollwerk: Don't be such a fool, if Berg is generous enough to sit here on your behalf. His father will have him released soon enough. But if you stay here, there'll be no hope for you; you'll just have to rot in gaol.

Pätus: Give me a sword..

Fritz: Away with him! -

Bollwerk: Away! -

Pätus: Have mercy on me and give me a sword -

Seiffenblase: Here, have mine..

Bollwerk: [*Grasps his arm*] Herr - wretch! No, don't - don't put up your sword! You won't have drawn in vain. I must first bring my friend to safety and then you may expect me here - Outside, understand, so for the present - get out! [*Throws him out of the door*]

Tutor: My dear Herr Bollwerk -

Bollwerk: Not a word. You - you can go with your young man and teach him to mend his ways. I will meet you wherever and however you wish.

[*Exit TUTOR*]

Pätus: Bollwerk! I'll be your second.

Bollwerk: You fool! You're acting as if - Do you want to hold my glove for me while I have a piss? - What use would seconds be? Come on now, weakling, and second yourself out of the city.

Pätus: But there are two of them.

Bollwerk: Would that there were ten of them, and not a Seiffenblase among them - Come on, you fool, don't add to your problems.

Pätus: Berg! - [*Bollwerk drags him off*]

☐

ACT THREE

Scene 1

Heidelbrunn

[*The MAJOR in a nightshirt. The PRIVY COUNCILLOR*]

Major: Brother, I am no longer the man I once was. In my heart I am ten times more frantic than you may see from my face - It's very good that you've come to visit me. Who knows for how much longer we will see each other.

Privy Councillor: You're always one for excess in everything. - Taking a trifle like this so much to heart! - If your daughter were to lose her beauty, she'd still be the same good girl she was before. She may have a hundred other endearing qualities.

Major: It's not just her beauty - Devil take me, it's not just that she's losing. I don't know, but I feel I'll go insane if look at her for long. Her health is gone, her cheerfulness, her sweetness; I don't know how to list all the things, but even if I can't list them, I can see them, I can feel them and I understand them. You know how I've made the girl my idol. And now I must watch while she's wasting away and dying under my care. - [*weeps*] Brother, Privy Councillor, you have no daughter. You can't know the feelings of a father with a daughter. I've fought in thirteen battles and been wounded eighteen times, and stared death in the face, and I've - Oh, leave me alone; take yourself off home; let the whole world disappear. I want to reject it, take my shovel in my hand and be a peasant.

Privy Councillor: And your wife and children..

Major: Is that meant as a joke? I know neither wife nor children, I am Major Berg of blessed memory. I'll take up the plough and be old father Berg, and whoever comes too close will get my pickaxe around his ears.

Privy Councillor: I've never seen him so fanatical-melancholy before.

[*The Major's Wife bursts in*]

Major's Wife: Help, husband - we're lost - Our family! Our family!

Privy Councillor: God forbid, sister! What are you saying? Do you want to drive your husband mad?

Major's Wife: Let him go mad - Our family - Infamy! -- I can't go on - [*Collapses onto a chair*]

Major [*Crosses to her*]: Out with it - Or I'll wring your neck for you.

Major's Wife: Your daughter - the tutor - Run off! [*Faints*]

Major: Has he made a whore of her? [*Shakes her*] What are you fainting for? Now's not the time for fainting. Out with it, or may lightning strike you. She's turned whore? Is that it? - Well let the whole world turn whore, then, and you Berg take up your dung fork. - [*Goes to leave*]

Privy Councillor: [*Restrains him*] Brother, if you value your life, stay here - I will investigate all this - Your rage is making you irrational.

[*He exits, locking the door*]

Major: [*Struggling in vain to open the door*] I'll irrational you - [*To his wife*] Come on, come on, you too! I want you to watch this [*Rips the door open*] I wanted to set an example - God has preserved me thus far to set an example to my wife and children - In vain, in vain, all in vain!

[*He drags his unconscious wife offstage*]

Scene 2

A school in the village. A dark and gloomy night

[*WENZESLAUS. LÄUFFER*]

Wenzeslaus: [*Sitting at a table, his glasses on his nose, drawing lines on paper*] Who's there? What's the matter?

Läuffer: Help me! Shelter me! Worthy Herr Schoolmaster! They want my life.

Wenzeslaus: Who are you then?

Läuffer: I'm tutor in the neighbouring castle. Major Berg is after me with all his servants; they want to shoot me.

Wenzeslaus: God forbid - Sit yourself down here beside me - Here, take my hand. You'll be safe here with me - And now tell me all about it while I write out this exercise.

Läuffer: Just let me come to myself again first.

Wenzeslaus: Good, catch your breath, and then I'll fetch you a glass of wine and we'll have a drink together. But in the meantime, tell me -Tutor - [*Puts his ruler down, takes off his glasses and looks at him for a while*] Well, to judge from your coat - Yes, yes, I do believe you are a tutor. You look so red and white. Now tell me, my dear friend, [*Puts his glasses back on*] how have you arrived at the unfortunate position of having your patron in such a rage against you? I simply cannot imagine how a man like Major von Berg - I know him of course, I've heard enough talk about him, he's the reputation of being of an irritable disposition, choleric, very choleric - Do you see, I have to draw the lines for my boys myself. There's nothing a lad finds more difficult to learn than to write well. - Not to write prettily, not to write quickly, but just to write well, for, as I always say, handwriting influences everything else; morals, knowledge, everything, my dear tutor. A man who cannot write well, I always say, cannot behave well either - Now, where were we?

Läuffer: Might I ask for a glass of water?

Wenzeslaus: Water? - You shall indeed. But - yes, what were we talking about? Good handwriting. No, the Major - hey hey hey - But you know something, Herr - What is your name?

Läuffer: My - my name's - Almond.

Wenzeslaus: Herr Almond - And you had to think about it? Well, well, we all have lapses of memory from time to time, particularly red and white young men - But you shouldn't be called Almond, you should be called Almond Blossom, because you're all red and white like almond blossom - I grant you, the profession of tutor is one of those, *unus ex his*[5], which is perennially strewn with roses and lilies, and in which one is but seldom pricked by the thorns of life. For what does one have to do? Eat, drink, and sleep, with nothing to worry about, sure of a good glass of wine, a roast dinner every day, and each morning one's coffee, tea, chocolate or whatever one drinks, and that continues on - Oh, yes, I was going to say: Are you aware, Herr Almond, that a glass of water is as detrimental to your health after violent emotion as after violent physical exercise. But of course, what interest do you young tutors take in matters of health? - But tell me, will you, [*Puts down his glasses and ruler and stands up*] how can it do your constitution any good if all your nerves and arteries are tense, and your blood is circulating most violently, and your life force is in a - fever, in a -

Läuffer: My God, Count Wermuth -

[*LÄUFFER leaps into the bedroom*]

[*Enter COUNT WERMUTH with a couple of servants with pistols*]

Count: Is there a fellow called Läuffer here - a student in a blue coat with braid on?

Wenzeslaus: Sir, in our village it is the custom to take off your hat when entering a room and speaking to the master of the house.

Count: The matter is urgent - Tell me, is he here or not?

Wenzeslaus: And what crime is he supposed to have committed that you come looking for him so heavily armed?

[5]One of those

[*The COUNT makes for the bedroom, WENZESLAUS stands in front of the door*]
Wenzeslaus: Stop, sir! This room is mine, and if you do not instantly quit my house, I have only to ring my bell and half a dozen burly peasant lads will beat you to a pulp. If you behave like highwaymen, you must be treated like highwaymen. And to prevent you getting lost, and to help you find the way out of my house as well as you found the way in –
[*WENZESLAUS takes his hand and leads him out of the door. The servants follow*]
Läuffer: [*Leaps out of the room*] Oh happy man! Excellent man!
Wenzeslaus: [*As previously*] In – your life force, I was saying, is in a – state of excitation, all your passions are likewise in tumult, in an uproar – Now, were you to drink water in this state, it would be like throwing water on a powerful flame. The strong movement of air, and the conflict between the two opposing elements produces an effervescence, a seething, an agitation, a state of ferment –
Läuffer: I admire you..
Wenzeslaus: Gottlieb! – Now you may drink, gradually at first – gradually – and then this evening you'll have to make do with some salad and knackwurst – Who was that uncouth lout who was looking for you?
Läuffer: He's Count Wermuth, the Major's future son-in-law. He's jealous of me because the girl can't abide him –
Wenzeslaus: But what's that supposed to mean? What can the girl want with you, then, Monsieur Callow Menial? To throw away her prospects for the sake of some young Siegfried with neither house nor hearth? Put that out of your mind and follow me into the kitchen. I see my lad's gone to fetch me some bratwurst. I'll fetch you the water myself, for I have no maid, and I haven't yet presumed to think about a wife, for I know I couldn't support one – never mind actually look for one, not like you young red and white gentlemen – But what they say is true, I suppose, the world is changing.

Scene 3
Heidelbrunn
[*THE PRIVY COUNCILLOR. HERR VON SEIFFENBLASE and his TUTOR*]
Tutor: We spent only one year in Halle, and then on our return from Göttingen we travelled by way of all the celebrated universities of Germany. We were therefore unable to spend long in Halle on our second visit. Besides your son was at that time most unfortunately incarcerated and there were but few opportunities for me to have the

honour of speaking with him. I can therefore give you no very detailed account of your son's demeanour there.

Privy Councillor: Heaven has laid a curse on all our family. My brother - I will not attempt to conceal it from you, for both the city and country are full of it - has had the misfortune of his daughter's disappearance without her having left so much as a trace. And now I hear this of my son - if he had behaved himself properly, how could it have happened that he be thrown into gaol? In addition to his generous allowance, I have sent him every six months something extra; in any case -

Tutor: The bad company and the bewildering range of distractions at an academy.

Seiffenblase: The strangest aspect of the whole affair is that he is there on someone else's account, the epitome of depravity, a man to whom I would refuse a groschen even were he to be starving on my dunghill. He's been here, you will have heard of him. He was looking for money from his father on the pretext of having your son released. Presumably he would have taken it to another academy and started his trickery all over again. Of course, I'm familiar with the way dissolute students carry on, but his father smelled a rat, and refused to see him.

Privy Councillor: Not young Pätus, the alderman's son, surely ?

Seiffenblase: I believe he's the one.

Privy Councillor: Everyone censured the father for his severity.

Tutor: What cause is there for censure, Herr Privy Councillor? When a son so sorely abuses his father's kindness, the father's heart must turn away from him. Eli the high priest was not harsh, yet broke his neck.

Privy Councillor: One can never be too harsh on the excesses of our children, but we should not punish their misery. It's said the young man was reduced to begging here. And my son is sitting there on his account?

Seiffenblase: Who else? He was his closest friend and could think of no-one better to act out Damon and Pythias. But there's more. Herr Pätus returned and wanted to resume his place, but your son insisted that he wished to remain there; you would soon have him released; while Pätus and some other archbraggart and gambler would make their escape and fend for themselves as best they could. Perhaps they'll put on masks and attack some other poor student in his room, put a pistol to his chest and steal his watch and purse, as they did once in Halle.

Privy Councillor: And my son is the third of this trio?

Seiffenblase: I don't know, Herr Privy Councillor.

Privy Councillor: Come and dine, gentlemen! I have already heard too much. God's judgement rests on certain families; in some certain diseases are hereditary, in others the children go astray no matter what the fathers do. Eat; I will fast and pray. Perhaps this evening is recompense for the dissipation of my youth.

Scene 4

The school

[*WENZESLAUS and LÄUFFER dining at a bare table*]

Wenzeslaus: Do you like it? There's a difference between my table and that of the Major's, no? But when schoolmaster Wenzeslaus eats his sausage, his digestion is aided by a clear conscience. And when Herr Almond ate roast capon with mushroom sauce, his conscience made every mouthful he swallowed stick in his throat with moral outrage. You are - now tell me, my dear Herr Almond - and don't take it amiss if I tell you the truth, it spices conversation as pepper does a cucumber salad - now tell me, isn't it craven of me if, convinced that I am an ignoramus and can teach my charges nothing, and being lax with them, allowing them to be lazy, robbing the Almighty of their time, I then proceed to take a hundred ducats - wasn't it that much? - God forgive me, but I've never seen so much money together at once! - to put a hundred and fifty ducats in my pocket for nothing, for absolutely nothing!

Läuffer: Oh, but that's not all. You're not aware of your advantages, or perhaps you sense them without being fully aware of them. Have you never seen a slave in a braided coat? Oh, freedom, golden freedom!

Wenzeslaus: What do you mean: freedom? I'm not as free as you might think. I'm tied to my school and must render account for it to God and my conscience.

Läuffer: That's true - But what if you had to account to some cranky eccentric who made your life a hundred times worse than yours with your schoolboys?

Wenzeslaus: Yes, well - then he would have to be as superior in intellect to me as I am over my schoolboys, and that, I do believe, one seldom finds nowadays, especially among the nobility. Perhaps you're right, though, at least as far as that uncouth fellow is concerned, the one who wanted to get into my bedroom without first asking my permission. What if I went to the Count's and demanded entry to his rooms without so much as a by-your-leave - but upon my soul, eat up; you look as if you'd just taken a laxative. You'd like a glass of wine too, no? I know I promised you one earlier but I have none in the house. Tomorrow I'll buy some more and then we will have a drink on Thursdays and Sundays, and when Franz the organist visits us too. Water, water my friend *ariston men to hudôr*[6]. I remember that still from my schooldays. I've added a pipe after eating and a walk in the fields. After that you sleep more soundly than the Great Mogul. You'll have a pipe with me this evening?

Läuffer: I'll try it. I've never smoked in my life.

Wenzeslaus: Yes of course, you red and white gentlemen, it would spoil your teeth, yes? and spoil your complexion, yes? I've smoked almost from the time I was weaned, swopped the nipple for a pipe hey, hey, hey! It's good against foul air and equally against foul urges. So that's my routine: in the morning cold water and a pipe, then school until eleven, then another pipe until my soup is ready, my Gottlieb cooks soup as good as any of your French chefs, and then a slice of roast meat and vegetables and then another pipe, then school again, then writing out exercises until dinner time; I usually eat something cold, sausage and salad, a piece of cheese, or whatever the Lord has provided, and then another pipe before I go to sleep.

Läuffer: God preserve me, I'm living in a tobacco shop.

Wenzeslaus: And I've grown thick and fat thereby, and live content, and have no thoughts yet of dying.

Läuffer: But it's inexcusable that the authorities have not taken the trouble to make your life more comfortable.

Wenzeslaus: Well, well, that's how things are, and one must be content. I am after all my own master and will have no-one accuse me of shirking as I know that each day I do more than I have to. I have to teach my boys to read and write. I teach them arithmetic, and Latin, and to read with understanding and to write good things too.

Läuffer: And what sort of salary do they give you?

[6]For water is best [ἄριστου μὲν τὸ ὕδωρ]

Wenzeslaus: What salary? - Aren't you going to eat up that little piece of sausage there? You won't be getting anything better. Don't expect anything better, or you'll have to go to bed hungry for the first time in your life - What salary? That wasn't a very clever question, Herr Almond. Forgive me: What salary? I have God's own salary, a clear conscience, and if I were to crave for a higher salary from the authorities I would lose that. Are you really going to let that cucumber salad go to waste? Go on, eat up; don't be bashful. Heaven knows, at a meagre table one cannot afford to be bashful. Wait, I'll cut you another slice of bread.

Läuffer: I'm overfull as it is.

Wenzeslaus: Well leave it then. But you'll have no-one to blame but yourself if it's not true. And if it is true, then you were wrong to eat until you're overfull, for that brings on evil urges and sends the intellect to sleep. You red and white gentlemen may believe that or not, as you like. It's true, tobacco is also said to contain a narcotic, sleep-inducing, stupefying oil. I have indeed from time to time found this to be true and have made the attempt to throw my pipe and all its accoutrements in the fire, but the persistent fogs we have in these parts in addition to the continual dampness in the air in autumn and winter, and the marvellous effect I feel from it, while it simultaneously lulls to sleep those evil urges - Hallo, where were you then, young man? Just as I was talking of lulling to sleep, you started nodding off. That's what happens when your mind's empty and grown lazy and never exerted. Allons! Buck up, smoke a pipe with me! [*Fills a pipe for himself and LÄUFFER*] Let's have a good old chat! [*Smokes*] I meant to tell you earlier in the kitchen that I can see you're weak in Latin, but as you write a good hand, as you said, you could assist me in the evenings, because I must start taking care of my eyes, and write out my boys' exercises. I'll give you Corderius's Colloquia and Gürtler's Lexicon as well, if you've a mind to apply yourself. You'll have the whole day to yourself, you could make some progress with your Latin, and who knows, if it were to please God today or tomorrow to take me from this world - But you must apply yourself, that I will say, because at the moment you're hardly fit to act as my assistant, let alone - [*Drinks*]

Läuffer: [*Lays his pipe down*] How humiliating!

Wenzeslaus: But...but...but... [*Wrenches the toothpick out of his mouth*] What's this, then? Hasn't the great man acquired enough knowledge to care for his own body? Picking your teeth is suicide, yes suicide, a wanton destruction of Jerusalem carried out on your teeth. Here, if you have something trapped between your teeth: [*Takes water and swills his mouth out*] That's what you must do, if you wish to keep your teeth healthy, to honour God and your fellows, and not run around in your old age like an old watchdog, who, having broken his teeth in his youth, can no longer keep his jaw shut. Good God, what a fine schoolmaster you'd make then, in old age, letting your words fall unformed from your mouth and snorting something between nose and upper lip that neither cock nor dog could understand.

Läuffer: He'll be the death of me with his advice - The worst of it is, he's right -

Wenzeslaus: Now how's that? Don't you like the tobacco? I'll bet you, another few days with old Wenzeslaus, and you'll be smoking like a boatswain. I'll lick you into shape, so you won't know yourself.

☐

ACT FOUR

Scene 1
Insterburg
[*The PRIVY COUNCILLOR. The MAJOR*]
The Major: Look at me, Brother - I'm wandering around like Cain, restive and fitful - Do you know something? They say the Russians are at war with the Turks. I'll go to Königsberg to find out some more details. I'll leave my wife and die in Turkey.
Privy Councillor: Your outrageous ideas take my breath away. - Heavens, are we to be attacked from all sides? - Here, read this letter from Professor M-r.
Major: I can no longer read; my eyes are all but blind from weeping.
Privy Councillor: Then I will read it to you, to show you that you are not the only father with cause to complain: "Your son was recently imprisoned on account of a surety. He had, he tearfully confessed to me the day before yesterday, after five letters all written in vain, given up hope of receiving forgiveness from Your Grace. I exhorted him to remain calm while I intervened in the affair. He promised me this, but notwithstanding his promise he slipped away in secret from the prison that very night. His creditors wanted to have warrants issued, and his name put in all the papers, but I prevented this and have made good the amount owed, as I was more than convinced that Your Excellency would not permit this affront to your family's reputation. In anticipation of your early resolution of this matter, I have the honour.."
Major: Write and tell him: they can hang him.
Privy Councillor: And the family -
Major: Rubbish! There is no family; we have no family. Poppycock! The Russians are my family. I'll become a Russian Orthodox.
Privy Councillor: And there's still no trace of your daughter?
Major: What did you say?
Privy Councillor: You've no word at all of your daughter?
Major: Leave me in peace.
Privy Councillor: But you're not serious about travelling to Königsberg, are you?
Major: When do you think the mail leaves Königsberg for Warsaw?
Privy Councillor: I won't let you leave; it's pointless. Do you imagine that reasonable people will be taken in by your insane notions? I'm placing

you herewith under house arrest. People of your sort need to be dealt with severely or your grief may turn into madness.

Major: [*Weeping*]   A whole year - Brother Councillor - a whole year - and no-one knows where she may have taken flight.

Privy Councillor: Perhaps she's dead -

Major: Perhaps? - Certainly she's dead - if I could only have the consolation of being able to bury her at least - but she must have taken her own life, as no-one can give me any news of her. - A bullet through the head, Berg, or a Turkish sabre; that would be a victory.

Privy Councillor: But it's just as possible that she met up with Läuffer somewhere, and has left the country with him. I had a visit from Count Wermuth yesterday, and he told me he'd been to a school that same evening, and that the schoolmaster had not wanted to let him into his bedroom. He still suspects that the schoolmaster had him hidden in there, and perhaps your daughter with him.

Major: Where's this schoolmaster? Where's the village? And the wretched Count didn't force his way into the room? Come on, where's the Count?

Privy Councillor: He'll no doubt have stepped out to "The Pike" as usual.

Major: If I could only find her - If I could only hope to see her once more   - Confound it, but old and pining and raving as I am, yes, Devil take me, I'd laugh just once more in my life, for the last time laugh out loud, and lay my head on her defiled bosom, and then just once more I'd cry and then - Adieu Berg! That would be the way to die, that's what I would call sleeping safe and sound in the Lord. - Come now, Brother, your lad's a swindler, that's a trifle, there are swindlers at every court. But my daughter's a whore, that's what I call bringing a father joy. Perhaps she already has the three lilies on her back - Vivat tutors, and may the Devil take them all! Amen. [*Exeunt*]

Scene 2

A beggar's hut in the forest

[*GUSTCHEN in a coarse smock, MARTHE an old blind woman*]

Gustchen: Dear Marthe, stay at home and take care of the child. It is the first time I've left you alone all year, surely you will let me take a walk by myself. I've left you food for today and tomorrow, so you won't have to venture out on the road.

Marthe: But where are you going, Grete, God love you? And you so weak and sickly. Just listen to me now. I've had children like you, and without a lot of pain, thank God! But once I did try to go out the second day after my confinement, but never again! I all but gave up the ghost. It's true, I really could tell you what it feels like to be dead - Take heed. If you need something from the next village, blind though I may be, I'll find my way there. Stay at home and build up your strength again. I'll sort out everything for you, whatever it may be.

Gustchen: Let me be, Mother. I'm as strong as a young she-bear - you look after my child.

Marthe: But how am I to look after it, Holy Mother of God? I'm blind! When it wants to suck, am I to put it to my black and withered teat? You haven't the strength to take it with you, so stay at home, dear Gretel, stay at home.

Gustchen: I can't, dear Mother, my conscience is driving me to leave here. I have a father who loves me more than his life and soul. In a dream last night, I saw him, with bloodshot eyes, tearing out his white hair. He must think I am dead. I must go to the village and ask someone to get news of me to him.

Marthe: But, God help us, who is driving you on? What if you collapsed on the way? You can't go..

Gustchen: I must - my father stood there faltering. Suddenly he threw himself to the ground - He will kill himself if he doesn't hear news of me.

Marthe: But don't you know that dreams mean the opposite?

Gustchen: Not mine - Let me go - God will be with me.

[*She exits*]

Scene 3

The school

[*WENZESLAUS, LÄUFFER sitting at a table. Enter the MAJOR, the PRIVY COUNCILLOR and COUNT WERMUTH with SERVANTS*]

Wenzeslaus :[*Dropping his glasses*] Who are you?

Major: [*With drawn pistol*] Damnation! There he is like a pig in muck. [*Fires and hits LÄUFFER in the arm. He falls off his chair*]

Privy Councillor: [*Who has tried in vain to restrain him*] Brother [*Pushes him angrily*] Now you've done it, you lunatic!

Major: What? Is he dead? [*Covering his face*] What have I done? Have you no more news of my daughter to give me?

Wenzeslaus: Gentlemen! What's this? The Day of Judgement? What is all this? [*Rings his bell*] I'll teach you to attack an honest man in his own house!

Läuffer: I beseech you: don't ring the bell! - It's the Major; I deserve it for his daughter's sake.

Privy Councillor: Is there no surgeon in the village, honest schoolmaster? He's only wounded in the arm; I would like to have him treated.

Wenzeslaus: Oh, treated, eh! Highwaymen! Do you shoot people down, just because you're so rich you can afford to have them treated? He is my assistant. He's been here in my house for a year now; a quiet, peace - loving, industrious fellow, with not a word ever said against him, and you come and shoot my assistant in my own house! - I'll know the reason why, or I'll be damned. Do you understand?

Privy Councillor: [*Busying himself bandaging LÄUFFER*] Why all this palaver, my dear man? We're sorry enough as it is - But he might just bleed to death, so go and find us a surgeon.

Wenzeslaus: Well well! If you go round inflicting wounds, you'll have to heal them too, highwaymen! I'll have to go and see my neighbour Schöpsen. [*He exits*]

Major: [*To LÄUFFER*] Where's my daughter?

Läuffer: I don't know.

Major: You don't know? [*Draws another pistol*]

Privy Councillor: [*Tears the gun away from him and fires it out of the window*] Do we have to put you in chains, you -

Läuffer: I haven't seen her since I took flight from your house. That I swear before God, before whose judgement I may shortly appear.

Major: So she didn't run away with you?

Läuffer: No.

Major: Well then, another charge of powder discharged in vain! I wish it had gone through your brains, so you wouldn't be able to utter another crafty word, you bastard! Leave him lying there and come with me to the ends of the earth. I must find my daughter again, if not in this life, then in the next. And I tell you, my so sensible brother and my even more sensible wife will not be able to prevent me. [*Runs off*]

Privy Councillor: I mustn't let him out of my sight. [*Throws LÄUFFER a purse*] Take this to pay for your treatment, and remember that you wounded my brother far more grievously than he did you. There's a bank note in there. Take care of it and get what you can with it.

[*Exeunt all except LÄUFFER*]

[*Enter WENZESLAUS with SCHÖPSEN, the barber and several PEASANTS*]

Wenzeslaus: Where's that brood of vipers? Tell me!

Läuffer: Calm down, I beg you. I have received far less than my actions deserved. Master Schöpsen, is the wound serious?

[*SCHÖPSEN examines it*]

Wenzeslaus: What's that? Where are they? I won't stand for that, no, I won't stand for that, even if it costs me my school, my position, and everything I have. I'll beat the dogs into a pulp - Just think, neighbour, where on earth *in iure naturae* and *in iure civili* and *in iure canonico* and *in iure gentium*[7] or where you like has it ever been sanctioned for an honest man to be attacked in his own home, and that a school too, a sacred place. - Serious, no? You've examined it? Well, is it?

Schöpsen: There is a good deal one could say on the subject - well, we'll just have to see - in the end we'll just have to see, won't we.

Wenzeslaus: Right, Sir, hey hey, *in fine videbitur cuius toni*[8]. You mean, only when he's died or when he's completely recovered, will you be able to tell us whether the wound was serious or not. I'm sorry, I didn't put that in the proper medical language. A competent doctor would know beforehand. If not, I'd say to his face that he'd only half-way learned his surgery or pathology, and had spent his time in brothels rather than in college. For in *amore omnia insunt vitia*[9]. And when I see an ignoramus, no matter what faculty he comes from, I'll always say he's a lady's man, a brothel creeper. I won't be gainsaid.

Schöpsen: [*After further inspecting the wound*] Well the wound is, it depends on how you look at it - we'll have to see, we'll have to see.

Läuffer: Here, Schoolmaster! The Major's brother left me a purse full of ducats and a banknote besides - We'll be all right now for a few years to come.

[7]Natural law... civil law... canon law... international law

[8]It will all become clear in the end

[9]In love, all vices are contained

Wenzeslaus: [*Picking up the purse*] Well, that's something – but a man still has rights in his own home and sacrilege is still sacrilege – I'm going to write him a letter, the Herr Major, the kind he won't want anyone else to see.

Schöpsen: [*Who meanwhile has been eagerly eyeing the purse, swoops on the wound*] We will be able to cure you eventually, but it will be very difficult, hopefully, very difficult –

Wenzeslaus: Oh, I hope not, neighbour Schöpsen. I was afraid of that. But allow me to say before we start, that if you take your time in curing the wound, we will take ours in paying you; but if you can put him back on his feet in two days, you'll be paid just as quickly; and you can count on that.

Schöpsen: We'll have to see.

Scene 4

Gustchen: [*Lying by a pond surrounded by bushes*] Am I to die here then? – Father! Father! I am not to blame for your having heard no news of me. I have spent the last of my strength – I am exhausted – His face, his face is ever before me! He is dead, yes dead – of grief for me. His spirit appeared to me last night, to bring me the news – to call me to account – I'm coming, yes, I'm coming. [*Gathers her strength and throws herself in the pond*]

[*Enter the MAJOR. THE PRIVY COUNCILLOR and COUNT WERMUTH follow*]

Major: Hullo, someone's gone into the pond – it was a woman, maybe not my daughter, but some unhappy woman nonetheless – After her, Berg! This is the way to Gustchen or to Hell! [*Jumps in after her*]

Privy Councillor: [*Entering*] God in heaven! What shall we do?

Count Wermuth: I can't swim.

Privy Councillor: On the other side! – I think he's got the girl. There, over there in the bushes – Can't you see? Now he's going down with her – After him!

Scene 5

On the other side of the pond

Major: [*Shouts offstage*] Help! It's my daughter! Great God in heaven! Count, reach me that pole, quickly now!

[*The MAJOR carries GUSTCHEN onstage, followed by the PRIVY COUNCILLOR and COUNT WERMUTH*]

Major: There! - [*Lays her down. The PRIVY COUNCILLOR and the COUNT attempt to revive her*] Cursed child! Was it for this I raised you? [*Kneels by her*] Gustel! What's the matter? Have you swallowed some water? You're still my Gustel? - The godless wretch! If only you'd told me about all this before, I could have bought the lout a title. Then you could have crept off together. God preserve us! help her, she's fainted [*Leaps up and paces about, wringing his hands*] If only I knew where we could find that damned village surgeon. - Is she still not awake?

Gustchen: [*Weakly*] Father!

Major: What is it you want?

Gustchen: Forgiveness.

Major: [*Crosses to her*] Let the Devil forgive you, wilful child. - No [*Kneels by her again*] don't leave me, Gustel - my Gustel! I forgive you; all is forgiven and forgotten - God knows, I forgive you - Will you forgive me! There's nothing more we can do now. I've blown the scoundrel's brains out.

Privy Councillor: I think we should take her now.

Major: Leave us alone! What's she to you? She's not your daughter. You concern yourself with your own flesh and blood at home. [*He takes her in his arms*] There, my girl - maybe I should take you with me back to the pond [*Turns her towards the pond*] - but we don't want to go swimming 'till we learned how to swim, do we - [*Clasps her to his breast*] Oh, my only, dearest treasure! I can carry you again in my arms, godless wretch! [*Carries her off*]

Scene 6

Leipzig

[*FRITZ VON BERG, PÄTUS*]

Fritz: There is only one thing I hold against you, Pätus. I have meant to tell you for a long while now. Just think about yourself for a moment. What has been the cause of all your misfortune? I'm not going to blame anyone for falling in love. We are the right age, we're on the sea, the wind is driving us on, but reason must be there at the helm, or we'll run onto the first rocks and be wrecked. The Hamster girl was a flirt who did with you just what she wanted. She cost you your last coat, your good name and the good name of your friends too. I thought that might have taught you a lesson. The Rehaar girl is an naïve, innocent young lamb. If you range all your batteries against a heart which neither can nor will defend itself, in order to, what shall I say? to destroy it, to reduce it to ashes, that is wrong, brother Pätus, that is wrong. Don't take this amiss, but as things are we will no longer be able to stay such good friends. A man who goes as far as he can with a woman is either a tomfool or a scoundrel; a tomfool if he can't control himself and show innocence and virtue the respect they deserve, a scoundrel if will not control himself and, like the Devil in paradise, only takes pleasure in ruining women.

Pätus: Don't lecture me, brother! You're right. I regret it, but I promise you, I'll swear an oath if you like, that I never touched the girl.

Fritz: But you did climb in through her window, and you were seen by the neighbours. Do you imagine their tongues will be as reticent as your hands may have been? I know you. You may give the impression of confidence, but really you're shy when it comes to women. I like that in you. But were it no more than the loss of her good name - she's a musician's daughter, she's no fortune, only what she's received from nature, and to rob her of her only asset, her good name - you've ruined her, Pätus-

[*Enter HERR REHAAR, a lute under his arm*]

Rehaar: Your humble servant, humble servant Herr von Berg. I wish you a very good morning. How did you sleep and how did you find our little concerto? [*Sits down and tunes his lute*] Have you played it though? [*Continues tuning*] I had an awful scare last night. I'll try to call it to mind - you probably know him, he's one of your fellow countrymen. Twang, twang. Damn this E-string! I can't get it to stay in tune. I'll bring you another this afternoon.

Fritz: [*Sits down with his lute*] I haven't looked at the concerto yet.

Rehaar: Well well, you're a lazy young chap, Herr von Berg, not looked at it yet? Twang! I'll bring you another this afternoon. [*Puts the lute down and takes a pinch of snuff*] They say the Turks have crossed the Danube and have trounced the Russians back to - what's the place called? - to Otschakov, I think. But how should I know? I can tell you, if Rehaar had been with them, you know, he would have run further than that. Ha, ha, ha! [*Picks up his lute again*] I tell you, Herr von Berg, I know of no greater pleasure than to read in a paper that an army has taken to its heels. The Russians are sensible to have run away. Rehaar would have run too, like any sane person. What's the point of staying and being killed? Ha, ha, ha!

Fritz: This is the first position, yes?

Rehaar: Quite right; the second finger a little further round and the little finger off the finger-board, that's it - now round out the trill, round it out, Herr von Berg - My late father always used to say that a musician must be devoid of courage, and that a musician with heart was a scoundrel. If he can just play his concertos and can blare out a good march tune - I said that to the Duke of Kurland, when I was on the way to Petersburg, the first time I was in the entourage of Prince Czartorinsky, and had to play for him. It still makes me laugh. When I came into the room and went to make a deep, deep bow, I hadn't noticed that the floor was made of mirrors, and the walls too, so I fell headlong like a block of wood and gave myself a huge cut on my head. The gentlemen of the court came over and started to tease me. "Don't stand for it, Rehaar", said the Duke, "You've a sword at your side. Don't stand for it". "Yes", said I, "Your Majesty, but my sword has not been drawn since the thirties. It's not a musician's place to draw his sword, for a musician with heart who draws his sword is a scoundrel who will never accomplish anything on any instrument". - No, no, the third course, and the ninth position, that's it - cleanly now, round out the trill and keep your thumb still, that's it -

Pätus: [*Who has kept to one side, comes forward and offers Rehaar his hand*] Your servant, Herr Rehaar, How are you?

Rehaar: [*Stands with his lute*] Your humble ser - How am I, Herr Pätus? *Toujours content, jamais d'argent*[10], that's old Rehaar's motto, don't you know. All my students know, and that's why none of them pays me - Herr Pätus still owes me for that last serenade, but it doesn't occur to him..

Pätus: You'll have it, my dear Rehaar. I expect my allowance in a week without fail.

Rehaar: Yes, you've been waiting some while now, but there's no sign of the allowance, is there. What is one to do? One must be patient. I always say that I treat no man with as much respect as I do students. Admittedly a student is nothing, that's true, but he might become anything. [*He puts his lute down on the table and takes a pinch of snuff*] But what have you done to me, Herr Pätus? Was it right; was it honourable? Climbing in at my window last night, into my daughter's bedroom.

Pätus: What's that, Grandad? I..?

[10]Always happy, never any money

Rehaar: [*Drops his snuff box*] I'll grandad you, and I'll make sure it's heard
about in the right places, sir, you can be sure of that. My daughter's
honour is dear to me, and she's a respectable girl, damn it! If only I'd seen
you yesterday, or I'd woken up, I'd have bundled you out of the
window, head over heels - Was that honourable, was that repectable?
Damn it, when I was a student, I behaved like a student, not a criminal.
When the neighbours told me about it today, I thought it would kill me.
The girl had to be put on the mail coach straightaway, to her aunt in
Kurland; yes, sir, Kurland, for she's lost her honour here. But who will
pay for her fare? I haven't been able to touch a lute all day, and I've
broken at least fifteen E strings. Indeed, sir, I'm still trembling all over,
and Herr Pätus, I've a bone to pick with you. Things can't stay as they
are. I'll teach scoundrels like you to seduce the children of honest folk.

Pätus: Don't insult me, sir, or -

Rehaar: Do you see that, Herr von Berg! do you see - if only I had heart, I'd
challenge him on the spot - Look at him standing there laughing in my
face. Are we among Turks or heathens then, that a father and daughter
are no longer safe together? Herr Pätus, you will not go unpunished, I
assure you of that, even if it has to go as far as the Elector himself. The
army's the place for lewd dogs like you! Following the colours, that's
what you should be doing! You're scoundrels not students!

Pätus: [*Boxes his ears*] Don't insult me; I've told you five times already!

Rehaar: [*Jumps up with his handkerchief to his eyes*] Well then. Just wait - if I
can keep this bruise until I see His Majesty - if I can keep it for a week
until I can go to Dresden and show it to the Elector - You wait, you'll
get your come-uppance, just wait, wait - is it permissible? [*Weeps*] to
strike a lutanist? because he won't give you his daughter to play on? -
Wait I'm going to tell His Majesty the Elector that you struck me in the
face. You should have your hand cut off - villain! [*Runs off. PÄTUS makes
to follow him but is restrained by Fritz*]

Fritz: Pätus! You have behaved badly. He was the injured party. You should
have been gentler with him.

Pätus: Why did the cur insult me then?

Fritz: If your behaviour is insulting, you deserve to be insulted. He has no
other way to avenge his daughter's honour, but there are people who
would -

Pätus: What? What people?

Fritz: You have dishonoured her, you have dishonoured her father. A swine who'll take liberties with women and musicians, who are less than women.

Pätus: A swine?

Fritz: You should offer him a public apology.

Pätus: With my cane.

Fritz: Then I shall answer you in his name.

Pätus: [*Shouts*] What do you want of me?

Fritz: Satisfaction for Rehaar.

Pätus: Surely you don't intend to compel me, you naïve fellow –

Fritz: Yes, I intend to compel you not to be a scoundrel.

Pätus: You're a – we'll have to come to blows.

Fritz: Gladly – if you will not render Rehaar satisfaction.

Pätus: Never.

Fritz: That remains to be seen.

□

ACT FIVE

Scene 1

The school

[*LÄUFFER, MARTHE with a child in her arms*]

Marthe: In God's name, help a poor blind woman and an innocent child who's lost its mother.

Läuffer: [*Giving her something*] How did you find your way here if you can't see?

Marthe: It was very exhausting. The mother of the child used to act as my guide. She left the house one day, two days after her confinement; she left at midday and was to return in the evening; she is yet to return. God grant her eternal peace and glory!

Läuffer: Why wish her that?

Marthe: Because the good woman's dead. She would never have broken her word otherwise. I met a workman from the hill who saw her throw herself into the pond. An old man went and threw himself in after her. I suppose that must have been her father.

Läuffer: Good heavens! Why am I trembling – Is that her child?

Marthe: Yes it is. See how plump it is, fed on nothing but cabbage and turnips. What could a poor woman do; I couldn't calm it, so, as my provisions were gone, I took the child on my back, and, like Hagar, set off, trusting in God's mercy.

Läuffer: Let me hold it – Oh my heart! – To be able to press you to my heart – I think I can explain this frightful mystery! [*Takes the child in his arms and crosses to the mirror*] Ah! Are these not my features? [*Faints; the child begins to cry*]

Marthe: Have you fainted? [*Picks up the child from the floor*] Precious, my little precious! [*The child calms down*] Hey! What's happened? No answer. I must call for help. I think he must be injured.

[*She exits*]

Scene 2

A small wood near Leipzig

[*FRITZ VON BERG and PÄTUS with drawn swords, REHAAR*]

Fritz: Are you ready?

Pätus: Will you begin?

Fritz: You must strike first.

Pätus: [*Throws down his sword*] I can't fight with you.

Fritz: Why not? Take up your sword. I have insulted you and must offer you satisfaction.

Pätus: You may insult me as you wish. I need no satisfaction from you.

Fritz: Now you insult me.

Pätus: [*Runs to embrace him*] My dearest Berg! Do not take it as an insult if I say that you are not capable of insulting me. I know your heart - the mere thought of which turns me into the most abject coward on earth. Let us remain good friends, I would fight with the Devil himself, but not with you.

Fritz: Well, give Rehaar satisfaction, or I shall not leave this place.

Pätus: Gladly, if he demands it.

Fritz: He is as worthy as you. You struck him in the face - Come Rehaar, draw!

Rehaar: [*Draws*] Yes, but he mustn't take up his sword.

Fritz: You can't mean that. Would you draw against a man who cannot defend himself?

Rehaar: Yes, let those with courage draw against armed men. A musician must be devoid of courage, and you, Herr Pätus, must give me satisfaction [*Lunges at him, PÄTUS steps back*] - Satisfaction. [*Lunges and hits PÄTUS in the arm. FRITZ disarms him*]

Fritz: Now I see, Rehaar, that you deserve to have your ears boxed. Shame on you!

Rehaar: But what am I to do if I've no backbone?

Fritz: Put up with having your ears boxed and keep your mouth shut.

Pätus: Stop it, Berg! It's only a scratch. Herr Rehaar, I beg your forgiveness. I should not have struck you when I knew you were not capable of demanding satisfaction of me. How much less should I have given you cause to insult me. I confess your revenge is far too mild for the outrage I have committed against your house. I will try another way to make good the wrong, if fate smiles on my resolve. I will ride after your daughter and will marry her. I'll find a position in my own country, and even if my father and I are never reconciled, I am sure of an inheritence of fifteen thousand guilders. [*Embraces him*] Will you give me your daughter's hand?

Rehaar: Well well, I've nothing against it, as long as you treat her honourably and repectably, and can provide for her - Ha ha ha, I've said all my life that good can come from students. They still have integrity in their souls, but officers - they'll get a girl pregnant and no-one cares two hoots about it; that's because they're all courageous fellows and must let themselves be killed. A man with courage is capable of any vice.

Fritz: You are a student too. Come now; it's too long since we made punch together; let's drink to the health of your daughter.

Rehaar: Yes, and then there's your little lute concerto, my young Herr von Berg. Look, I've missed three hours of your lessons, but as I'm a man of honour too, I'll spend three hours this evening in your room playing the lute until it's dark.

Pätus: And I'll accompany you on the violin.

Scene 3

The school

[*LÄUFFER lying in bed, WENZESLAUS*]

Wenzeslaus: Good God! What's happened for you to have me called from work? Are you unwell again? I think that old woman must have been a witch - You haven't been at all well since she was here.

Läuffer: I don't think I'll last much longer.

Wenzeslaus: Shall I send for neighbour Schöpsen?

Läuffer: No.

Wenzeslaus: Have you something weighing on your conscience? Tell me, confess it, without reservation - You're looking about you so full of fear that it fills me with horror; *frigidus per ossa*[11] - Tell me, what is it? - As if you'd killed someone - What is it distorting your features like that? - God preserve us, I must fetch Schöpsen -

Läuffer: Stay - I don't know if I've done right - I've castrated myself..

Wenzeslaus: Wha - castrat - Let me offer you my heartfelt congratulations, you splendid young man, a second Origen! Let me embrace the favoured, chosen one! I cannot conceal from you that I can barely - barely resist the heroic resolve to imitate you. You've done right, dear friend! This is the way for you to become a light of the church, a star of the first magnitude, even a church father. I congratulate you, I'll shout "Jubilate" and "Evoe" for you, my spiritual son - Were I not past those years when the Devil in his guile sets his nets for our foremost and best powers, I would certainly not hesitate a moment. -

[11]Chilled to the bone

Läuffer: Be that as it may, Herr schoolmaster, I regret it.

Wenzeslaus: What do you mean, regret it? Banish such thoughts, dear brother! Surely you won't cloud such a noble act with inane remorse and sully it with base tears? I can see some rising to your eyes even now. Swallow them down and sing with with joy: "I'm set free from triviality, now give me wings, wings, wings". You don't want to turn like Lot's wife and look back at Sodom, now you've at last reached the peace and tranquility of Zoar. No, Herr colleague, I must inform you that you are not the only person to have had this idea. Even among the benighted Jews there was a sect, whom I would gladly have acknowledged publicly, were I not afraid of offending my neighbours and my poor lambs in the school. On the other hand I must admit they did have some idiotic and asinine ideas, which I really couldn't have gone along with. For example they refuse to answer a call of nature on a Sunday, and that's against all the rules of a healthy regimen. I rather hold with our blessed Doctor Luther: "What goes up is for God, what goes down, Devil, is for you" – Yes, where was I?

Läuffer: I'm afraid the motives for my actions were of quite another sort... remorse, despair –

Wenzeslaus: Yes, now I have it – The Essenes, I was saying didn't take wives either; it was one of their fundamental precepts, and thus they lived to a great age, like those we read of in Josephus. How they set about taming the flesh, whether they did as I do, living in sobriety and moderation and smoking honest tobacco, or choosing your way – this much is certain *in amore, in amore omnia insunt vitia*[12], and hail, hail to a joung man who manages to negotiate such obstacles, and whom I will crown with laurels; *lauro tempora cingam et sublimi fronte sidera pulsabit*[13] .

Läuffer: I'm afraid I am going to die of the wound.

Wenzeslaus: Nonsense, God will provide. I'll call on Schöpsen straightaway. He will certainly never have seen a case like this before, but he cured your arm, which was, after all, a wound which did not enhance your welfare, God will surely grant him his grace to effect a cure which will further your soul's eternal salvation.

[*He exits*]

[12]in love, in love all vices are contained

[13]I shall wreathe his temples with laurels and his elevated forehead will strike the heavens

Läuffer: His jubilation wounds me more deeply than my knife. O innocence, what a pearl you are! Since losing you I have gone step by step deeper into passion and have ended in despair. If this latest step does not lead to my death, perhaps I may start my life anew and be reborn as a Wenzeslaus.

Scene 4

Leipzig

[*FRITZ VON BERG and REHAAR meeting in the street*]

Rehaar: Oh, Herr von Berg, young sir, a little letter; it arrived care of me. It's from Herr von Seiffenblase; he studied the lute with me a while ago. He asks me to give this letter to a certain Herr von Berg in Leipzig, if he's still here – How I've been scurrying about!

Fritz: Where is Seiffenblase to be found now then?

Rehaar: I'm to give this to Herr von Berg, he writes, if I happen to know this worthy fellow. Oh, how I've been scurrying about – Herr von Seiffenblase is in Königsberg. Well, what do you know, and my daughter's there too, in lodgings just across the street from him. Katrinchen writes that she can't compliment him highly enough for the courtesy he shows her, and all for my sake; he studied with me for seven months.

Fritz: [*Takes out his watch*] My dearest Rehaar, I must go to the college – Tell Pätus nothing of all this, I beg you –

[*He exits*]

Rehaar: [*Calling after him*] 'Till this afternoon – our little concerto! –

Scene 5

Königsberg, Prussia

[*PRIVY COUNCILLOR, GUSTCHEN, the MAJOR at the window in their house*]

Privy Councillor: Is it him?

Gustchen: Yes, it's him.

Privy Councillor: I see now the aunt must be a vile creature, or else she's conceived a hatred for her niece and is intent on seeing her ruined.

Gustchen: But uncle, she can't ban him from the house.

Privy Councillor: After what I told her? – Who would take it amiss were she to say to him: "Herr von Seiffenblase, you have let it be known in a coffee house that you intend taking my niece as your mistress, go and seek other company in the city; you are wrong to call on me; my niece is a foreigner, entrusted to me; with no other support; were she seduced, the blame would fall on me. I would be condemned by both God and Man".

Major: Quiet, brother! He's coming out now with his tail between his legs. Ho, ho, ho, He's fit to be tied. My word he's pale.

Privy Councillor: I'll go over straight away and see what's happened.

Scene 6

Leipzig

[*PÄTUS at a table writing. Enter FRITZ VON BERG with a letter in his hand PÄTUS looks up and continues writing*]

Fritz: Pätus! – Are you busy?

Pätus: Just a minute – [*FRITZ paces up and down*] Right – [*Lays his pen aside*]

Fritz: Pätus! I have received a letter – and haven't the courage to open it.

Pätus: Where is it from? Is it your father's hand?

Fritz: No, von Seiffenblase – but my hand trembles as soon as I go to open it. Open it, brother, and read it me. [*Flings himself into a chair*]

Pätus: [*Reading*] "The memory of so many pleasant hours, which I still remember having enjoyed with you, compels me to write to you to remind you of those pleasant hours" – What an extravagant style he has.

Fritz: Just read it –

Pätus: "And as I feel myself compelled to send you word of my arrival here and the news of occurences hereabouts, I must tell you of your family who have suffered a great many misfortunes during the year, and thanks to the friendly reception I have always received from your parents, I feel compelled, as I know that you and your father are estranged and that he will not have written to you for some considerable time, to tell you of the misfortune with the tutor, who has been ejected from your uncle's house for having violated your cousin, which she took so much to heart that she jumped into a pond, which tragedy has left your whole family in the most appalling..." – What is it, Berg! – [*Splashes him with lavender water*] How are you, Berg? Tell me, are you unwell – If only I hadn't read this damned – It's sure to be a fabrication – Berg! Berg!

Fritz: Let me be - It will soon pass.

Pätus: Should I fetch someone to bleed you?

Fritz: Nonsense - stop acting like a Frenchman - read it again.

Pätus: Yes, I'll - I'll take this wicked, malicious letter this instant and - [*Tears it into pieces*]

Fritz: Violated - drowned. [*Strikes his forehead*] My fault! [*Stands*] my fault and mine alone -

Pätus: You're being irrational. Are you responsible for her letting herself be seduced by the tutor -

Fritz: Pätus, I swore I'd return to her, I swore it - The three years have flown by, I have not returned, I've left Halle, and my father has had no news of me. My father has dispaired of me, she has learned of this, and her grief - you know her propensity for melancholy - her mother's strictness, her isolation in the country, and a faithless love - Can't you see, Pätus, can't you see? I am a villain. I am responsible for her death. [*Throws himself back into the chair and covers his face*]

Pätus: You're deluded! - It's not true, that's not what happened stamps his foot Damnation. How can you be stupid enough to believe it all? That lazy, good-for-nothing rat Seiffenblase is playing a trick on you - Just let me lay my hands on him - It's not true that she's dead, and if she is dead, she hasn't taken her own life..

Fritz: But he can't have made it up - taken her own life - [*Jumps up*] Oh, that's dreadful!

Pätus: [*Stamping his foot again*] No, she's not taken her life. Seiffenblase is lying; we must find more to substantiate this. You remember you told him once when you were drunk that you were in love with your cousin. You see, that gave the scoundrel the idea - but do you know, do you know what you should do? Tell him where to go; show him you don't care; make him eat his words, write to him: "I am most obliged to your honour for your news, and would ask you" - No the best idea would be to write back to him: "You are a villain". That's the most sensible thing for you to do.

Fritz: I want to go home.

Pätus: I'll go with you - I'm not going to leave you on your own, Berg.

Fritz: But how? Travelling is out of the question - If I wasn't afraid of being rejected, I'd try at Leichtfuss et Companie, but I owe them a hundred and fifty ducats already -

Pätus: We'll go together - Wait, we'll have to pass the lottery office. The Hamburg mail arrives today, I'll ask on our way, just in fun -

Scene 7

Königsberg

[The PRIVY COUNCILLOR leading on MISTRESS REHAAR by the hand, GUSTCHEN, the MAJOR]

Privy Councillor: Here, Gustchen, I've brought you a companion. You're of an age and your situations are the same - take each other's hand and be friends.

Gustchen: I have long been yours, dear Mamselle! I can't tell you how my bosom rose and subsided each time I saw you from my window, but you were always involved with diversions, with carriages and serenades, that I feared a visit from me might come at an inopportune time.

Mistress Rehaar: I would have anticipated you, my dear young lady, had I had the courage. I thought it injudicious to intrude on my own into such an imposing house. I was therefore compelled to resist the urging of my heart that has led me so often to your door.

Privy Councillor: Just think, Major, Seiffenblase has resonded to the warning I gave to Frau Dutzend and which she, as I requested, passed on to him in my name: he will soon find a way to be avenged on me. He denied any responsibility in the affair and straightaway arrived the next day with Minister Deichsel. The poor woman didn't have the heart to prohibit his visits. Last night he had two carriages waiting in the street and another at the Brandenburg Gate which remained open on account of the fireworks. But Madam Dutzend found this all out yesterday morning. In the afternoon he tried with all his might to convince the Mamselle to accompany him and the Minister to the assembly, but Madam Dutzend smelled a rat and sent him packing. He twice drove past the door but had to turn back. His cards were now on the table, so he tried once more today, but not only did Madam Dutzend refuse him entry to the house, but also informed him that she felt constrained to ask the Governor for a watch to be kept on her house. He started fuming and threatened her with the Minister - To set her mind at rest, I offered to take Mamselle into our house. We'll take her with us to Insterburg for six months, until Seiffenblase has forgotten her, or for as long as she wishes -

Major: The horses are harnessed and ready. When we go to Heidelbrunn, we won't forget you, Mamselle. You shall come with us, or perhaps my daughter will remain with you in Insterburg.

Privy Councillor: That would probably be best. Besides, the country doesn't agree with Gustchen, and I want to be able to keep an eye on Mamselle Rehaar.

Major: It's as well your wife can't hear you – or have you plans for your son?

Privy Councillor: Don't make the poor girl blush. She must have seen him often enough in Leipzig, the wicked lad. Gustchen, you're blushing in front of us all. He doesn't deserve it.

Gustchen: Now my father has forgiven me, is your son to find your heart less generous?

Privy Councillor: He has yet to jump in a pond!

Major: If only we had been able to find the blind woman with the child, about whom the schoolmaster wrote to me. I'll not rest until we do – Come on! I must start for my estate today.

Privy Councillor: There's no point. You must spend the night in Insterburg.

Scene 8

Leipzig. Fritz von Berg's room

[FRITZ VON BERG sitting, his hands under his chin. PÄTUS bursts in]

Pätus: Triumph, Berg! Why are you miserable? – God! God! [*Grasps his head and falls to his knees*] Fate! Fate! – Leichtfuss wouldn't make you an advance, would he. Forget him – I have money, I have all of it – Three hundred and eighty Friedrichsd'or won at a stroke [*Leaps up and shouts*] Hididdledum, off to Insterburg! Start packing!

Fritz: Are you mad?

Pätus: [*Pulling out a purse and emptying it on the floor*] There's my madness. It's you that's mad not to believe me – Now help me pick them up. Come on, bend down – and it's off to Insterburg today, hooray! [*They pick up the money*] I'll give my father eighty Friedrichsd'or, that's what my last allowance came to, and I'll say to him: "Now Papa, what do you think of me now?" We can pay all your debts, as well as mine, and then we'll travel like princes. Hooray!

Scene 9

The school

[*WENZESLAUS. LÄUFFER, both in black*]

Wenzeslaus: How did you like my sermon, colleague? Did you find it edifying?

Läuffer: It was good, very good [*Sighs*]

Wenzeslaus: [*Taking off his wig and putting on a nightcap*] That won't do. You must tell me from which part of the sermon you drew particular benefit. Listen - Sit down. I must tell you something. I noticed something in church which shook me. You were sitting there day-dreaming, and, if the truth be known, I was ashamed of you before the whole congregation; indeed, ·I frequently came close to losing the thread of my argument. What, I thought, this young champion, who has so valiantly triumphed, and has, so to speak, been victorious in the fiercest of battles - I must confess, you have vexed me, *skandalon edidous, hetaire!*[14] I could see what was going on, I could see you forever looking at the centre door, the one under the organ.

Läuffer: I must confess, there's a painting hanging there which has quite unsettled me. The evangelist Mark with a face not a whit more human than the lion sitting by his side, and the angel by Matthew the evangelist looking more like a winged serpent.

Wenzeslaus: It wasn't that, my friend! Don't try to tell me it was. Admit it, one looks at a picture and then looks away, and that's that. Did you hear what I said? Can you quote me one word from my sermon? And it was intended just for you, quite casuistically - Oh! oh! oh!

Läuffer: I was particularly taken with the idea that there exists a considerable similarity between our souls and their rebirth and the growing of flax and hemp; and as hemp can only be released from its old husks by violent pounding and beating on the cutting board, so too must our souls be prepared for heaven by means of all manner of suffering and affliction and mortification of sensuality.

Wenzeslaus: It was intended casuistically, my friend -

Läuffer: However, I can't conceal from you that your catalogue of devils and how they were thrown out of heaven, and the whole story of the revolution there, and Lucifer considering himself the most beautiful of the

[14]You have caused scandal, colleague

angels - The modern world has long ago outgrown such superstition, why bring it all up again? Throughout today's rational world nobody believes anymore in devils -

Wenzeslaus: And for that very reason, the rational world of today will go to the Devil. I am not given to censure, my dear Herr Almond, but we truly live in pernicious times; it is the last, evil time. But I shall say no more about this. I can see that you are a sceptic, and such people too must be endured. It must come soon, and you are still young - but even assuming, posito even, while not admitting, that our religious doctrines were all just superstition, about spirits, Hell and the Devil - what's it to you, what's biting you to make you fight against it tooth and nail? Do no wrong, do right, then you will have no cause to fear devils, even if there were more of them than tiles on the roof, as our blessed Luther says. And as for superstition - Hush, hush, dear me. Consider first with mature reflection how much benefit superstition has brought with it and then see if you have the heart to cast your rational jibes at me. As far as I'm concerned, if you root out superstition, then the true faith will die too, and you will be left with a barren field. But I can think of someone who said that they should be left to grow together, and that the time would surely come when the wheat would be separated from the tares. Superstition - if you were to take their superstition from the mob, they'd be freethinkers like you and hit you over the head. Take their devils from the peasants and they'll turn into devils against their superiors, and prove then that such things exist. But let's put that to one side - What was I talking about? Ah yes, tell me, who were you looking at throughout the whole of my sermon? Don't try to conceal it from me. It certainly wasn't me, unless you have the most appalling squint.

Läuffer: The painting.

Wenzeslaus: It wasn't the painting - It was under it, where the girls sit, the ones who come to you for catechism classes - my dear friend! Surely there can be none of the old leaven still in your heart - Well, well, he who has once tasted the glories of the world to come - I ask you, it made my hair stand on end - It's the one with the yellow hair so carelessly pushed up under her red bonnet, yes? with light brown eyes twinkling so mischievously under dark eyebrows, like stars from behind rain clouds. - It's true, the girl is dangerous; I caught sight of her just once from the pulpit, and thereafter had to shut my eyes tight if they happened to fall on her, or I would have been like the wise men on the Areopagus, who forgot truth and justice for the sake of base Phryne. - But tell me, what are you doing succumbing to evil urges now that you lack the wherewithal to satisfy them? Do you want to surrender yourself to the Devil for nothing? Where is the vow you swore to the Lord? - I'm speaking to you now as your spiritual father, - you, who with so little effort could triumph over all sensuality, take flight over the earth and soar to better lands. [*Embraces him*] Ah, my dear son, with these tears, which I shed out of heart-felt concern for you, I beg you, not to turn back to the flesh pots of Egypt now that you are so near Caanan! Hurry, hurry! Save your immortal soul! There is nothing in the world now to hold you back. The world has nothing more to offer you to recompense you for your faithlessness; not even sensual pleasure, never mind spiritual peace - I'll go and leave you to your resolutions.

[*He exits. LÄUFFER remains seated, deep in thought*]

Scene 10

[*Enter LISE, a hymn book in her hand, without him noticing. She looks at him silently for a long time. He springs up and goes to kneel but, seeing her, stands for a while in confusion*]

Läuffer: [*Approaching her*] You have stolen a soul from heaven. [*Grasps her hand*] What brings you here, Lise?

Lise: I've come, Herr Almond - I've come, because you said there'd be no catechism class tomorrow - because you - so I came - you said - I've come to ask if there's a catechism class tomorrow.

Läuffer: Oh! -- Look at these cheeks, you angel! How they burn with innocent fire, then would damn me if they could -- Lise, why is your hand trembling? Why are your lips so pale and your cheeks so red? What is it you want?

Lise: Is there a catechism class tomorrow?

Läuffer: Sit here by me - put your hymn book down - Who puts your hair up for you when you go to church? [*Sits her on a chair next to him*]

Lise: [*Goes to rise*] Forgive me. My bonnet's probably not straight, there was such a terrible wind as I was coming to church.

Läuffer: [*Taking both her hands in his*] Oh, you're - How old are you, Lise - Have you never - What is it I want to ask you - Have you never had an admirer?

Lise: [*Cheerfully*] Oh yes, just the last few weeks; and the shepherd's girl Grete was so jealous and kept saying: "I don't know why he's taking so much notice of that simple girl"; and then I had an officer too, that was three months ago.

Läuffer: An officer?

Lise: Oh yes, and a very distinguished one too. I'm telling you, he had three stripes on his arm; but I was too young still, and my father didn't want to give me to him on account of the soldier's way of life.

Läuffer: Would you - Oh, I don't know what I'm saying - Might you - Wretched creature that I am!

Lise: Oh yes, with all my heart.

Läuffer: Enchantress! - [*Goes to kiss her hand*] But you don't know yet, what I was going to ask you.

Lise: [*Pulling her hand away*] Oh don't do that, my hand is so dirty - Shame on you! What are you doing? You see, I've always wanted a clerical gentleman. As long as I can remember I've always preferred educated men. They're always so courteous and polite, not all blood and thunder like soldiers; although I do like them too in a way, that I can't deny, on account of their colourful coats. I tell you, if clerical gentlemen were to wear colourful coats like soldiers, I'm sure I'd die!

Läuffer: Let me seal your mischievous lips with a kiss! [*Kisses her*] Oh, Lise! If you but knew how miserable I am.

Lise: Shame on you, Sir. What are you doing?

Läuffer: Once more and then never again for all eternity! [*Kisses her*]
[*Enter WENZESLAUS*]

Wenzeslaus: What's this? *Pro deum atque hominum fidem!*[15] How now, you false, false, false prophet! Ravening wolf in sheep's clothing! Is this the care, you owe your flock? Seducing the very innocence, which you should be saving from temptation? It must needs be that offences come; but woe to that man by whom the offence cometh!

Läuffer: Herr Wenzeslaus!

Wenzeslaus: No more! Not one word more! You have shown yourself in your true colours. Out of my house, Lothario!

[15]By the faith of men and gods

Lise: [*Kneeling before WENZESLAUS*] Dear Herr Schoolmaster, he has done me no harm.

Wenzeslaus: He has done you more harm than could your worst enemy. He has led your innocent heart astray.

Läuffer: I acknowledge my guilt – but who could resist such temptation? If my heart were ripped from my body, and I was torn limb from limb, so that but one vein full of blood was left me; that perfidious vein would yet beat for Lise.

Lise: He has done me no harm.

Wenzeslaus: Done you no harm – Heavenly Father!

Läuffer: I told you she was the most charming creature ever to have graced creation; I have imprinted that on her lips; I have sealed with my kisses this innocent mouth which by the magic of its words would have lured me to far greater crimes.

Wenzeslaus: And is this no crime? What do you young men nowadays call a crime? *O tempora, o mores!* Have you read Valerius Maximus? Have you read his essay *de pudicitia?* In it he cites the case of Maenius who struck his freedman dead for once kissing his daughter; his reasoning: *ut etiam oscula ad maritum sincera perferrent*[16]. Doesn't that apply to you? Don't you find that to your taste? *Etiam oscula, non solum virginitatem, etiam oscula*[17]. And Maenius was a heathen; what should a Christian do, who knows that the state of matrimony was instituted by God, and that to poison the rapture of such a state at the roots, to deprive a future husband of the joy and consolation of his wife, to profane his heaven – Away, out of my sight, miscreant. I wish to have nothing further to do with you! Go and find a sultan and act as overseer of his harem, but not as shepherd to my sheep. You hireling! You ravening wolf in sheep's clothing!

Läuffer: I wish to marry Lise.

Wenzeslaus: Marry? – oh, of course – as if she could be happy with a eunuch.

Lise: Oh yes, I'm really and truly happy, Herr Schoolmaster.

Läuffer: Oh, what a wretched creature I am!

Lise: Believe me, Herr Schoolmaster, I shan't let him go. Take my life but I shan't let him go. I like him, and my heart tells me I couldn't like anyone in the world as I do him.

[16]that she may bring pure kisses to her husband

[17]kisses too, not simply virginity, kisses too

Wenzeslaus: Well - but - Lise, you don't understand the problem - Lise. I can't tell you why, but you cannot marry him; it's impossible.

Lise: Why should it be impossible, then? Herr Schoolmaster? Why is it impossible, if I want it, he wants it and my father does too? Because my father always said to me, if I could ever find a clerical gentleman -

Wenzeslaus: But damn it, you see he can't - God forgive me, you tell her

Läuffer: Perhaps she has no need for that - Lise, I can't sleep with you.

Lise: Then we can spend our waking time together, as long as we're together, laughing and kissing hands - By God, I like him! God knows I like him!

Läuffer: You see, Herr Wenzeslaus! She desires only love from me. And is it really necessary for the success of a marriage that one satisfies one's bestial urges?

Wenzeslaus: What's that? - *Connubium sine prole, est quasi dies sine sole*[18]... Be fruitful and multiply, it's there in God's word. In a marriage there must be children.

Lise: No, Herr Schoolmaster, I swear I want no children in my life. Yes, children! With all that they entail! It would be of no use to me to have children. My father has ducks and chickens enough that I have to feed every day. If I had children in addition to those..

Läuffer: [*Kisses her*] Divine Lise!

Wenzeslaus: [*Tearing them apart*] What! What! Before my very eyes? - Go and crawl away together then; for all I care; for it is better to marry than to burn - but it's all over for us, Herr Almond; all the great hopes I had for you, all the great expectations, which your heroism inspired in me - Gracious Heaven! How great is the gulf between a father of the church and a capon. I thought, he would be Origen the second - *O homuncio, homuncio*[19]! It will have to be a man of a very different sort, a man of firm intentions and principles, to take the path leading to his being a pillar of our sinking church. A very different man! Who knows when there might be another!

[*He exits*]

Läuffer: Let's go to your father, Lise! His consent and I will be the happiest man on earth!

[18]A marriage without children is like a day without sun

[19]Oh little man, little man

Scene 11

Insterburg

[*PRIVY COUNCILLOR. FRITZ VON BERG. PÄTUS. GUSTCHEN. MISTRESS
REHAAR. GUSTCHEN hide as the others approach in another room. The PRIVY
COUNCILLOR and FRITZ run to meet each other*]

Fritz: [*Falling on his knees before him*] Father!

Privy Councillor: [*Raising him up and embracing him*] My son!

Fritz: Have you forgiven me?

Privy Councillor: My son!

Fritz: I am not worthy to be called your son.

Privy Councillor: Sit down. Think no more about it. But how did you
support yourself in Leipzig? More debts added to my account? No? And
how did you get away?

Fritz: This generous young man paid off everything for me.

Privy Councillor: How's that?

Pätus: This far more generous - Oh, I can't speak.

Privy Councillor: Sit down, children. Now speak more clearly. Are you
reconciled with your father, Herr Pätus?

Pätus: I've not heard a word from him.

Privy Councillor: Then how did you both manage?

Pätus: We won the in the lottery, a small amount - but it came in useful as
we wanted to come here.

Privy Councillor: I can see that you wild young fellows think more clearly
than your fathers. What must you have thought of me, Fritz? But you
were sorely maligned to me.

Pätus: Seiffenblase, no doubt?

Privy Councillor: I shan't name him. That might lead to brawling, which
would be out of place here.

Pätus: Seiffenblase! I'll hang for him.

Privy Councillor: But what led you to return, just now - ?

Fritz: Go on - that "just now", Father! That "just now" is what I've come to
fathom.

Privy Councillor: What then? What do you mean?

Fritz: Is Gustchen dead?

Privy Councillor: Ah ha, the lover! What leads you to ask such a question?

Fritz: A letter from Seiffenblase.

Privy Councillor: He wrote to you that she was dead?

Fritz: And dishonoured too.

Pätus: More of his wretched slanders!

Privy Councillor: Do you know a Mistress Rehaar in Leipzig?

Fritz: Why yes, her father was my lute teacher.

Privy Councillor: He wanted to dishonour her. I saved her from his machinations, and now he's my sworn enemy.

Pätus: Mistress Rehaar - Devil take him!

Privy Councillor: Where are you going?

Pätus: Is he in Insterburg?

Privy Councillor: No, he's not - Don't be too eager to rescue the princess, Sir Knight of the Round Table! Or are you acquainted with Mistress Rehaar too?

Pätus: I? No, I don't know her - Yes, I know her.

Privy Councillor: So I see -Would you care to step into the next room for a moment?

[He takes him to the door]

Pätus: [*Opens it, and steps back, holding his head in both hands*] Mistress Rehaar - Let me kneel at your feet - [*Offstage*] or is this all a dream? Am I transported? - bewitched? -

Privy Councillor: Let us leave him! - [*Turns to Fritz*] And you still think of Gustchen?

Fritz: You have yet to resolve the awful mystery. Was Seiffenblase lying?

Privy Councillor: I think we should talk about that later. Let's not spoil the joy of this moment.

Fritz: [*Kneeling*] Oh Father, if you feel any tenderness for me still, don't leave me suspended between heaven and hell, between doubt and hope. That was why I returned here. I could no longer suffer the agony of uncertainty. Is Gustchen alive? Is it true that she's dishonoured?

Privy Councillor: That is, I'm afraid, all too sadly true.

Fritz: And she threw herself into a pond?

Privy Councillor: And her father threw himself in after her.

Fritz: Then let the executioner's axe fall - I am the most miserable of men.

Privy Councillor: Stand up! You were not responsible.

Fritz: I will never stand [*Beats his breast*] I was responsible; I and I alone responsible. Gustchen, blessed Gustchen, forgive me!

Privy Councillor: What have you to reproach yourself with?

Fritz: I swore to her, falsely swore - Gustchen! Would that I could leap in after you! [*Stands up hurriedly*] Where is the pond?

Privy Councillor: Here! [*Leads him into the next room*]

Fritz: [*Offstage, shouting loudly*] Gustchen! - Is this a phantom? - Oh Heaven! Heaven what joy! - Let me die! Let me die in your arms!

Privy Councillor: [*Wiping his eyes*] What a charming group! - Would that the Major were here!

[*He exits to join them*]

Last Scene

[*The MAJOR, a child in his arms. OLD PÄTUS*]

Major: Come in, Herr Pätus. You have restored me to life. That was the last worm eating away at me. I must introduce you to my brother, and set your blind old mother, like a jewel, in gold.

Old Pätus: Oh, my mother has made me far happier by her unexpected visit than she has you. You have merely recovered a grandson, who will serve to remind you of unhappy times; but I a mother, to remind me of the most delightful days of my life, and whose maternal affection I have until now, I am ashamed to say, repaid with nothing but hatred and ingratitude. I drove her from my house after she had made over to me my father's fortune and her own. I have behaved towards her more abominably than a tiger - What a blessing it is, thank God, that she is still alive, to grant me forgiveness in her saintly mercy! Thankfully it still lies in my power to atone for my despicable crime.

Major: Brother Berg! Where are you? Hey! [*Enter PRIVY COUNCILLOR*] Here is my child, my grandson. Where is Gustchen? My beloved little grandson! [*Fondles him*] my beloved, funny, little doll!

Privy Councillor: How splendid! - and you, Herr Pätus?

Major: It was Herr Pätus who discovered him for me - His mother was the blind old woman, the beggar woman, about whom Gustchen has told us so much.

Old Pätus: And a beggar woman thanks to me — Oh, the shame of it binds my tongue. But I shall tell the whole world, how monstrously I behaved -

Privy Councillor: Have you heard the news, Major? A suitor has been found for your daughter - but don't press me to tell you his name.

Major: A suitor for my daughter! - [*Throws the child on the sofa*] Where is she?

Privy Councillor: Gently now! He's with her now - will you give your consent?

Major: Is he a fellow from a good family? Is he an aristocrat?

Privy Councillor: I doubt it.

Major: But not someone too far beneath her? She was to marry into one of the finest families in the kingdom. That was an ill-fated dream! If only I could banish that thought. It could still drive me into the madhouse.

Privy Councillor: [*Opens the door. At a sign from him FRITZ and GUSTCHEN enter*]

Major: [*Embracing him*] Fritz! [*To the PRIVY COUNCILLOR*] Is it Fritz? Do you wish to marry my daughter? - God bless you. Do you not yet know, or do you know it all? Look how my hair has gone prematurely grey! [*Leads him to the sofa*] Look, there is the child. Are you a philosopher? Can you forget it all? Is Gustchen good enough for you still? Oh, how she's repented. I swear to you, young man, she has repented more than any nun or saint could. But what's to be done? Even the angels fell from heaven - but Gustchen has raised herself up again.

Fritz: Give me a chance to speak.

Major: [*Embracing him still*] No, Son - I want to squeeze you to death - for being so forgiving, for being so noble-minded - for being - my son -

Fritz: When I'm in Gustchen's embrace, I envy no king.

Major: Right, that's right - So she's confessed it all to you, then; she's told you everything -

Fritz: This mistake only makes her more precious to me - her heart all the more angelic - She need do no more than look in the mirror to assure herself that she will be the source all my happiness, and yet she trembles before the thought, what she calls her unbearable thought, that she might make me unhappy. What prospect can there be for me with such a woman but heaven itself?

Major: Yes, heaven indeed; if it's true that it is not the righteous alone who enter there, but also those sinners who repent. My daughter has done penance, as I have too for my stupidity in not taking the advice of a brother whose understanding of the affair was superior to mine. She has returned to our society, and, thank God, because of this, happily so have I.

Privy Councillor: [*Calling into the next room*] Herr Pätus, come on out. Your father is here.

Old Pätus: What's that I hear – my son?

Pätus: [*Embraces him*] Your unhappy, outcast son. But God was kind to me, poor orphan that I was. Here is the money, Papa, which you paid for my education away from home. Here it is again, with my thanks. It has attracted double interest, the capital has increased, and your son has become an honest fellow.

Old Pätus: Must you all vie with each other today to shame me with your generosity? My son, embrace again you father who, for a while, cast off his humanity and degenerated into a wild animal. Your grandmother suffered as you did. But she is returned, has forgiven me, and has taken me back as her son, as you have as your father. Take all my fortune, Gustav! Dispose of it as you please, as long as you spare me the ingratitude I showed your grandmother when she made me such a gift.

Pätus: Allow me to use it to bring happiness to the sweetest, the most virtuous girl –

Old Pätus: What's this? You in love too? I will joyfully allow you anything. I am old and, before my death, would like to know grandchildren to whom I may show the devotion your grandmother has shown to you.

Fritz: [*Embraces the child on the sofa, kisses it and takes it to GUSTCHEN*] Now this child is mine too; a sad token of the weakness of your sex and the folly of mine; but most of all of the advantages of young ladies being educated by tutors.

Major: Yes, but my dear son, how then should they be educated?

Privy Councillor: Are there no institutes, no sewing-schools, no convents, no colleges for them to attend? – – But let us talk of this another time.

Fritz: [*Kisses the child again*] And infinitely precious to me as being the image of his mother. At least, dear child, I will never entrust your education to a tutor!

THE END